The
Work/**Stress**
Connection

By James Spradley

Guests Never Leave Hungry: The Autobiography of James Sewid,
  A Kwakiutl Indian
You Owe Yourself a Drunk: An Ethnography of Urban Nomads
The Cultural Experience: An Ethnography in Complex Society (with
  David W. McCurdy)
Anthropology: The Cultural Perspective (with David W. McCurdy)
Deaf Like Me (with Thomas S. Spradley)
Culture and Cognition: Rules, Maps and Plans
Anthropology Through Literature (with George McDonough)
The Ethnographic Interview
Participant Observation
The Cocktail Waitress: Woman's Work in a Man's World (with Brenda
  Mann)

By Robert Veninga

Interpersonal Effectiveness and Health Administration

By Robert Veninga and James Spradley

The Work/Stress Connection: How to Cope with Job Burnout

The Work/**Stress** Connection:
How to Cope with Job **Burnout**

Robert L. Veninga/PhD
James P. Spradley/PhD

LITTLE, BROWN AND COMPANY **L|B** Boston / Toronto

FIRST EDITION

The quotation on page 122 from *Learn to Relax: 13 Ways to
Reduce Tension,* by C. Eugene Walker, © 1975, is reprinted by
permission of Prentice-Hall, Inc., Englewood Cliffs, New Jersey.
The letter on page 171 to Ann Landers, copyright Ann Landers,
is reprinted by permission of Ann Landers and Field Newspaper
Syndicate.

Library of Congress Cataloging in Publication Data

Veninga, Robert L.
  The work/stress connection.

  Includes bibliography.
  1. Job stress. 2. Burn out (Psychology)
I. Spradley, James P. II. Title.
HF5548.85.V45   158.7   81–522
ISBN 0–316–80747–8   AACR2

BP

Designed by Janis Capone

*Published simultaneously in Canada
by Little, Brown & Company (Canada) Limited*

PRINTED IN THE UNITED STATES OF AMERICA

To Karen Smit Veninga and Barbara Walton Spradley,
who generously gave their ideas,
offered their insights,
and shared their experiences
for this book

Acknowledgments

This book has been a collaborative effort in the fullest sense. Each of us brought to the writing and research the perspectives and investigative methods of our respective disciplines. Dr. Spradley is a cultural anthropologist who specializes in the study of urban subcultures. Dr. Veninga is a behavioral scientist who specializes in communications research in large health organizations. Dr. Spradley has studied stress among Native Americans, Peace Corps volunteers, cocktail waitresses, and bums on skid row. Dr. Veninga has investigated the stress faced by nurses, probation officers, and hospital administrators. Together we designed a conceptual framework for studying job burnout. We collected additional data for this book, conducting in-depth interviews, making observations, and using survey questionnaires. Together we analyzed the meaning of our data and selected the major issues for each chapter. Then we spent two years working jointly in planning, writing, criticizing, and revising the manuscript. Every chapter and paragraph reflects this full collaboration.

This book would not have been possible without the cooperation of hundreds of people who told us about their jobs. We are indebted to all the people who participated in an interview, filled out a questionnaire, and allowed us to observe their work situation. They taught us how the modern workplace can devastate lives, destroy hopes, and deplete energy. But they also taught us how to manage work stress and live free from job burnout. In a very real sense, this book is also their book. The many examples cited in this book have been carefully disguised to protect the anonymity of those who shared their work lives with us.

We owe a debt of gratitude to our students, who listened to us lecture on many of the ideas in this book. We deeply appreciate the interest, support, and suggestions made by many others, including Brent Veninga, Sheryl Spradley, Deborah Spradley, Laura Spradley, Tom Correll, Joan Correll, Mary Lou Burket, Tom Spradley, Louise Spradley, Otila Veninga, Frank Veninga, Suzi Ehrman, Jane Cowan, Joyce Anderson, Gerald Anderson, Catherine Veninga, James Veninga, Katherine Smit, Peter Smit, Marilyn Shaw, Robert Shaw, Janice Thayer, Jack Thayer, Jane Lancaster, Lou Johnson, Jim Johnson, Calvin Roetzel, Caroline Roetzel, Nina Verin, Jeff Nash, Anedith Nash, Jean Kruft, Andrew Bloom, David McCurdy, Carolyn McCurdy, Rachel Goldman, Ruth Warland, Dale Warland, Marty Rossmann, and Jack Rossmann. Laura Evans and Peggy Freudenthal made helpful comments on this manuscript. We are indebted to Bill Phillips whose editing, suggestions to improve the manuscript, and enthusiasm for this project were extremely valuable. We deeply appreciate the encouragement, ideas, and confidence in the project that Susan Lescher gave us.

Finally, this book would not have been possible without the contributions made by Barbara Spradley and Karen Veninga. We count them as our intellectual colleagues who participated in many discussions about our research and writing. They listened to us talk endlessly about job burnout; they critically evaluated our research ideas and suggested many improvements in the manuscript. Their faith in this book before it became a reality supported our efforts at every stage of the project.

Contents

Part One
The Nature
of Job Burnout

Chapter One
What Is Job
Burnout?

Sally Swanson, a thirty-eight-year-old mother of four, works as a bank teller in Des Moines, Iowa. Like many women, she feels the pressure of running a home, raising children, managing a job, and carving out leisure time for herself. "I did fine until we got a new supervisor last year," she says with an exhausted sigh. "Within two months I had started to burn out." Sally takes antacid pills several times a day. She worries that she may have an ulcer. "I feel as if he's looking over my shoulder all the time," she says. "He never has a good word to say to anyone. Sometimes the tension at the bank is so thick you could cut it with a knife."

Bob Mackler taught biology in a rural North Dakota high school for ten years. "With inflation and a teacher's salary, I saw my earning power going down, down, down. So I quit." Bob and his wife moved to Minneapolis, where he found a higher-paying position. He started as an assistant manager at a Wendy's Old-Fashioned Hamburger store. In a few months he had moved to associate manager and taken responsibility for supervising five assistant managers. "A year and a half later I was completely burned out," Bob told us a few weeks after he had resigned. "My wife and I had split up. I felt tired all the time and was drinking more than ever before. I had to work rotating shifts and usually put in more than fifty hours a week. I'd get off at midnight and some days have to open up at seven the next morning. I started getting headaches on my day off."

After three years as an executive secretary, Liz Keifer wants to quit. Jackson Electronics is a good company and she enjoys the status of working for the vice-president, but at twenty-six, Liz feels trapped in a demanding job that has lost its challenge. "In six months you can do this work blindfolded. After a year you realize you're making a lot of decisions your boss gets credit for. There's just no place to go on this job."

Like many college graduates, Liz feels overqualified. The job itself is only part of the reason she feels burned out. "I guess I'm partly to blame," Liz says philosophically. "The other secretaries who do the same things I do love their work. I guess I just didn't go to college to spend my life as somebody else's servant. For months I've been so tired when I come home I can only watch a little TV and then fall into bed exhausted." Liz told us she gets depressed frequently. She cries over inconsequential things. And that makes her angry at herself. "How would I feel if I had to do this job for the rest of my life? Never! Never! I'd go insane."

The Reverend Bill Hansen graduated from seminary twenty-five years ago. He has spent the last sixteen years at Treemont Methodist Church, where, except for a secretary and part-time youth minister, he carries all the responsibilities for parish activities. "I'm really running dry," he said in a quiet manner. "It's as if I've used up all I have in this church. I sometimes think I don't want to hear one more problem or preach one more sermon." Plagued by chronic fatigue, Mr. Hansen finds it increasingly difficult to make decisions, prepare sermons, and go to church dinners. "When I go home at night," he told us, "I'm too tired to move. There's tension all around my neck, down my shoulders, and over my arms."

Sally and Bob and Liz and Mr. Hansen make up only the tip of the job-burnout iceberg. "Down at the bank," says Sally Swanson, "some of the other employees seem more burned out than me." In both of his jobs, Bob Mackler observed the same symptoms. "Teacher burnout must have hit half the teachers in my high school; they had lost interest in kids and the subjects they taught. And now when I get together with other restaurant managers, about all we talk about is how burned out we are from our jobs." The secretaries at Jackson Electronics compare notes almost every day about their bosses' moods and angry outbursts that come from constant pressure. Bill Hansen said, "I know at least a dozen people in my congregation with serious problems caused by the stress of their jobs."

Many occupational hazards are limited to a few industries. Black-lung disease, for instance, strikes workers who spend their lives in coal mines. Radiation affects nuclear-power-plant workers. Job burnout, on the other hand, is not a job-specific hazard. It can devastate the lives of college professors and chimney sweeps. It can drain the energy of housewives and taxicab drivers. It can leave waitresses and corporation presidents feeling listless and unable to make the smallest decisions.

When we began our investigation of job stress more than a dozen years ago, we focused on Peace Corps volunteers and police officers. Both groups experience a high level of stress in their work. Then we turned to other occupations—more than one hundred in all. We talked to nurses, college professors, fishermen, painters, service-station attendants, veterinarians, window washers, psychologists, housewives, social workers, teachers, assembly-line workers, judges, counselors, prison guards, newspaper editors, and publishers—to name only a few of the other fields. We found that job burnout, while more prevalent in some occupations, cuts across all of them.

We had a single purpose in all of our scientific investigations: to get beneath the surface of everyday jobs, to probe the *feelings* people had about their work. We looked for the hidden meanings that work takes on for all of us. We sought to discover why some people suffered from job burnout while others, doing the same tasks, remained free of its symptoms. We studied how people cope with the frustrations of their jobs. In addition to anthropological fieldwork that involved on-the-job observations, we conducted in-depth interviews and asked people to fill out open-ended questionnaires. Our goal was not to study a random sample and make statistical generalizations; rather, we hoped to describe some of the cultural patterns associated with work in our society.

We wanted to identify the range of job pressures, trace out their consequences, and find out how people managed stress on the job.[1]

One of the most important facts revealed by our data, though not new, struck us with new urgency. It is simply that *your job can be hazardous to your health.* Stress in the workplace can give you negative fringe benefits you never bargained for. Physical illness. Emotional exhaustion. Ulcers. High blood pressure. Drinking too much. Headaches. Depression. In short, your job can burn you out. It can leave you listless and angry, upset with your spouse and kids, unable to enjoy your evenings and weekends. Like a thief in the night, work stress robs millions of workers of their health and happiness, then goes scot-free while the blame is laid elsewhere.

But we learned an equally important lesson from the people we studied: *you can avoid job burnout.* You can prevent the damage caused by unrelieved work stress. You can find ways to release the pressure. It's possible to humanize the workplace, to match people with jobs, to equip workers to cope with stress. Again and again we talked with people who had learned to live with high levels of stress in their jobs. They knew how to identify and avoid the hazard and had discovered ways to renew themselves. They were workers who lived in pressure-cooker jobs from eight to five, yet remained free from job-burnout symptoms.

In this book we will have a great deal to say about both of these findings. Drawing on the data from our own studies of job burnout, we hope to provide you with a clear understanding of this malady, as well as show you how to avoid it altogether or recover if you become a casualty. From time to time we will draw on the literally thousands of recent scientific studies related to work, stress, and health. Let's begin with a definition of job burnout.

Job Burnout: A Definition[2]

In this book job burnout refers to *a debilitating psychological condition brought about by unrelieved work stress, which results in:*

1. depleted energy reserves
2. lowered resistance to illness
3. increased dissatisfaction and pessimism
4. increased absenteeism and inefficiency at work.

This condition is debilitating because it has the power to weaken, even devastate, otherwise healthy, energetic, and competent individuals. Its primary cause is unrelieved stress, the kind that goes on day after day, month after month, year after year. It manifests itself in these four major symptom areas, ones we will look at briefly here, but examine in more detail in chapter 3.

Every kind of work creates some type of stress. You must work overtime to complete a report by a deadline imposed by someone else. You have to stand in the same two-by-three-foot area for eight hours a day, packaging tiny computer parts that come down the assembly line. You sit at your desk with nothing to do, watching the clock, unable to leave, unable to do what you would like. Each of these situations can place special demands on you—a stress to which you must respond. Some workers will find these stresses a challenge, even enjoyable, while others evaluate them in more negative terms.

For Sally Swanson, in her job as a bank teller, it was the unrelenting criticism of her supervisor that became a chronic irritant and stress. Bob Mackler's stress came, in part, from the fifty-five to sixty hours a week he spent at Wendy's. But more important, he continued to feel responsible even when not at work. On his day off he found himself calling in to see how things were going. The chronic nature of the pressure took its toll and, as Bob freely admitted, "I just burned out from that job." Both Bill Hansen and Liz Keifer felt the continuing stress that came from feeling trapped in jobs they had outgrown. Liz Keifer's frustration centered on an unchallenging job. Bill Hansen had come to doubt his own ability to find another church: "I feel used up here but don't see any hope of [being assigned to] another parish."

One of the first consequences of unrelieved work stress takes the form of depleted energy reserves. When people talk about burning out, they usually report feelings of exhaustion, weariness, loss of enthusiasm. They feel bone tired, when they go to bed and also when they wake up. A nurse told us, "I'm constantly preoccupied with the problems at work. I require more sleep and cannot drag myself out of bed in the morning." A purchasing agent confided, "I become emotionally exhausted and I just can't face going to work. I've even called in sick, just because I couldn't stand the thought of facing that place. I get depressed and forgetful." When your energy runs low, it can affect leisure-time activities. Bob Mackler loved to read books, but job burnout took away his interest, made his mind wander, and robbed him of his pleasure. "In three months I've only finished reading a couple chapters," he said, shaking his head.

Depleted energy reserves also can spoil your time with other people or wipe it out altogether. As the nurse mentioned above remarked, "I'm no fun to be with anymore." A middle-aged veterinarian said, "I used to enjoy playing with my son in the evening. Now I'm too tired. I get impatient with him. I just want to get alone."

The second result of the stress that causes job burnout is *lowered resistance to illness.* "I began to get more colds," said a school principal, reflecting on the start of his own experience of job burnout. This is a common complaint among those who suffer from job burnout, but more serious problems can follow. Dr. Carroll Brodsky, a physician at the University of California Medical School in San Francisco, studied the way work stress led to illness in prison guards and teachers. He found that two-thirds of those he studied suffered from diseases such as ulcers, hypertension, arthritis, and depression.[3]

Dr. Walter Menninger, senior staff psychiatrist at the Menninger Foundation, Topeka, Kansas, believes there is a clear relationship between stress and the aches and pains of everyday life. He says, "A chronic backache may signal the load is getting too heavy; the ulcer may suggest dealing with a situation you can't stomach. . . . Some degree of exhaustion is observed along with the development of other symptoms such as migraine headache, gastrointestinal upset, canker sores, and flu."[4]

The exact manner in which work stress lowers your resistance to illness and contributes to disease is not fully understood. Yet we do know that scientific studies have shown that stress is implicated in many serious illnesses. Take the nation's number-one killer: coronary heart disease. In one investigation, a group of experts rated overall stress of specialties in medicine, dentistry, and law, then studied the health records of professionals in these fields. They discovered that people in high-pressure jobs, such as trial lawyer and oral surgeon, not only smoked more (a stress-related activity), but had a higher incidence of coronary heart problems. In another study, tax accountants' cholesterol levels increased as the income-tax deadline drew near and their workloads increased. After work tapered off, cholesterol levels also declined. What they ate made little difference in this fluctuation. Another scientific study, this one of NASA personnel working on space flights, showed a direct relation between coronary-artery disease and stressful jobs. Researchers studied the health and work stress of managers, scientists, and engineers. The managers had to cope with the most work stress, especially in the form of conflict and overload. Among these three groups, the managers had a significantly higher incidence of coronary heart disease than the others.[5] Later, in chapter 3, we will examine more carefully how work stress increases our susceptibility to other illnesses as well.

The stress of job burnout also leads to *increased dissatisfaction and pessimism.* Again and again we found that as people lived with unrelieved stress, the jobs they once enjoyed turned sour. Many looked back wistfully to an earlier era of contentment with their work. A housewife suffering from job burnout said, "For the first five years I loved being a housewife. It was meaningful and fun, but that seems like a long time ago. Now when my husband comes home I'm ready to climb the walls. I get headaches almost every day. I feel guilty, but I just hate the feeling of being a trapped housewife." The head of personnel in a large company, who recognized his own symptoms of job stress, said, "I started noticing a definite change in how I felt about my job. Like staff meetings. I used to look forward to them eagerly, but now I dread them like the plague. I'm just too tired to put up with the hassles."

With amazing regularity we found that when people did learn to cope with work pressures, when they recovered from job burnout, their satisfaction level went up dramatically. A college professor is typical of many others. "I used to go around angry all the time at the administration of this college. I had lost my first love for students and for teaching. I came within a hair's breadth of giving it all up and trying some other career. I know now it was a case of burnout, and when I got that under control, my old enthusiasm returned. This college is a great place—and it really hasn't changed. But I sure have."

For many of those we studied, dissatisfaction had slowly turned to dark pessimism. We asked one sample of workers in a variety of occupations, "How would you feel if you had to continue your present job for the rest of your life?" Here are some of their candid answers, which reveal the tragedy of unrelieved stress:

- "I would be worn out at fifty."
- "Very depressed. Would probably require professional help."
- "I couldn't face it. I would be very depressed."
- "If my position were not to improve . . . I don't feel that I could stand it much longer, let alone for the rest of my life."
- "Horrible. I would feel pinned down, locked into a position where there would be very little sense of achievement."
- "I'd kill myself. I could not take it."
- "Totally defeated. There would be little to look forward to."

Finally, job burnout leads to *increased absenteeism and inefficiency at work.* This may occur because of actual stress-related illness or simply lowered morale. As Jerome Rosow, head of the Work in America Institute, says, "Workers who are turned off will stay out under any pretext."[6] In 1976, the Bureau of Labor Statistics reported that Americans lose 3.5 percent of work hours through absenteeism. It has been estimated that one out of three workers on any particular day has called in sick because of a stress-related problem.[7] And when job burnout sets in, even those days on the job are less efficiently spent. Workers under stress take longer coffee breaks, take longer to accomplish tasks, make more mistakes, and put off tasks that require immediate attention. Many observers see a direct link between job burnout and our national decline in worker productivity.

Job Burnout Isolation

When workers experience any of these symptoms, they often feel a sense of isolation. We have observed something akin to a cultural taboo against admitting to ourselves or others that a mere job has depleted our energy reserves, brought on severe headaches, or made us angry and dissatisfied. It's as if such an admission implies personal failure in one of life's most important activities. After all, work consumes nearly one-third of our lives and gives us one of our primary identities. No one wants to announce to others in so many words, "I can't handle my job anymore. I'm not a very competent person." The net result of this taboo against admitting we have become victims of work stress was summed up by one worker who said, "In this company it's an unwritten policy that you work together but burn out alone."

A trip to your family physician can also leave you feeling isolated and wondering if you've become a hypochondriac. We talked with numerous people who had experiences of this sort. Al Richardson worked as a copywriter for a large ad agency in Tucson. Deadline pressure and work overload took their toll and Al became tired, jumpy, and irritable. He found himself waking up at four or five in the morning, unable to get back to sleep. As the months dragged by, he found it increasingly difficult to come up with concepts or write the kind of copy he had produced in the past. At his wife's insistence, Al went in for a physical and talked to his doctor about his problems. "Can't find a thing wrong," said his doctor. "I think you're worrying too much. Maybe need a few days off." Because job burnout, at least in the beginning stages, involves more a *loss of health* than *the onset of a disease,* Al's doctor provided little help. Al went back to the office with little reassurance, questioning even more seriously what was wrong, why the others at work didn't seem to suffer as he did from the job.

Like Al, many workers suffering from job burnout have almost no way to find out if colleagues have similar problems. We have observed work groups where half a dozen people or more shared responsibilities, talked almost daily, yet suffered in silent isolation from one another. Work stress strikes far more people than most of us realize. In 1979, for example, the American Academy of Family Physicians released an extensive study of six occupations. They surveyed 4,473 people who worked as farmers, garment workers, business executives, secretaries, and teachers. The study sought to find out what percentage in each occupation experienced significant work stress. The number who usually or always worked under stress was startling:

> −80 percent of the business executives
> −66 percent of the teachers and secretaries
> −44 percent of the garment workers
> −38 percent of the farmers

These workers reported four typical kinds of job pressures: work overload, pressure from superiors, deadlines, and low salaries. Perhaps the most important finding of this study had to do with the effect of stress on health. Those workers who reported high levels of work stress had two, three, and even four times the number of health problems. They had allergies, migraines, backaches, nervousness, headaches, depression, insomnia, and other classic job-burnout symptoms.[8]

Another study, released in 1979 by the National Commission on Working Women, also showed that job burnout is not an uncommon problem. This study surveyed 150,000 women workers, 80 percent of whom fill clerical, service, and factory jobs. The results showed that the average woman worker is isolated and lonely. She works at a tedious, dead-end job. She feels trapped and seethes with frustration over her lot.

One of the most telling responses that pointed to job burnout among these women comes from the fact that 55 percent reported they had *absolutely no leisure time.* Exhausted from unfulfilling routine, they could not recoup their energy losses through rest or recreation. They could not use their off-the-job time for improving skills through education. Elizabeth Duncan Koontz, chair of the National Commission on Working Women, said, "These findings focus on the fact that most women have two jobs, the unpaid work goes on before, during, and after the paid work. Sometimes these double responsibilities keep women isolated and lacking in energy to solve their work-related problems."[9]

This book offers remedies for those workers feeling trapped, guilty, and alone, caught in their struggle with work stress. We hope to show not only the widespread nature of job pressures in our society but also ways to reduce your sense of isolation and any sense of personal failure that may accompany job burnout.

In the next two chapters we will diagnose both the causes and symptoms of job burnout. We begin with a careful examination of stress, our biologically inherited response patterns to stress, and why these response patterns no longer relieve the pressures and demands created by our jobs. Work stress, although the primary risk factor in job burnout, combines with several other risk factors, such as family stress and environmental demands, to create havoc for many people. A clear understanding of all the risk factors will give you a sound basis for coping with job burnout.

In our research we found that this condition can progress through five distinct stages, each with specific symptoms. If you want to deal effectively with work stress, understanding these stages is necessary; both prevention and treatment depend, in part, on how far job burnout has progressed. This discussion ends part 1 of the book and sets the stage for a detailed consideration of the treatment strategies.

In part 2, "The Treatment of Job Burnout: Personal Strategies," we want to examine specific ways you can relieve work stress. Each strategy lies within the power of almost any worker to employ. Indeed, most were discovered by asking ordinary people how they handled the stress, tension, and pressure that came from their jobs. Our goal is to provide you with strategies to help you control your responses to your job, rather than letting your job control you. We close this part of the book with an examination of the most common ineffective coping strategies. These constitute "blind alleys" that burned-out workers mistakenly believe will lead to relief of the symptoms of job burnout. In reality, they only lead to more advanced stages of the malady.

In part 3, "The Treatment of Job Burnout: Organizational Strategies," we will shift our attention from your *response* and focus on the ultimate *cause:* work stress itself. In addition to controlling your response to stress, it is also possible to get control of your job, to change the things that bring on tension. Oftentimes a very small adjustment in the workplace can lead to better jobs for whole groups of workers and increase productivity at the same time. We will show you how to identify the source of work stress in your job, how to deal with bosses who create frustration and strain, and how to cope with dead-end jobs. Finally, we will describe the special problems of those high-risk occupations called the "helping professions." Those who must take care of the needs of other people, such as social workers, teachers, nurses, physicians, dentists, counselors, psychiatrists, and attorneys, are more prone to job burnout than many others. We will examine the special nature of these occupations and point to specific treatment measures that can prevent job burnout.

In part 4, we have included a special chapter for those who seek to help someone suffering from job burnout. In our research we found that spouses, friends, and bosses, in their attempts to help someone caught in the throes of work stress, often contributed unwittingly to the problem. We will examine why this happens and give specific recommendations for effectively helping job burnouts.

Finally, we are quick to admit that the scientific study of job burnout has only begun.[10] Many researchers, from the fields of anthropology and primatology to medicine and public health, are searching for answers to many questions on work stress, our response to it, the nature of jobs, burnout symptoms, and strategies for treating this malady. We invite you to contribute to this ongoing investigation by participating in the National Job Burnout Survey presented in the last chapter.

Chapter Two
The Stress
Response

Job burnout results from unrelieved work stress. But the connection between such stress and our health problems does not yield a simple cause-and-effect model. For this reason many people remain puzzled and unconvinced that work stress causes their headaches, backaches, insomnia, ulcer, or hypertension. They continue to treat the symptoms and ignore the cause; in time, job burnout turns into a cluster of chronic diseases.

"Sure, I work under pressure," said one attorney. "But I've done that for years and this back problem only came on recently. All this stuff about work stress just doesn't add up in my case." A young housewife looked honestly puzzled. "I don't work under pressure at all," she said. "I even hire someone to do the heavy cleaning. It just doesn't make sense that my work at home could make me tired all the time." Some people think that because they enjoy their work it couldn't adversely affect their health. Others look around and see coworkers who live with the same work pressures, yet abound with energy and live free from burnout symptoms.

We've all heard the popular prescription that oversimplifies the work-stress connection. It says: "Stress is bad for you. It can affect your health, so slow down! You're working too hard, running too fast, burning the candle at both ends. If you don't take it easy you'll wear out." Although it may sound plausible, and even work in some cases, job burnout does not often follow the logic of this argument. Hard work, long hours, and even insufficient rest, *in themselves,* seldom lead to job burnout.

In this chapter we will show how work stress causes both physical and psychological distress. Understanding this work-stress connection is essential if you want to get control of job burnout. We must first examine the concept of stress and then our response to it.

Stress

We all engage in activities to meet our needs, fulfill our wants, and deal with the *normal demands* of life. We prepare food in order to eat; we wear cool clothing to avoid becoming overheated in warm weather; we balance the checkbook to stay within our budget; we fill the gas tank when the car runs low on fuel. We realize that certain demands are normal and develop routines for dealing with them.

But life seldom makes only normal demands. Unanticipated situations arise almost every day. We shall define stress as *anything that places an extra demand on you.* The demand requires an adjustment on your part. The car runs out of gas and you have to call and cancel the doctor's appointment. The extra demand required a change in plans. The bank calls to say you've overdrawn your checking account. You must now deal with this new situation. Gasoline supplies run low in your city and you have to wait for hours in long gas lines; the stress makes you tense and irritable.

Sheryl Tinkham works from nine to five every day, then hurries home to have dinner ready for the family by six o'clock. She has little trouble with this schedule, but now and then a stressful event occurs. One afternoon Sheryl's boss rushes up to her desk. "I need you to stay a couple hours later today and finish this report. The vice-president wants to see it before he leaves!" If Sheryl says no, her boss will explode. But

Sheryl's husband expects dinner to be cooked and on the table no later than six o'clock. Sheryl knows he will sulk all evening if she works overtime again. An extra demand is made on her; she feels caught, but must deal with this stress in some manner.

Some extra demands create stress because they block the satisfaction of basic human needs. Many forms of work stress operate in this manner. Working a double shift of sixteen hours can cut into your body's need for rest. So can working on a job that requires rotating shifts. If you have to work in a cramped, unventilated place, it can thwart your need for movement and oxygen. Working under any threat to your personal safety undercuts your security needs. In 1978, there were 60,000 acts of violence in our nation's schools, most of them against teachers. They ranged from threats of pulling off an elderly teacher's wig to rape and murder. A New York City schoolteacher describes this kind of stress: "It just isn't worth it. The classes are overflowing with kids who demand and deserve full-time attention. Staff morale is low. Then there is the pervasive threat of violence. Teaching is a twenty-four-hour occupation. I don't care how good you are, after seven to ten years you burn out."[1]

Stress can come with an extra wallop whenever a crisis occurs. After fifteen years as foreman, Jim Shelton found himself unemployed when the meat-packing plant where he worked closed down. Two hundred others also lost their jobs. The unsettling event created the most tension and anxiety Jim had experienced since he had divorced his first wife more than twenty years earlier. Here's how he described it: "It was as if the bottom dropped out of all my plans. I started looking for a new job and, at my age, it was one of the toughest things I'd ever done."

Some stress events place special demands on us even though we anticipate them. Your father has a weak heart and you've worried about him for years. Then he has a heart attack and, after three months in the hospital intensive-care unit, he dies. All the grief and mixed emotions you feel represent some of your reactions to this stress event. It will take months, perhaps years, to adjust to the death of such a close relative, even though it was anticipated.

The extra demands of life that we call stress come in bright, cheerful colors as well as dark, somber ones. You've looked forward to a promotion for three years, expecting it to come, wanting the higher salary, the new responsibilities. Then the good news arrives and you move up the company ladder. Nevertheless, the promotion does place new demands on you and constitutes a major stress.

Alex Haley, author of *Roots,* worked more than twelve years researching and writing his bestselling book. The enormous success, though something he had worked hard to achieve, placed extra and often overwhelming demands on him. Reflecting on that experience in an interview with Jeffrey Elliot, Alex Haley said, "I hope to God I never have anything like the *success* of *Roots* happen to me again."[2] Any positive experience, when it places new demands on us that require an adjustment, will involve stress. In order to understand work stress and its role in job burnout, we must recognize that things we seek and enjoy have as much power as things we shun and dislike. Your body can't tell the difference between going to the dentist or falling in love, between being promoted or losing your job. When stress occurs, the stress response is never far behind.

How the Stress Response Works

One of the most remarkable discoveries of modern science is that human beings have a general response to all forms of stress. Your body switches on the stress response whether you suffer from third-degree burns or receive an eviction notice. The pattern follows a similar course and it has a single goal: *to bring relief from the stress.* The stress response has evolved over millions of years and gives us, along with other mammals, a definite survival advantage.

During an earlier period of human existence, many daily stresses posed a direct threat to survival. One's life depended on an appropriate response executed with the greatest speed. The vast majority of strategies used by the earliest humans for dealing with threat depended on *muscular activity.* Like our primate ancestors before them, early hunter-gatherers depended exclusively on immediately available natural resources. They roamed about within a specific territory, chasing game animals, moving with wet and dry seasons to sources of food and water, fighting off predators, and protecting themselves against severe weather. The ability to use physical strength, speed, agility, and stamina was an important selective advantage. Through the long process of evolution, human beings came to share with other mammals this generalized stress response. It seeks to bring relief from stress *by means of vigorous muscular activity.*

Dr. Walter Cannon, an American physiologist, initiated the study of this stress response during the 1920s. Scientific research since then has supported the general outline of his theory, although we now know far more about the biochemical nature of this response pattern. Dr. Cannon called it the "fight-or-flight" response. He argued that it played an important role in survival. "If fear always paralyzed it would result in danger of destruction," he wrote. "But fear and aggressive feeling, as anticipatory responses to critical situations, make ready for action and thereby they have had great survival values."[3]

The stress response actually involves four closely related processes. It begins when your body undergoes a rapid *mobilization,* a preparation for muscular activity. Consider the stress response of Ron Dorsey, a patrolman on the graveyard shift of a large city police department. On a cold night in January 1979, shortly after three o'clock, a call came over his radio. "Burglary in process at Sixteen hundred Grand Avenue." "That's mine!" he shouted to himself and at the same instant felt his heart begin to pound. Tense with fear, even though he had been on the force for six years, Ron sped to the address, an apartment building a few blocks away. As he skidded into the snow-covered alley behind the apartment, he saw a dark figure rush out the back door, dash across the alley, and run between two houses. "Stop or I'll shoot!" Ron yelled as he jumped from his car and started after the person. "I had no intention of shooting," Ron admitted later, "but I wanted to scare that guy into stopping." And stop he did, hands high in the air.

In a moment Ron had him pushed up against the side of the house, frisked him for weapons, and then walked him back to his patrol car where he radioed for help. Less than four minutes had passed since Ron had first heard the call.

Like all of us under stress, Ron was keenly aware of his feelings, thoughts, and actions—what we call the behavioral aspects of the stress response. However, hidden from view, a host of endocrine and autonomic-nervous-system functions had also taken place. A dramatic biochemical change had coursed through Ron's body. Hundreds of scientific studies have confirmed that the human body, anticipating the necessity of fight or flight, begins to mobilize almost instantly. And this happens whether you're chasing a criminal, denied a promotion, working under unrealistic deadlines, or ground down by an autocratic boss. This biochemical mobilization stands at the very heart of the burnout process.

It all starts in the hypothalamus, a tiny bundle of nerve cells at the center of the brain. Messages race from that command post and spread the alarm throughout the nervous system. Muscles tense. Blood vessels constrict. The tiny capillaries under the skin shut down altogether. The pituitary gland sends out two hormones that move through the bloodstream to stimulate the thyroid and adrenal glands. Thyroid hormones increase the energy supply you need to cope physically with the stress. The adrenals send some thirty additional hormones to nearly every organ in the body. This automatic stress response causes the pulse rate to shoot up; blood pressure soars. The stomach and intestines stop all the busy activity of digestion. Hearing and smell become more acute. Hundreds of other physical changes occur without us even knowing it.

The second process, one which starts immediately, is a sharp *increase in energy consumption.* The alarm reaction that puts the entire body in a state of readiness burns up considerable energy. That's why, in the aftermath of an auto accident or other sudden stress, even people who suffered no injuries will feel completely drained. It also helps to explain why people can sometimes perform feats of exceptional strength in stress situations. Ron Dorsey's body began to burn up energy at a rapid rate the moment he received the call. His feelings of lassitude from several hours of dull routine disappeared with the changes in body chemistry.

Dr. Hans Selye, the pioneering endocrinologist and father of stress research, believes that under stress we use up a special fuel source, what he calls "adaptation energy."[4] This energy provides power to mobilize the body; it also appears to give us strength for the fight-or-flight reaction. The way our body consumes this adaptation energy is critical to our understanding of job burnout. After four decades of stress research, Dr. Selye concluded that each human being has a finite amount of adaptation energy available at the time we encounter stress. After burning up part or all that is available, we need an opportunity to replenish the available supply by removing ourselves from the stress. When stress continues for a prolonged period, the available adaptation energy burns up and exhaustion sets in.

The third process that makes up part of our stress response is the *muscular action involved in fight or flight.* All the mobilization and energy consumption has this end in sight: taking some vigorous action to eliminate or escape the stress. The fight-or-flight adaptation worked well for early human beings, and it works well for us today, but only in certain situations. Taking quick and skillful action enabled Ron Dorsey to apprehend a suspected criminal. His stress response could hardly have been designed to carry out its job more efficiently. If you've ever had to jump out of the way of an oncoming automobile, swerve or hit your brakes to avoid a collision, stay up all night with a sick child, or rush someone to a hospital emergency room, you know the value of the fight-or-flight response.

Finally, the stress response ends with the *return of the body to a state of equilibrium.* Within a few hours Ron was back on the street, cruising in his patrol car. He felt tired but relaxed. That morning Ron went to bed early and slept for nine hours. He woke up feeling great. His adaptation energy had been renewed. Once again he was prepared to respond calmly to emergency situations. During the next few days, his body would continue to build up the supply of adaptation energy. Fortunately, nature has designed these relatively stable periods, including sleep, to restore our adaptation-energy level, leaving us prepared for future stress.

Is the Stress Response Obsolete?

For millions of years the success of the human fight against stress has depended on a single battle plan: *relieve stress by fight or flight.* This single strategy remains with us today, deeply etched into our genetic code. Whether effective or not for a particular stress, our bodies automatically mobilize, consume adaptation energy, and urge us to take some vigorous physical action.

At the same time, we live in a radically different world from the one experienced by early humans. Machines have replaced muscle power in almost every conceivable task, from washing clothes to constructing buildings. Work has become highly specialized. In the United States there are more than 30,000 different kinds of jobs, each with its own form of stress. Every day millions of people encounter threats to their well-being, such as sex discrimination, excessive overtime, deadline pressure, assembly-line boredom, too little work, emotional overload from client problems, uncertainty about job security, a boss who grinds them down, health hazards in the workplace, and many more. Yet in every different type of job and each particular kind of work stress, we all share the same standard response. We are living in the Space Age, with all its novel forms of stress, equipped with only our Stone Age biochemistry and physiology to contend with them.

Consider the work of air-traffic controllers. In this occupation we can see how our biological fight-or-flight response has not evolved to keep pace with our changing social institutions. Their work demands constant vigilance, but hardly more muscular activity than pressing a button or focusing their eyes; yet, one mistake could result in the death of hundreds in an air crash. Every tiny light that blips across the radar screen has to be watched. Controllers have to clear a never-ending stream of jets for landing and take off, sometimes with pea-soup fog shrouding the runways.

One air-traffic controller watched in horror as a Boeing 747 missed a commuter airliner at Washington's National Airport by less than 100 feet. His body, which had mobilized again and again in the face of the continual stream of smaller stresses, seemed to leap into high gear as it prepared for fight or flight. Yet the last thing he could do at that moment was run from the control tower or engage in any kind of aggressive activity. He described the way the stress and his innate response to it made him feel: "My stomach was up against my backbone. I began to perspire profusely. My mouth and throat were desert dry. Sharp and tingling sensations were shooting up my spine to my brain, which seemed to be saying, 'Run, run.' But I had other traffic to direct. . . . While driving home I was distraught and tears rolled down my cheeks while I recalled my part in the near tragedy. At home I consumed too much liquor for several days. . . . Two months passed before I really regrouped. The incident was in my dreams for several weeks."[5]

Studies of air-traffic controllers have revealed a higher than usual incidence of advanced job-burnout symptoms, including hypertension and peptic ulcers. One study revealed that air-traffic controllers working at extremely busy airports such as Kennedy International and O'Hare had significantly higher blood pressure than those who cleared runways at airports in Topeka and Chattanooga.[6] As stress increases, mobilization occurs more frequently, draining our reserves of adaptation energy.

We believe that our stress response has become obsolete and this is the basic cause of job burnout. Work stress goes unrelieved for several reasons. First, on many jobs, workers experience long-term stress because their innate fight-or-flight response has been rendered ineffective. The stress goes on year after year; nothing provides the necessary interruption so they can restore themselves. Second, because every form of work stress stimulates our biochemical response, our bodies experience the energy-draining mobilization again and again. It may happen once a day or dozens of times, depending on the stress. However, the modern workplace allows little room for vigorous physical activity. Prodded into a state of readiness in the face of stress, we must then remain inactive, never discharging the tension that has built up. As Dr. David

Hamburg has observed, "The net effect seems to be that the contemporary human organism frequently gets mobilized for exertion but ends up doing little or nothing—preparation for action, without action. . . . These stress responses may be less useful than they once were, and in some circumstances may actually be harmful."[7] Third, although scientific research has uncovered strategies for coping effectively with work stress, many people ignore them or don't realize they exist. These strategies aim to give people control over their jobs and also to live more in harmony with their Stone Age biochemistry. We will examine many of them in parts 2 and 3 of this book.

Because each of us must live with an obsolete stress-response mechanism, we face the everpresent danger of living also with a magnitude of unrelieved stress. Perhaps the most stressful job invented by modern man is that of the combat soldier. The way unrelieved stress has affected men in combat gives us an important lesson on how other kinds of stress can lead to job burnout.

Unrelieved Stress and Combat Fatigue

The stress of military combat often results in using up all available adaptation energy and brings on serious health problems. The stress of combat has had disastrous effects during most American wars. And for too long it went unrecognized. During the Civil War, doctors diagnosed those who collapsed as suffering from "nostalgia." Thousands of soldiers were afflicted. Without sign of injury they simply could not continue fighting. The most severe cases were discharged as "insane" or having "paralysis."

The trench warfare of World War I brought new horrors. When large numbers of men developed symptoms of fatigue, it mystified army physicians. They concluded that these men suffered from "shell shock," brain damage caused by the loud concussion of explosives above the trenches. During World War II, psychiatrists rejected the shell-shock theory. They diagnosed the hundreds of men who collapsed in battle as mentally ill. They had "combat psychoneurosis." Intensive studies of these casualties revised the diagnosis again. The experts then discovered what almost any combat soldier could have told them: the problem was *combat fatigue.*

Job burnout has had a similar history of misunderstanding. Physician and layman alike have referred to it as a "character weakness," the mark of a "sickly individual," or a "nervous breakdown." In some cases, one of the symptoms of burnout becomes the focus of attention. We say that "John has an ulcer," or "Marvin is an insomniac," or "Fred is lazy and an unreliable employee." All these labels, because they ignore the destructive power of unrelieved stress, often lead to placing blame on the individual. They seldom provide a solution. But once we recognize that such diverse problems are part of a "burnout syndrome" with a specific underlying cause, prevention and cure become possible.

It wasn't until the Vietnam War that the United States armed forces made significant breakthroughs in dealing with combat fatigue. How did this come about? They recognized that burning out on the battlefield came from *unrelieved stress;* this opened up avenues for relieving the pressure. Jungle fighting in Vietnam created the usual combat stress. However, most operations lasted for a relatively short period of time, only a few days in many cases. Within minutes helicopters whisked exhausted soldiers back to base for hot showers, steak and baked potatoes, movies, and access to the PX. Unrelieved combat stress became a thing of the past. The tour of duty in Vietnam never lasted longer than thirteen months, and every soldier had a week's vacation outside of Vietnam during that time. Up to 1969, with half a million servicemen in Vietnam, the incidence of combat fatigue was less than one hundred cases per year. This dramatic reduction in a debilitating stress disease that had baffled army physicians in previous wars came about by relieving the chronic nature of the stress. It prevented the soldiers from burning up all their immediately available adaptation energy. It also gave them periods away from the stress to restore their supply of available adaptation energy.

This experience with combat fatigue holds an important lesson for those struggling with job burnout. Although work stress seldom reaches the intensity of combat stress, it does go on month after month without relief. It is the continuous nature of stress that, in part, bankrupts your life and leads to all the symptoms associated with both combat fatigue and job burnout. But if you can take the pressure off, even for brief periods, you can increase your chances of avoiding a personal energy crisis. We shall return to this insight later when we discuss personal strategies for coping with job burnout.

Job-Burnout Risk Factors

Although we have argued that our obsolete stress response is the underlying cause of job burnout, that only takes us partway to an understanding of this malady. Since we all come into the world endowed with this fight-or-flight response, we still don't know why some people burn out and others do not. This brings us again to unrelieved stress: those exposed to prolonged periods of unrelieved work stress run a high risk of suffering from job burnout.

But, you may ask, why do some people exposed to work stress burn out, and others do not? In our research we observed cases where two individuals worked under the same stressful job conditions, yet one experienced job burnout and the other did not. In searching for an explanation of this, we had to shift away from thinking about single causes to examining a number of risk factors that affect the incidence of job burnout.

The way heart specialists understand coronary-artery disease can provide us with a useful model for understanding burnout. Probably everyone who reads this book has had his life touched by our nation's number-one health problem, heart disease. When someone we know has a heart attack, we all wonder what caused it.

Mr. Jones retired at age sixty-five after years on the assembly line at the Chrysler plant in Detroit. Before retirement he had paid for a tiny lot on a lake in northern Michigan; now he looked forward to building a cabin and enjoying endless hours of fishing. With help from his son he poured the foundation and erected the walls. Cross-beams went into place and the outline of inner rooms took shape. Eager to shut out the driving rain of the north woods, Mr. Jones undertook the job of nailing shingles on the roof by himself. After a morning of carrying bundles of asphalt shingles up the ladder and pounding nails in the hot sun, he collapsed near the steps of his half-completed cabin. An hour later at a small country hospital, Mr. Jones was pronounced dead of a heart attack.

"What caused it?" his son asked the attending physician.

"He had a massive myocardial infarction. His heart stopped because the muscle became starved for oxygen; it couldn't get enough blood to function properly." The physician shook his head sadly as Mr. Jones's son told of his father's dreams of retirement.

But the family and friends, unsatisfied with the doctor's answer, continued to ask the same question: What caused his heart attack? One member of the family, a nurse, added to the explanation: "It's really the coronary artery, the blood vessel that supplies the heart muscle. It becomes clogged and that causes the heart attack. If you can discover it early enough, it's sometimes possible to replace that artery in a process called "coronary-bypass surgery." But no one suspected that Bill Jones had any problems with clogged arteries.

The question is carried one step further: What caused the artery to become clogged? Too much cholesterol, a fatty substance found in many foods and produced by our bodies. It forms plaques on the walls of the blood vessels, restricting the flow of blood. Maybe Bill Jones's diet, always rich in such high-cholesterol foods as red meat, eggs, and cheese, caused his heart attack. And what about smoking? Yes, Bill had smoked for years, and that has a damaging effect on the heart. Overexertion could also be blamed; after all, Bill Jones was not in any condition to try the roofing job by himself. How can we find our way out of this maze of multiple causes? Can we ever find the one responsible?

Researchers who specialize in the study of heart disease no longer think in terms of single causes.[8] They seek instead to identify "risk factors," those things that together affect the human heart. Each risk factor varies from high to low; two packs of cigarettes a day means high risk; abstinence from smoking means low risk. But single risk factors in themselves can't cause a heart attack or give immunity. That's why most of us have heard of chain smokers who live well into their nineties. Risk factors always work in combination. The primary risk factors implicated so far in the case of heart disease include:

1. high cholesterol level
2. high blood pressure (hypertension)
3. cigarette smoking
4. overweight
5. lack of exercise
6. overexertion
7. advanced age
8. family history of heart disease
9. insufficient vitamin B-6
10. stress

We also know that men in our society have a higher risk of heart disease than women. Some studies also indicate that moderate drinking of alcoholic beverages lowers your risk of a heart attack. In the future we can expect more risk factors to join the list.

Let's go back to job burnout, that debilitating psychological condition brought about by unrelieved stress. The primary risk factors that will increase your chances of burning out are well documented by scientific research. No single risk factor can lead to burnout by itself. That's why we all know individuals who work at highly stressful jobs who do not burn out. Conversely, if you have a low-stress job, it does not give you immunity to burnout. The primary risk factors include:

1. individual perception of stress
2. family pressures
3. environmental demands
4. work problems
5. faulty stress safety valves

Although unrelieved stress stands as the basic cause of burnout, in the same way that a blocked coronary artery causes a heart attack, these risk factors take us farther down the road to understanding burnout. As we will see, each risk factor contains within it powerful forces which, if left unattended, will dissipate our adaptation energy. Let's look more closely now at each one.

Individual Perception of Stress

Each person learns to see the world through "stress-colored glasses." But the character of the lens differs for each of us so that an event that brings intense, unrelieved stress for one individual may affect another in only minor ways. John and Fred both worked for a large manufacturing firm for more than twenty-five years, rising together to responsible management positions. They retired in the same year and both had to adjust to the stress and demands of this change. But John perceived this change as a new opportunity; Fred saw it as a great loss. One would hardly know they had experienced the same event. During his lifetime, John had acquired a consuming interest in photography. Evenings and weekends found him roaming the countryside photographing birds and wildlife or locked in his basement darkroom developing pictures. He never found enough time to enter photo contests or try to market his best pictures. Retirement meant endless days of sharpening his skill and enjoying his hobby. Fred had no hobbies; his life had been devoted exclusively to his family and his job. He spent hours with his children as they grew up, then with his grandchildren. But in the year before retirement, both his sons and their families moved to large cities more than three thousand miles away. For months after retirement Fred was at a loss. It was two years before he began to find new interests and adapt to his change in status.

Every culture teaches people what to define as stressful, what to interpret as a minor adjustment. Even such a profound experience as the death of an infant can have different meanings. For an American couple, if their infant daughter dies, it will be one of the most shattering, stressful events they will ever experience. But for an Australian aborigine, the death of an infant merely postpones the day it will enter the human family. This tribe of people believes that the soul of the infant merely returns to the "churinga," or common world of spirits, to await a better time to be born. On the basis of this deeply held religious belief, a mother may put her newborn child to death if she has another infant to feed. The stress associated with death and infanticide depends upon our cultural background and how we have learned to perceive these events.

Our "stress-colored glasses" influence the way we perceive stress on the job or in the family. Not all assembly-line workers are bored by the time-paced monotony. Not all air-traffic controllers find the tension of clearing runways during stormy weather a dreaded task. In 1971, the *Wall Street Journal* set out to find the most "physically draining and mentally numbing" jobs. Working at a foundry furnace, selling subway tokens, lifting lids on a steel-mill oven, and removing the hair and fat from hog carcasses headed their list. Yet some people in all these jobs enjoyed the challenge of their work and did not perceive them as highly stressful. Manuel Decena of San Antonio can clean a hog carcass in forty-five seconds. And he beams with pride at the fact that most men couldn't even hold their breakfast down if they tried it.[9]

Our perception of stress directly affects the burnout process. As we will see in later chapters, almost anyone can alter her perceptions of stress events. We can learn to redefine retirement, the loss of a loved one, even the dead-end job, and thereby reduce the stress. Some people who are especially prone to burnout seem to write "disaster" over every unwanted event at home and at work.

In June of 1979, thousands of people across the United States were forced to wait in long gas lines. This single event was perceived in hundreds of different ways, resulting in varying degrees of stress. For some, it was a time to visit cheerily with others caught in the same predicament. Others felt ground down by the frustration of waiting. One man in California struck a pregnant woman who he thought had crowded in front of him. Another man in New York saw his car sideswiped by a driver trying to get ahead of him. He perceived this event as the height of injustice, leaped from his car with a gun, and killed the driver who had damaged his car.

Our perception of stress is a major risk factor in burning out. High stress perceivers will find less relief and burn out more easily; low stress perceivers run less risk. But this is only one risk factor, and we must always consider the way all factors work together. The next three risk factors are the primary sources of pressure: family pressures, environmental demands, and work problems.

Family Pressures

Families are alive and well in our country, despite dire predictions that they would become unimportant. For most of us, what happens in our families brings great joy as well as the most intense forms of stress. Conflict between husband and wife, arguments with teenage children, failing health of a parent, adjusting to new schools, feeling isolated in a new neighborhood, and death of a family member can all bring unrelieved stress. Family pressures inevitably affect our lives at work and vice versa. Sometimes we can't tell which came first, work stress or family pressure. The pharmacist who worked in a big city hospital and blamed his job for burning him out confided, "The pharmacy where I work is open twenty-four hours a day, three hundred and sixty-five days a year and it requires that many various shifts be covered. My wife finds it hard to accept that once a month I work an evening and weekend shift. All I can tell her is she shouldn't have married a pharmacist."

Liz Keifer, whom we discussed in chapter 1, felt trapped by her secretarial job, but her mother's long bout with cancer and her eventual death meant long months of additional stress. Even as she worked through her own grief, she realized that family pressures had not disappeared. Her aging father now depended on her more than she wanted, hampering her plans to move to another town and find a better job. In her case, family pressures and work stress jointly contributed to burnout.

In a far-reaching study of stress, Dr. Thomas Holmes in the department of psychiatry at the University of Washington Medical School set out to identify the most stressful life events that people face. He asked thousands of people to rate the events most frequently reported, thus discovering a yardstick for measuring their intensity. Among the fifteen most stressful events (out of a total list of forty-three), the majority involved family pressures. Death of a husband or wife, marital separation, death of a close family member, getting married, changes in the health of a family member, pregnancy, and gaining a new family member were rated by most people as the most difficult stresses.[10]

As children progress through the normal stages of life, new family pressures emerge. In some cultures adolescence is a time of relative tranquillity as children begin working alongside their parents, assuming adult roles. In our society, physical maturity occurs years before we allow our youth to assume social maturity, and the conflicts often become translated into family stress. Many young men and women strike out to gain an adult identity in ways that anger and frighten their parents. Tension within the family represents a major stress point for many people. If not controlled, this risk factor can undermine one's health and well-being.

Environmental Demands

Beyond the family and our lives at work, all of us are connected to the wider social and physical environment. The government raises taxes and we feel the pinch. Gas shortages occur and we have to wait in long lines. We look forward to Memorial Day weekend after a long, cold winter and thunderstorms ruin our camping trip. All of us encounter such short-term stresses that come from the wider environment: impersonal, beyond our control, yet they can invade our lives and create unrelieved stress.

Up until the accident in early 1979, George and Molly Anderson saw the Three Mile Island nuclear-power plant as a boon to the local economy. "Radioactive wastes" and "reactor meltdown" were words that never entered their vocabulary. Then the warnings came, a few days after they had planted a large vegetable garden. Molly, three months pregnant, left town immediately to stay with her parents in Boston, taking the two children with her. George stayed behind for two days even though their house was less than three miles from the power plant. Then he joined Molly and their children. They read the papers and watched the television news, and slowly the enormity of the problem swept over them. Should they go home? Had they already been exposed to radioactive fallout? Would it affect their unborn baby? Could they eat the food from their garden? Should they go back to their home or move away? The tension went on month after month, eating away at their energy, leaving them frustrated, anxious, worried, and angry. George lost money because he had to miss work. They both watched their young children for any signs of illness. Their anxiety subsided somewhat after Nancy was born six months later, but then a new fear arose: could radiation have caused some birth defect missed by the doctor? Unrelieved stress engulfed their lives because of an environmental change—the Three Mile Island accident. And this risk factor pushed both George and Molly closer to burnout. It increased both family pressures and work stress. It had become a major risk factor.

Environmental demands often influence the level of work stress. In May of 1979, diesel-fuel prices skyrocketed. One independent truck driver recalled, "I stopped at this truck stop, got a bite to eat, and when I came out to fill up, the price of diesel had jumped three cents a gallon." The first week in June the price rose by nine cents a gallon and supplies became increasingly short. Independent truckers, restricted by government regulations from passing the increase on for thirty days, felt the stress. Even a change in the regulation that shortened the time to ten days cut deeply into their profits. Three hundred truckers parked their semis on all lanes of the Indiana toll road trying to get their message to government officials. One driver angrily told a news camera, "We tried to do it the right way but people just ignore you. They step on you. It's just the dumb truck driver going down the highway!"

Work Problems

Even without the added pressures of rising prices, diesel shortages, and nuclear disasters, most jobs involve some stress. In many ways, the small but continuous frustrations of our jobs have more power to cause burnout than the dramatic, short-term stresses. Most jobs do not carry the stress of a combat zone or an airport control tower. But small doses of stress, if unrelieved, can build up and produce a toxic effect.

During the last decade, the U.S. Department of Labor conducted three nationwide studies on work conditions, including stress.[11] All three studies probed twelve kinds of work problems, such as health hazards, sex discrimination, age discrimination, and excessive overtime. In 1969, the year of the first study, 85 percent of all workers reported problems in one or more areas. By 1970, that figure had risen to 90 percent, and the most recent study, released in 1978, revealed that 95 percent had problems in one or more areas of work.

One kind of work stress often overlooked is too little stimulation. A senior secretary said, "Ultimately my work isn't very responsible, my tasks are unimportant. This job doesn't challenge me enough. I view my job as a still life. It moves neither forward nor backward but is always basically the same. It provides me few opportunities for growth."

The assembly line, the dull, routine factory job, the work of a housewife can all create the stress of *understimulation.* The housewife, bored at home with nothing to do, can be the same bundle of nerves at the end of the day as her husband who comes home after a frantic day in his executive office. Both of them can burn out from very different forms of job stress. Dr. Robert Seidenberg, a psychiatrist, found that suburban housewives dreaded the dullness of their secure, stable lives. The daily "eventlessness" was as stressful to them as performing a ten-hour open heart surgery was to a cardiac surgeon.[12]

Faulty Stress Safety Valves

Faulty stress safety valves, or an insufficient number of them, make up the last job-burnout risk factor. Most people have some safety valves, even if only to get angry and complain to a friend or spouse. Those who run a higher risk of job burnout have developed far fewer ways to release the pressures that build up from stress and don't seem to make good use of the stress safety valves they do have.

When our primal stress response is triggered, the mobilization process creates many different tensions within our bodies. The skeletal muscles tense in readiness for strenuous action. Emotions of fear and anger well up within us. Rapid breathing, increased pulse rate, and the dramatic changes in body chemistry add to an overall sense of tension and readiness. Faulty safety valves do not adequately release these bottled-up feelings. They don't allow for relaxation of muscles. They restrict our ability to release all the other pressures that build up. If you work on a job where stress occurs over and over again throughout the day, a single safety valve such as a drink in the evening falls far short of serving your needs. This risk factor is one of the most important because people can repair their faulty stress safety valves and add many new ones by changing their life-style, a point we will return to frequently in the last half of this book.

There are hundreds of potential stress safety valves, some more constructive than others: meditation, physical exercise, support from friends, reading, blaming others for failure, a change of activity, prayer, crying, vacations, eating, drinking, sleeping. A supervisor in a public health department told us, "On the way home from work I do therapy with myself. I say: 'It's just your job!' I don't believe a damn word of it but it does help."

Let's sum up the way these job-burnout risk factors work. It's as if each of us lives connected to a complex system of pipes and pressure valves. Unrelieved stress builds up from family pressures, work problems, and environmental demands. Our stress response, stimulated by each stress, mobilizes us for fight or flight over and over again. The tensions build. Our perceptions can raise or lower all these pressures, as can our ability to make effective use of multiple safety valves. Because families, our jobs, and the world in which we live constantly change, all of us face the danger of burning out. Yet no one needs to experience the debilitating symptoms of this condition. In the next chapter we will look more closely at the progression of symptoms through the stages of job burnout.

Chapter Three
Stages of Job Burnout

Like the human life cycle, job burnout goes through distinct stages. It begins when your stress response mobilizes your body so frequently in the face of chronic work stress that you deplete available adaptation energy. This can happen a few weeks into a new and demanding job or after twenty years working on an old job. In our research we discovered that this malady progresses through five basic stages, each more serious than the last. However, no two people experience these stages of job burnout in exactly the same way. One person might stay in one of the early stages for many years, then rapidly progress to a later crisis stage. Another will move quickly through all five stages, then recover and remain free from job burnout symptoms the rest of his life.

Although we observed a strong tendency for certain symptoms to occur in each stage, wide individual variations exist. One person begins to have mild tension headaches during an early stage; another doesn't get headaches at all; still another has painful migraine headaches that start in a late stage of job burnout. These individual variations in the way we go through the stages, as well as differences in symptoms, make it all too easy to ignore job burnout and only treat one or another symptom. Job burnout is a complex but elusive condition. No lab test can reveal it. You can't look in the mirror for a rash or other evidence. You can't tell simply by the fact that you have a high-stress job; low to moderate work stress can lead to burnout if you haven't learned to handle it. If you want to cope with this malady effectively, you will need to have a broad picture of the stages it goes through and the symptoms that tend to appear at each stage.

Consider a married couple, each caught in a struggle with job burnout, yet each at a different stage with different symptoms. Seven years ago Jeanette and Carter Nicholson met during their last year of graduate school at the University of Washington. The award of PhD's and marriage came in the same week. "We decided to take the first job that either of us found; the other could look for work in that city." Carter dreamed of teaching at a prestigious Big Ten University, but when Jeanette was offered a position first, at the University of Indiana, they moved to Bloomington. A few months later Carter landed a job with Bell Telephone; he's in charge of management-training programs for middle-level executives. With each year that passed, his salary rose steadily, while nothing opened up at the university. He slowly accepted the fact that he would remain an industrial psychologist.

Unlike teaching, Carter's job involves constant deadlines. He plans meetings, lectures at training conferences in other cities, and tries to live within a tight travel budget. He has two weeks' vacation a year. Unrelieved stress grew steadily from his first year on the job. Fired by feelings of resentment at missing out on a university position, Carter's own lack of adequate safety valves added fuel to the slow, smoldering fires of job burnout. After seven years he feels trapped by a demanding job; in reality he is trapped by the most serious stage of job burnout. He suffers from irregular heartbeats, a chronic peptic ulcer, and high levels of muscle tension.

Jeanette, Carter's wife, also feels burned out. Together they work hard at "trying to juggle two careers, raise two kids, and enjoy some family life." Even though they share many of the same frustrations, Jeanette and Carter are burning out in different ways, for different reasons, with different symptoms, and at different rates of speed.

Jeanette gets headaches and has trouble sleeping; Carter fights the tension that knots his stomach and makes him irritable. He struggles with bouts of depression and can't remember when he wasn't plagued by emotional exhaustion. "When I fall way behind and things start exploding around the office, my heart starts skipping beats like it's trying to catch up."

Jeanette has burned out several times before; Carter is well into the job-burnout process, but it's his first experience with the problem. Each time Jeanette starts to burn out she quickly changes gears, cuts back on committee work at the university where she teaches English literature, and recovers before the process goes very far. For the past three months the early warning signals, headaches and insomnia, have set Jeanette in motion making plans to cut her losses. For Carter, several years have passed since job burnout actually began. He used up his adaptation energy slowly, ignored the early warning signals, and now has fallen prey to an advanced stage of job burnout.

The Nicholsons recognize that, like many dual-career families, they have a high-pressured life-style. Both seek challenging, stress-filled experiences; any other way of life would bore them. But when pressures won't let up, they respond in sharply contrasting ways. Jeanette talks about her problems, feels discomfort quickly, and swings into action to get her life back in order. Carter, on the other hand, even though he knows a great deal about work stress and how to deal with it, becomes moody and withdrawn. This upsets Jeanette, who unwittingly adds to his stress by nagging him, "Don't just sit there and mope; do something!"

The Nicholsons have yet to grasp the most significant fact about their situation: they are at different stages in the burnout process. What works for Jeanette's mild job burnout won't help Carter's more advanced case. If they knew how to locate themselves in the stages of job burnout, they could not only adopt strategies to relieve their own stress, but they could give valuable support to each other.

Job burnout almost always begins with *The Honeymoon* stage, a period of high energy and job satisfaction. In one sense, this appears to occur before job burnout, but because even during this stage we use up adaptation energy, we consider it the start of the process. Stage two,

the *Fuel Shortage,* begins quietly and many people don't realize any- ②
thing has changed. Toward the end of this stage people begin to experience a set of symptoms: the early warning signals. If recognized,
prevention at this point becomes much easier than later forms of
treatment. The *Chronic Symptoms* stage occurs next; earlier symptoms ③
become habitual and new symptoms emerge. It's at this point that
many people recognize something has gone awry in their work and their
lives. Stage four, the *Crisis* stage, begins when symptoms become ④
critical. At this stage people become obsessed with their problem; job
burnout dominates their lives. Finally, some people enter a fifth stage,
Hitting the Wall, at which time victims of job stress can no longer ⑤
function on their jobs and their lives deteriorate in one of several ways.

Stage One:
The Honeymoon

When the Nicholsons first started their jobs, the challenge invigorated
their lives. Jeanette, excited by teaching, worked past midnight on
many days to prepare her Shakespeare seminar. Even with little sleep
she bubbled with energy. Carter, disappointed at first, quickly became
immersed in applying psychology to the "real world." It stretched his
mind and opened up new areas of teaching. He loved the travel and
reveled in the status of lecturing to corporate executives. The stress
of this honeymoon period used up vast amounts of adaptation energy,
but neither felt depleted.

Most workers begin their jobs with enthusiasm and a desire to make
them work. And they often enjoy the exhilarating stress of learning
new things, meeting new people, and proving their competence. Big
Jim Bujarski drives his rig more than 100,000 miles each year. "I'll
never forget when I first got the job. I was so excited before my first
run that I could hardly sleep. And then, when I cranked her up to
sixty-five heading south on Interstate Thirty-five, I felt like a million
bucks. That rig was all mine."

Even the battle-scarred executive can easily recall the first day in the new office. Added responsibilities and opportunities create a sense of pride and challenge. Bob Fitzgerald had started in sales with Southeast Plastics, Inc. He worked hard and traveled all over the country. "It's a great company to work for," he would say whenever anyone asked him about his job. He moved up to sales manager, then spent several years in the new-products division. He still remembers the first day after his promotion to executive vice-president. "I went into the office. It was the first time I had ever seen it. I sat in the plush chair and my eye caught the telephone console. Every vice-president's number was listed. I could have called a meeting and had them all in there in two minutes. I felt that I had made it, that all the hard work had paid off."

The enthusiasm we often feel during the honeymoon stage comes, in part, from a strong desire to succeed. No one sets out to become a loser, especially after only a few weeks on the job. Most of us approach new jobs eager to learn the ropes and learn them fast. The neophyte short-order cook wants to master the art of flipping hamburgers, even if only to avoid the wrath of the owner. The eighteen-year-old just hired to sell used cars will strive to demonstrate he can close deals as well as the veterans. The newly appointed college president will labor sixteen hours a day to prove to the board of trustees that they selected the best person. Carter Nicholson had studied only a smattering of industrial psychology in graduate school, but he did his utmost to read every book on personnel management and occupational mental health he could find.

Even when the deck is stacked against us, we want to succeed in new jobs. Sometimes the stacked deck becomes the bait that attracts us to a position and increases our satisfaction in the work. When Liz Keifer, the executive secretary mentioned in the first chapter, took the position at Jackson Electronics, the personnel officer said, "Look, you may as well know the facts. That position is a graveyard for secretaries. They last about two months." That was all Liz needed to hear. She took the job.

The first month she reorganized the office. She updated the complex filing system that others had left in shambles. Any letter her boss dictated found its way to his desk for a signature by eight o'clock the next morning, even if it meant she worked late. The second month she persuaded the company to give her an assistant to handle the workload. Periodically her boss exploded in routine fashion; unruffled, she stood her ground. Within four months the office hummed with unheard-of efficiency. Perhaps the greatest satisfaction came when Liz heard through the grapevine that her boss had told the personnel officer, "She's the best damn secretary you ever got me!" Not long after that she told a friend, "You know, it is possible to work for a male chauvinist pig and like it."

If the honeymoon stage continues, we often feel perfectly matched with our jobs. What stress we do feel only gives meaning to our work and adds to our sense of fulfillment. But two significant things take place in this stage and they can have long-range consequences. First, in spite of our enthusiasm, even enjoyable stress uses up adaptation energy. Though the psychological bills may not come due for many months or even years, unless we've learned to cope with stress, sooner or later we will have to pay.

Second, during this phase, we develop habits of dealing with stress. If successful, the honeymoon period can go on and on. However, if the strategies we develop are ineffective, the burnout process begins in earnest. More important, we have missed an opportunity to equip ourselves to deal with unforeseen stress that can erupt at any time from our job, family, or the wider world.

Some people become almost invulnerable to stress during this period and sail along for years, perhaps the rest of their lives, no matter how rough the seas. We all know people of boundless energy who work creatively until they reach eighty or ninety and never burn out. Even after the high excitement of the honeymoon wears off, many people stay in this stage indefinitely. In 1977, Dr. Robert Quinn and Dr. Graham Staines headed a research project for the U.S. Department of Labor to find out how workers felt about their jobs. They found that more than 60 percent of those interviewed worked at tasks they did best, their work was interesting and required them to be creative, and they had opportunities to develop their own special abilities.[1] This kind of match between workers and their jobs can lead to lifetime fulfillment.

Fred Nord has coached young speedskaters in Milwaukee for more than sixteen years. Some of his teams have won national titles and at least one woman picked off a silver medal in the Olympics. When asked about his job, Fred's eyes sparkled: "It's a love affair," he said. "I love my work. I'm doin' exactly what I want to be doin'."

Willie Elma James lives in an old ghetto of Saint Louis. For nearly twenty years she has caught the bus to the suburbs at seven-thirty each weekday morning. When she arrives at the Petersons' air-conditioned home in Colonial Village, she changes into the maid's white uniform and begins her work. At sixty-two she has made more than 40,000 beds, scrubbed out innumerable toilets, and washed enough floors to stretch from Chicago to New York. "I'm happy," she says matter-of-factly. "There are some things I want that I don't have, but I'm saving. My job isn't tiring, and really I don't think about it. I think about my church and my grandchildren, and about going to the Holy Land one day."[2]

In summary, the honeymoon stage leaves us satisfied, even exhilarated. But we also expend valuable energy; and if we do not replenish that energy we will slip inevitably into the next stage.

Stage Two:
Fuel Shortage

Any of the five job-burnout risk factors can lead you into the second stage of burnout. It begins when you overdraw your account of ready adaptation energy, but you probably won't know a fuel shortage has started. Sometime during this second stage, something will happen to let you know the shortage is real.

For many people, the fuel-shortage stage arrives with a vague feeling of loss. The honeymoon has ended. The disappointment often centers on your job. The challenge of work and your enthusiasm for it have waned. A typical comment was made by an attorney who had joined a law firm a year earlier: "Well, I thought it was going to work out better than it has. But I suppose I was a little naive. Not many clients appreciate what you do for them and most of your colleagues don't care." Sometimes individuals who have entered the second stage of burnout stand back amused by those who still charge around in the honeymoon stage. When a young, idealistic law student came to the firm to gain practical experience, the same attorney smiled and muttered to himself, "He'll get over it."

We call some people in stage two "tightrope walkers," for they seem constantly on the verge of losing their balance. The risk factors keep fluctuating. It's as if the force of gravity kept pulling the tightrope walker between fatigue and confusion, on the one hand, and maintaining control and enthusiasm, on the other. Exhaustion and discontent never become chronic; the highly creative burst never lasts long. When unrelieved stress builds up and almost pushes them off the high wire, they go into immediate action to recover and quickly regain their balance. It can happen every few weeks or only a couple of times a year.

Jan Olson, a real-estate saleswoman in Atlanta, exemplifies the tightrope walker. Congenitally optimistic and energetic, Jan never completely escapes this second stage of burnout, but constantly moves back and forth between its starting gate and finish line. Sunday she wakes up feeling torn between her family and the pressure to show houses to prospective buyers. Open houses keep her tied up most of the afternoon and evening. Monday morning tours of new houses on the market take her all over Atlanta and its suburbs; in the afternoon and evening she follows up on prospects met the day before. Monday can often stretch into a seventeen-hour day, and by Tuesday afternoon Jan feels the strain.

"If I take a nap, then disconnect my phone for the evening, I'm ready to go by Wednesday morning. If I push all day and show a house after supper, by Wednesday or Thursday I'm a wreck." About once a month Jan really collapses, usually after an argument with her teenage daughter, after losing an important sale to another real-estate office, or when phone calls have interrupted every meal for two weeks, called her in from the garden six times on Saturday, and made her late for church on Sunday. "I just go to bed for a day or my husband and I go away for a weekend. That's all it takes and I feel great again." Tightrope walking has become a way of life for Jan. She sometimes feels as if she's on the verge of burning out; at other times she races through her days on a full tank. In between she swings back and forth.

At some point late in this stage, many of the most frequent symptoms of job burnout make their appearance. These symptoms serve as important early warning signals that you have used up most of your available adaptation energy. They are your body's way of saying, "This stress has gone on too long!" Although the specific symptoms vary from one person to another, we have found five early warning signals that commonly appear in the second stage of burnout: (1) job dissatisfaction, (2) inefficiency at work, (3) fatigue, (4) sleep disturbances, and (5) escape activities. These symptoms often seem innocuous at first, but in later stages they will grow more intense if they go unheeded.

Job Dissatisfaction

Everyone has ups and downs on the job. It's normal to feel let down occasionally, disappointed with your work. Most of us have experienced a blue Monday or asked at the end of a tiring day, "Why am I in this rat race?" But an occasional feeling that "there must be more to life" is not the same as week after week of discontent.

When blue Monday turns into blue Tuesday and Wednesday and Thursday, an early warning signal for job burnout has flashed on. Dissatisfaction can begin innocently, like the mist that slowly turns to rain and ends with a downpour. It might begin in speculation, like the 1700 bank employees who were asked, "If you had enough money to live comfortably, would you continue working?" Seven out of ten said they would continue working but *not* at their present jobs.[3] When a national sample that included blue-collar workers was asked this question in a 1977 Labor Department survey, 80 percent said they would continue working, but only 9 percent would do so because they enjoyed the work they did.[4]

Workers who feel the dissatisfaction of burnout express it in different ways. "My work is not very challenging," said a dental hygienist. "I sometimes feel like I'm working in a factory. I'm not always given time enough with patients, so they don't make progress and I can't feel rewarded." After fifteen years, a college professor's love for teaching has worn thin: "I'm bored to death of hearing myself say the same old things semester after semester. I'm tired of these adolescent kids and their problems. I sometimes wish I could get into another line of work." When we asked a woman who held a supervisory position in a government agency how she would feel if she had to remain on her present job for the rest of her life, she said, "I would sell real estate first or even hire out to pick dandelions!"

Although job dissatisfaction can be an important barometer of burnout, you can fall into several traps related to discontent and satisfaction. Those in the first trap say, "I need to be one hundred percent satisfied with my work or it isn't worth it." Few people reach this ideal. Instead of striving for total joy in work, make up a kind of job balance sheet. If things come up fifty-fifty or better, count yourself lucky. If you are free from the other signs of burnout, you've probably learned to handle the stress of work.

Those we found in the second trap say, "Everyone hates his job." This philosophy led them to perceive their jobs as more stressful than necessary. An attitude of gloom and dislike for their work had eventually led to a slow burnout. Instead of trying to find some way to relieve their stress, these workers became mired in pessimism as they moved into later stages of job burnout. This philosophy is actually based on false information. Most workers do not hate their jobs. In survey after survey, the majority always indicate some level of satisfaction. In 1977, *Psychology Today* magazine surveyed 23,000 of its readers and found that 68 percent were at least somewhat satisfied with their jobs.[5]

The third trap in which some workers seemed caught was based on another premise: "If I enjoy my work, I won't burn out." Again and again in our research we found evidence to the contrary. A chemist who felt burned out from his work still liked his job: "The staff is flexible; the pay is more than adequate; it's a demanding schedule, but I love my work." A personnel manager who recognized he was exhausted and burning out said, "I like my job. I enjoy working with staff development and designing new projects. But I do come home tense most of the time." Unrelieved stress, whether you enjoy it or dislike it, can result in job burnout.

Inefficiency at Work

One of the first signs of impending burnout comes when a worker's efficiency noticeably drops. The service-station attendant takes longer and longer to change the oil and give lube jobs. The secretary has to retype letters more and more often because of mistakes. The executive finds it increasingly difficult to make prompt decisions.

You can see the signs of inefficiency and slackening productivity as you walk through office corridors. They show up deeply etched into the faces of bored workers who grind through their workday. The signs are reflected in the hassled look of executives who run from meeting to meeting according to frantic schedules. You can see inefficiency in the lifeless expressions of middle managers who listlessly open their mail, in the clerk who avoids the customer until the last possible moment, and in the blank stares of workers who gaze at the office clock and wonder why the day crawls along at a snail's pace.

It would be impossible to catalog all the many different ways inefficiency appears. But again and again in our interviews we came across five expressions of lost productivity directly related to burnout: *jadedness, cynicism, lowered creativity, avoiding decisions,* and *increased accidents.*

A hospital administrator said, "I guess I have been hitting it too hard. I don't have any spunk. I feel jaded and indifferent." He repeatedly complains that "there are just too many things to do and not enough time to do them." He feels that he is "never caught up," which is a common feeling among burned-out workers. They are psychologically out of breath. Caught in organizational quicksand, they struggle and struggle to get on top of their jobs only to find that they sink lower and lower into the sea of unfinished tasks.

Joe Moringo, an assistant city manager, fits the profile of the jaded employee. "You can't believe how much work there is around city hall. My in-box gets higher and higher. You just can't keep on top of things." We asked whether a vacation might help. "Oh, no," he replied matter-of-factly. "I couldn't take time off now. My in-box would be three times as full when I got back."

When people become jaded they often work harder but accomplish less. Unable to complete enough in eight hours, they stay nine. But slowly, as stress takes its toll, nine hours isn't enough and they put in ten or twelve, and then take work home. Unfortunately, if you're burning out, you may find an inverse correlation between the amount of time spent in your office and the *quality* of your work. One high-level executive in a major corporation says, "I'll fire anyone who works more than forty-five hours a week. If you have to spend more time than that, something's gone wrong with your efficiency."

Of course, not all jaded workers respond by putting in longer hours. Some put in fewer hours. A group of secretaries kill thirty minutes of productive time by talking to one another at the start of the day until the boss arrives. Tex Sansfield, a janitor, usually takes forty-five minutes to go to a hardware store for supplies when it should take only half that time. While at the hardware store he will browse and look over new tools. Sometimes he stops for a cup of coffee. He rationalizes his unauthorized break by saying, "The big boys take time out for their martini lunches, don't they? Why can't I take five minutes for a cup of coffee?" The janitor is correct: the three-martini lunch is a way that executives waste time under the auspices of conducting business. Many executives recognize the martini lunch as a time waster but will quickly defend the need for it. As an advertising executive said, "If you had my job, you would want a little bump at noon too."

Burned-out workers squander productive time in other ways. Take John Fellington, a loan officer at a California bank. While he will never do anything that would result in getting fired, he will fritter away at least a third of his work day by swapping stories, teasing secretaries, and arranging bets on the week-end football games. He has long conversations on the telephone, is gladly interrupted when the mail comes in, and religiously reads the *Wall Street Journal,* for, after all, "You got to keep on top of things." He uses the last thirty minutes of the day to tidy up his desk because he doesn't like to come into a cluttered office in the morning. When he comes to work in the morning it takes him at least fifteen minutes to get things organized for the day.

Lest we sound too hard on John Fellington, we recognize that all of us have our less productive days, but when burnout leaves a worker listless, jaded, and unmotivated, unproductive days string together into unproductive weeks. And those weeks can turn into unproductive months.

Inefficiency at work also shows up in a cynical attitude. Most organizations have their "house cynics," persons quick to tell you why something will never work. They long for the "good ol' days" when things seemed simpler. They delight in shooting their most powerful guns at creative young employees who are brimming with enthusiasm and new ideas.

The cynics slow down progress for themselves and others by saying, "We have tried that before," "That would never work around here," or "After you have been here as long as I have then you will know how foolish that idea is." This can even fuel the burnout process in other workers. As Jane Bettindors, a staff nurse, said about her boss, "I dread those staff conferences. She is so negative. I am completely drained after being with her only thirty minutes."

In addition to jadedness and cynicism, inefficiency shows up in a lack of creativity. The copywriter in an advertising firm must come up with new ideas for marketing products every day. An early warning sign of burnout can come with the feeling, "It's harder and harder to come up with ideas, to generate concepts. I feel like I'm running dry." A computer salesman who suffered from headaches and exhaustion said, "I feel burned out from the pressures of my job. I used to be very creative and aggressive on my job. I welcomed new ideas and change. Now I've become a passive, compliant person."

Alan Whyte worked as an editor for the college division of one of the largest publishing houses in the country. He started as a traveler, but after two years in the Midwest, the managing editor brought him to New York to build the list of textbooks for English courses. Alan loved his work. He traveled three weeks out of every month, contacting potential authors, offering contracts for new textbooks, going to meetings of the Modern Language Association, and developing new ideas for books. Within five years he had developed the best English list among major publishers.

But Alan had also begun to burn out. He drank more than he had in the past. He gained thirty pounds. And most of all, his flow of creative ideas and ability to encourage new authors began to fade. "Something had happened to me after about ten years. I became jaded. I couldn't tell a good proposal for a book from a bad one. I had seen so many, I wasn't getting any new ideas. I lost my enthusiasm for the job. I knew the head of almost every freshman English program in the country, but I got bored out of my mind. I hated to go to conventions. I'd stand at the book booth and smile at every English teacher and hate every minute of it."

Then Alan began calling in sick, calling in to say that he was working on some manuscripts at home. Authors sent in chapters for forthcoming books and Alan wrote them back saying, "I'll send them out immediately for review." But more often than not, the chapters piled up in his office and never found their way out to the reviewer. Because he had built a profitable list of books earlier, sales in his field remained steady in spite of his inefficiency. A change in vice-presidents of the college division enabled him to hide his problems for nearly two years. When discovered, Alan had reached the edge of complete burnout. After he was fired, the next editor found several completed manuscripts that should have gone to production nine and ten months earlier. The files were in complete disarray and it took months to bring order out of the chaos left behind.

Burnout also cuts into work efficiency when normally self-confident people begin avoiding decisions and tough issues. "As I look back on that period in my life," said Alan, "I see how fearful I was to make decisions. I avoided meetings with prospective authors. I was afraid that I would pick a new book that would turn out to be a dog. I found myself avoiding my boss. I was afraid he would pin me to the wall with questions I couldn't answer. I became sick at the time of crucial staff meetings. But most of all, I just doubted myself and my abilities."

If you were to look at Alan's personnel file you would find the following notation: "Between 1964 and 1977, Mr. Whyte was a competent, hardworking, and productive employee. One of our best. Mr. Whyte's contract was terminated, however, on June 30, 1979, due to total ineffectiveness." The file does not try to explain the glaring contradiction. Unfortunately, Alan was a victim of occupational burnout that cost him not only his job but a good share of his future.

Sometimes inefficiency at work is most dramatically reflected in the number of accidents that employees have. Dr. Leon Brody, director of research at New York University's Center for Safety, believes that all of us become more accident-prone when under stress. When the pressure goes on month after month, it can significantly affect the accident rate of an individual or even an occupation. In one large study of high- and low-stress jobs, the difference in accident rates was striking. In the high-stress jobs, twice as many workers reported an injury. And it wasn't merely that high-stress jobs are more dangerous, because these same people reported striking differences for off-the-job accidents. Those who held low-stress jobs had an accident rate of 13.7 percent. Those who held high-stress jobs had an accident rate of 22.4 percent.[6]

For people in some jobs, the stress of work overload can lead to accidents with far-reaching consequences. In October of 1976, a U.S. Boeing 707 freighter took off from Santa Cruz, Bolivia. It lifted off the runway, then crashed, tearing through trees and rooftops before it came to rest on a playing field. The crew and seventy-seven people on the ground were killed. Investigators found that the controls of the Boeing 707 had been improperly set. They blamed it on the exhausted state of the crew, who had only had three hours of sleep after coming off twenty-three hours of duty. This kind of work overload is within the Federal Aviation Administration's safety regulations and some suggest it may be a common occurrence.[7]

One kind of inefficiency at work, more difficult to measure, shows up in occupations that serve people. Social workers, psychiatric aides, lawyers, nurses, teachers, and counselors become drained by carrying other people's problems. One of the first signs of burnout occurs when these workers become callous, indifferent to another tale of woe from another welfare mother, and withdraw emotionally. This happens so frequently in some people-helping professions that they become known as "burnout jobs." One young counselor said, "After three years in a halfway house for mental patients I became so burned out I had to quit. I felt as if I was on the verge of a breakdown myself." Because of the high frequency of burnout in the helping professions, we will later devote an entire chapter to it.

Fatigue

Like hunger and thirst, the sensation of fatigue is one of the body's most valuable mechanisms for self-protection. If we did not have feelings of exhaustion and tiredness, we would quickly use up all our energy and collapse. Fatigue is nature's way of calling a halt to physical and mental exertion. It signals a need for rest, a change in activity.

After a period of vigorous exertion people feel mostly *muscle fatigue,* a common experience for most of us. But a more important kind, called *general fatigue,* occurs early in job burnout. Caused by the accumulation of chronic stress, it comes from depleting our adaptation energy. General fatigue can leave us feeling more tired than if we'd taken a five-mile hike even if we have done nothing more strenuous all day than lift a few paper clips. Because our muscles tense up during periods of stress, muscle fatigue and general fatigue may occur simultaneously, creating a kind of keyed-up tiredness. General fatigue is the body's first line of defense against too much stress and it can take many forms, from feeling tired all the time to needing more sleep.

Fred Blake, a sandy-haired, lanky mechanic of thirty-six, owns a

Shell service station on Figueroa Street in Los Angeles. His father has pumped gas on this corner since gasoline cost sixteen cents a gallon, and Fred can't remember a time when he didn't help around the station, washing windows, sweeping out the shop, stacking cans of oil, putting air in tires. He learned to rebuild carburetors and replace worn gears as naturally as most of us pick up family mannerisms and local accents. Since he graduated from high school Fred has put in at least fifty-five hours every week. He opens up at seven-thirty every morning, catches a quick lunch between repair jobs, and leaves for home at six every night. Saturdays he works from eight to two, and until the oil crisis of 1973, he worked four or five hours on Sunday. But the long hours are less a problem than the stress of gas shortages, customers always wanting their cars fixed yesterday, and the break-ins and thefts of tools.

The gas shortages of 1979 only increased his frustration. Day after day Mr. Edwards, an elderly customer of long standing, calls. "Do you have enough premium for me today?" he asks on the edge of panic. "Yes!" Fred almost shouts into the phone. Shaking his head and crawling back under a grease-dripping engine, Fred explains. "Mr. Edwards don't drive more than eight miles a week, but every day it's the same phone call. 'Do you have enough premium?' When he does come in, his tank can only take one or two gallons."

Sally Rafael is a regular customer; her husband brings in several trucks from his landscape company for Fred to service. Sally pulled up to the pumps on Memorial Day weekend at the height of the shortage. Pointing to extra cans and several boat gas tanks in the back of the truck, she said, "I need fifty gallons; we're going up to Lake Arrowhead for the weekend."

"Can't do it," Fred told her reluctantly.

"After all the years we've been coming here?" Sally demanded angrily.

"I'm sorry, I just can't give you fifty gallons for your boat when some people can't get enough for their cars."

"Well, go to hell!" Sally screamed at him as other customers looked on. She gunned her pickup and took off at top speed, shouting, "We'll take our business somewhere else!"

When asked about his job, Fred practically blurted out the feelings of weariness that dogged his life day after day. "It used to be, when I was younger, before I married, I could work late and go out 'til eleven or twelve every night. I'd still be down at the station feeling great the next morning. Now I go home, eat dinner, read the paper, and by eight-thirty I'm ready for bed. If I go out on weekends, by ten o'clock I'm ready to go home and go to bed. It's like you're in a rut. I'm tired all the time. Get up, go to work, go home tired, day after day, year after year. It's as if I'm doing the same old thing all the time."

The fatigue of burnout from work stress is hardly an isolated problem. A national survey conducted by the Survey Research Center at the University of Michigan in 1977 asked workers in all industries about their energy level after work. Like Fred Blake, a whopping 64 percent said they did not have a lot of energy left over when they got off work. More than one in four said they became very tired in what they considered a short period of time. When asked if they would rather have a 10 percent pay raise or work fewer hours per week, 37 percent said they would rather have a shorter work week. Even in a period of double-digit inflation, nearly one in five said they would opt for less tiring work over a 10 percent raise in pay.[8]

Sleep Disturbances

For many people, instead of feeling exhausted, their burnout takes the form of feeling tense, keyed-up, speeding along faster in high gear. Forty percent of all workers report periods of feeling nervous, fidgety, and tense.[9] They can't turn off their motors. This tension often expresses itself in sleep disturbances. Nearly one-third of all workers report difficulty falling asleep and many have trouble staying asleep.[10] One engineer who felt burned out said, "Sunday evenings I literally was depressed about having to work the next morning." His sleep was disturbed as a result of job stress. "I even sleepwalk or do something in my sleep like take the pictures off the walls."

Sleep is nature's way to refuel, to resupply the body cells with energy. A need for *more* sleep can signal job burnout, but so can a need for *less* sleep. Many people who burn out ignore the early warning signal of changes in sleeping habits. They find it more difficult to fall asleep, but simply start taking medications to help them. They may wake up before the alarm goes off or even wake up during the night, unable to stay asleep. Consider a typical case.

Sandy has worked as a cocktail waitress at the Lamplighter Restaurant for the past four years. With two young children and growing Visa and Master Charge bills, it became necessary for her to start working. George, her husband, works as a roofer, laying asphalt and cedar shingles all day in the hot sun of Phoenix, Arizona. Sandy works only weeknights and her schedule allows time to spend with the children. George and Sandy feel lucky. The extra money has made the pinch of inflation less painful and their schedule is not unmanageable. Sandy leaves for work at six, so George takes care of the kids in the evening. She sleeps from one-thirty until eight-thirty or nine; George and the kids get their own breakfast and he drops them off at school on the way to a construction job.

It surprised Sandy at first that she didn't feel more tired working the evening shift. She felt new energy and looked forward to getting out of the house. Even after fighting through crowds balancing her tray of drinks on a Friday night, she usually felt rested by Saturday morning. "I need seven or eight hours of sleep," she'd tell other waitresses. "If I get that, I don't mind working." But Sandy's feelings didn't register the long-term stress of her job. Research scientists at the National Institute of Occupational Safety and Health ranked waitress as one of the ten most stressful jobs in a study of 130 occupations. And like many women, Sandy worked two jobs. All day she cleaned, did laundry, picked up the kids after school, helped out with the cub scout troop, and ran the house. Sandy was slowly running down without any fuel gauge to warn her.

The first signal came with a change in her sleeping habits. She came home at one-thirty keyed-up from a busy evening and found it difficult to fall asleep. At first she'd crawl into bed and try to sleep, then would get up quietly so as not to wake George and go to the kitchen to have another cigarette and a shot of brandy. Even after she went back to bed, it would sometimes take her an hour to fall asleep.

"I guess I just don't need as much sleep as I thought," she told George when he began asking when she came to bed. Soon, every night it was closer to three in the morning when she finally fell asleep. "I don't understand it. I used to be dead to the world the minute my head touched the pillow. And it isn't like I'm not tired. I just have trouble sleeping."

Then her pattern shifted again. Sandy started taking Sominex; her doctor wouldn't prescribe anything stronger. She had always slept through George's alarm and never heard him in the bathroom. Now she fell asleep more easily but began waking early. The slightest noise in the morning woke her and she couldn't get back to sleep. Then she started waking with a start before George's alarm went off, worried he might sleep through it. The slow climb out of sleeplessness had changed to chronic early-morning wakefulness. And with it came fatigue that affected her work. A new bartender irritated her; the customers no longer seemed interesting; even the other waitresses were bitchy. More than once she woke up in the middle of the night feeling angry, reliving the hassles of the previous evening at work.

Whether you are a housewife and waitress or a physician, working two jobs as Sandy did can lead to the early warning signals of burnout. Dr. Herbert Freudenberger, an authority on burnout, had no greater immunity. "I know for a fact," he recalled, "that one of the reasons I burned out the first time was that I worked a complete day (perhaps ten to twelve hours) in my independent practice as a psychoanalyst, and then left my office to work in the free clinic until midnight or later, only to return to my office the next morning at eight. Exhaustion or collapse was sure to follow. I found that it just was not easy to leave the clinic at night. There was just too much to do."[11]

Escape Activities

Unrelieved stress can make you feel as if you're in a combat zone. All you want to do is run, flee, escape. If your stress safety valves don't work very well, you may find yourself trying to escape by eating more, reaching for another martini, going through an extra pack of cigarettes, or going on shopping sprees. It isn't the amount you eat, drink, or smoke that signals the start of burnout, but a *noticeable increase* in some escape activity.

Alan Whyte, the burned-out textbook editor, considered himself a moderate drinker when he started work as a traveler. Even after moving to New York, he seldom had more than a glass of white wine at lunch while others downed a couple of martinis. After three years of unrelieved work pressure, his drinking habits began to change. Alan had never learned many effective ways to relieve stress. His glass of white wine gave way to a scotch and soda at lunch, then two before dinner. At the end of his fourth year working out of the New York office, he sometimes consumed four or five drinks a day, a practice that would have shocked him several years earlier. Alcohol is one of the most frequently used escapes. When a U.S. Labor Department survey asked a sample of workers if they had noticed an increase in their drinking during the preceding year, one in ten said yes.[12]

A management consultant who deals with stress among executives says, "It's frightening the amount of alcohol, Valium, and Librium you see at the executive level. If you look at the statistics on alcoholism, you'll find the senior-level business executives near the top of the occupational rankings."[13]

In a survey by *Psychology Today* magazine of 23,000 readers, the most frequent methods reported for coping with stress were eating, daydreaming, and buying something for themselves. The same study found that managers and executives were more likely to drink after work to handle tension; foremen and skilled workers were more likely to use drugs, both on and off the job.[14] In one factory we studied, where workers were numbed by the routine of manufacturing, they escape through illicit drugs. "Guys will go out back and smoke dope every chance they get—on their breaks, at lunch. They hate their jobs and do everything they can to fuck off," one worker told us. On any day of the year a number of workers will show up drunk or with hangovers. Drinking after work is a collective social activity that occurs almost daily.

Perhaps the most frequent escape activity for many people under stress is smoking. "Sally tries to cut back and even stop," said one husband. "She knows it's a real health hazard, but then things build up at work and she'll go through a pack and a half a day." When asked if they had noticed a definite increase in the number of cigarettes they smoked during the past year, 27 percent of those workers polled in a national survey were smoking more.[15]

Shopping sprees become a signal for some that stress has increased. One woman found she had run up bills of more than $4,000. "I reached the limit on my first credit card; it was three hundred dollars. Then with impulse buying I found myself running up bills on other cards. When I reached the limit, I knew I could take out another credit card at another store. I would purchase anything. I even charged my dog! I didn't see it coming and it seemed so easy."

All the early warning signals that appear during the fuel shortage stage of job burnout can alert us to the fact that work stress has begun to erode our health. It is during this stage that we have an unparalleled opportunity to make use of all the treatment strategies discussed later in this book. The individual in this stage still has enough reserves to carry out his or her own stress-relief program. Yet we found in our investigations that all too many people pass these early warning signals off as "part of modern life." They refused to recognize or simply didn't know that these symptoms were part of a much larger process, one that was slowly depleting their adaptation energy. It became only a matter of time before they had moved into the next stage of job burnout.

Stage Three:
Chronic Symptoms

The third stage of job burnout usually begins with a rather profound feeling that "something is happening to me." The physical and psychological symptoms of earlier stages now become more pronounced so that you can't easily dismiss them. It is during the chronic symptoms stage that many people suffering from job burnout first visit their physicians to discuss one or another symptom. Whatever the symptoms that affect a particular individual, and wide variations occur, they become much more difficult to shake off. It is especially during this stage that people experience *chronic exhaustion, physical illness, anger,* and *depression.*

When tiredness turns into *chronic exhaustion,* the normal rhythm of tiredness-rest-recovery goes out of your life. In its place comes an endless flat plain of exhaustion. People not only feel run down, they also move slower, their shoulders slump, they lose interest in hobbies and friends, they become irritable. A clerk in a large law firm who had entered this stage of job burnout said, "I'm exhausted. I can't seem to get enough rest to be able to do the things I want at home." A factory worker put it simply: "I feel lifeless inside." A counselor at a drug rehabilitation center said, "I feel sucked dry. I don't want to hear one more problem."

When burnout fatigue goes on day after day there often seems little difference between how tired you feel on going to bed and on waking up. Your attention span decreases. A good book can't hold your interest. You may fall asleep watching TV. Your desire to explore new things wanes. Whatever form it takes, the fatigue of burnout should not be taken lightly. It signals deep inner changes as chronic, unrelieved stress does its damage.

As job burnout progresses it frequently leads to *physical illness.* Dr. Hans Selye calls such illness the "diseases of adaptation." The facts are not all in, but sufficient evidence exists to identify many physical illnesses connected with work stress. Much of the problem lies in the fact that, as we said earlier, your body mobilizes for vigorous action over and over again; at the same time your job frustrations can't be solved by physical action. The fight-or-flight responses induce actual chemical changes. You use up energy supplies to cope; your immunity to infectious disease drops. Muscles tense. The entire gastrointestinal system is affected. Your mouth can become dry, your stomach aches, nausea can make you vomit, diarrhea or constipation can occur. Stress can affect your eyes, making it difficult to focus. The tiny blood vessels under the skin contract and may result in itching, hives, or eczema. The central pumping station speeds up; blood chemistry changes.

A U.S. Air Force officer, talking about his stressful job, said, "I become almost physically ill. My body aches as if I have a viral illness. I get tension headaches and am nauseated." When our immunity to disease is lowered, we may find that, instead of an average of two or three colds a winter, we now get three or four. The flu comes more frequently. Our resistance has dropped.

Backaches and headaches are two of the most frequent symptoms of burnout. In the United States, the seven million disabled by lower-back pain and the twenty-five million suffering from recurring headaches spend more than one billion dollars a year for over-the-counter pills to relieve these pains. A finance officer in a bank said, "About three o'clock almost every day I'd need an aspirin; my head would pound. And after a meeting my head would throb. I knew it was coming; our meetings usually came in the afternoon and afterwards we were all burned out."

A prison guard, who talked to Dr. Christina Maslach in California, described his burnout experience. "On the way home from my first day on the job I realized that my neck hurt. The muscles were tight, and that caused me to have a headache. Later on I realized that my neck and back would begin to get stiff and sore and painful just before I went to the prison—and it would last until I got home again."[16]

Skin conditions, from acne and eczema to hives and itching, are frequently symptoms of stress. Jim Jackson's eczema began during his second year as youth director at Memorial Presbyterian Church. When we interviewed him, the tension and frustration spilled out. "I don't know if I can take it much longer! I've got to get out of this church. Reverend Olgivie is living in the 1920s. He's so uptight about the morals of today's youth that I can hardly talk about anything. I started two years ago trying to reach kids who didn't come to church.

It worked. Pretty soon they were bringing their friends to church and their problems to me. I was knee deep in counseling them about everything from sex and dope to quarrels with parents."

Jim planned weekend retreats and took busloads of kids to summer camp. He taught Bible classes and tried to share his faith informally. One weekend early in his second year he told a few college students that he thought the marijuana laws should be revised. The conversation then turned to abortion and other topics never discussed from the pulpit of Memorial Presbyterian Church.

On Tuesday afternoon the minister called Jim into his office. After a long discussion he said, "This church is not in favor of abortion or changing the marijuana laws. I can't believe you read the same Bible I do! If those are your opinions, it'd be best if you kept them to yourself."

The months that followed brought a long series of confrontations. Increasingly Jim felt watched, suspected, controlled, and compromised. He found himself avoiding controversial questions from high school students and prefacing his answers with "Well, this church believes . . ." Within six months he had developed several small red patches on his legs that itched most of the time. His family physician referred him to a dermatologist, who said, "It looks like psoriasis or maybe eczema." He prescribed cortisone cream, which reduced the itchiness, but the red, flaky patches spread to his back and arms. When the Reverend Mr. Olgivie took his month's vacation, almost all the itchy patches cleared up, but within a month after he returned, Jim went back to his dermatologist in even worse condition. "I knew my skin problem was directly related to my situation at the church," he said. "I was burning out, not from being too busy with those kids, but from the pressure to conform to what the minister and some of those conservative old-timers wanted."

The gastrointestinal system can also feel the effects of stress. Some people have difficulty swallowing. For others, recurrent heartburn, acid stomach, diarrhea, colitis, or constipation can result. In time, the wear and tear of work stress can lead to ulcers, one of the most widespread occupational diseases in America today.

Dr. Richard Grayson, a physician in Illinois who helped found the American Academy of Stress Disorders, says, "Ulcers are an occupational hazard of great importance when you consider that at any given time there are half a million Americans disabled by peptic ulcers and perhaps another fifteen to twenty million who are being treated for or who are suffering from ulcers. If workers throughout all industries were encouraged to apply for workman's compensation benefits for peptic ulcers, the economic impact would be tremendous."[17]

Job burnout can also show up early with cardiovascular symptoms. Dizzy spells, shortness of breath, pounding heart, and irregular heartbeat often come from work stress. In one study, researchers discovered that burned-out workers noticed slight changes in blood pressure that made them dizzy. As these spells became more frequent they worried about having a stroke. Their anxiety about what was happening to their bodies increased the stress.[18]

Physical symptoms caused by work stress are more widespread than most people realize. In a recent survey of Chicago teachers, 25 percent reported that they suffered from physical problems caused by the pressures of their jobs. No one knows for sure how many of the seven million Americans with lower-back pain or the twenty-five million with headaches are actually suffering from job burnout. We do know that work stress is a major cause of such physical complaints. We do know that doctors estimate at least 50 percent of all their patients come with problems caused by one kind of stress or another. We do know that each year, 15 percent of the nation's adult population takes tranquilizers. If we pay attention to the aches and pains of everyday life, they can help us search out more effective ways to deal with stress. But if we ignore these physical symptoms or manage them exclusively with medications, the fires of stress will continue to burn away inside, doing irreversible damage.

During this third stage of job burnout, many people find themselves with almost perpetual feelings of *anger*. They resemble volcanos always on the verge of eruption. It takes little to make them upset at other people; they have what Dr. Walter Menninger calls a "short fuse." The calm, accepting, easygoing person becomes chronically angry.

You may find yourself suddenly reacting with anger in situations that surprise you.

Virginia Thompson, a nurse on a cancer ward, described her own reaction one night after three years on the job: "I had never lost my temper with a patient," she recalled. "To me that was the height of losing control. But that particular evening this patient was in pain and wanted his medication. I was busy running up and down but I went in to give it to him. As I was pouring it down his nasogastric tube, which wasn't easy, he hit me over the head. It caught me off guard, and I screamed. Then I shouted, 'Do you want this?' He just looked at me with those eyes; he couldn't even talk. I finished off with, 'Cut that out,' the way you do when you've said something wrong and you can't take back the words. I just stood there. I was thinking, I don't believe I did this. I really felt bad, and I remember apologizing."[19]

When work stress continues unabated, a person's anger often becomes more focused. Instead of feeling upset at people in general, be it clients, students, bosses, the company, the government, people suffering from burnout often take on a single conflict. Hatred can center on one or two individuals.

Dick Bradford, a social worker, found himself deep in a running battle with the head of security at an alcoholism treatment center. "He doesn't know shit from shinola," he would mutter to himself after a bitter exchange in a staff meeting. At night, Dick would lie in bed feeling angry at this one man, going over and over again their disagreements of the day. Sandy found her anger focused on the new bartender. "I can't work with Gene," she confided to one of the other waitresses. As her burnout became chronic, she couldn't hide her hostility from Gene or the other bartenders. Waitresses who worked the bar at the Lamplighter selected one of two stations where they placed orders and picked up drinks. Usually Sandy could avoid the waitress station where Gene worked, but occasionally, another waitress arrived early and Sandy was forced to work with Gene. When he filled a glass so it ran over on her tray, she glared at him. If he opened a bottle of beer too quickly so it foamed over on her tray, she swore at him under her breath. A night working with Gene sent her home seething with anger, unable to sleep, moving ever deeper into job burnout.

Finally, for some people the pressures of their work and the unrelieved stress result in *depression.*

Ruth Rogers, a black woman in her mid-forties, runs her own laundromat-cleaning business. Tall and heavily built, Ruth loves her tiny laundry with its fourteen single-load Speed Queen washers, the six double-load machines, and the seven variable temperature dryers. Ten years ago she quit her job as a maid, and with the small insurance left by her husband's sudden death, she opened up the laundry. She takes in dry cleaning and finished laundry and sends them out each day. Customers come in to use the coin-operated machines or leave their dirty clothes for the wash-dry-fold service that Ruth says takes up most of her time.

Ruth has a string of regular customers who often stop to talk. "When I first started coming in here eight years ago," one woman says, "Ruth Rogers was so full of fun! She'd have all her customers smiling or laughing when they left. I just don't know what's happened to her lately." Ruth isn't sure herself, but many days she feels like she has to drag herself to the bus—she arrives every morning between seven and seven-thirty. She wakes up in the morning not only tired, but also feeling down. "I'm in a blue funk at the start and ending of every day." Once in the shop, Ruth starts taking in wash-dry-fold orders and dry cleaning from early customers. Betweentimes she sorts and weighs the clothes and loads the machines. As soon as all the machines are humming, she starts mopping the floors, cleaning the surfaces of all the machines, and then, one by one, loading the damp clothes into the dryers.

The cloud that hangs over her seems to lift by about ten when she stops to have coffee with one of the women from the beauty shop next door. Delivery men with soap or dry cleaning interrupt her work. Most days are so busy she hardly thinks about herself. She checks in dry cleaning, matches ticket numbers, searches for orders when customers come in, rushes back to finish wrapping the latest wash-dry-fold order. She eats lunch and dinner in her little "kitchen" in the back, keeping an eye out for customers. It will be nine or nine-thirty before she closes and ten-thirty before the bus finally deposits her two blocks from home. "I find myself crying a lot at home in the evenings," she says. Sundays are spent cleaning house and visiting friends.

Depression has numerous causes and can range from that "blue Monday" feeling to serious mental illness. Unrelieved stress is only one of the sources, but as it depletes our energy reserves, the continuous pressures of job, family, or the environment can leave us depressed. At first Ruth Rogers merely felt moody and blue once or twice a month; then it increased to every week and would last a day or two. The way Ruth perceives her life as a widow, the unrelieved pressures of the laundromat-cleaning business, and, perhaps most of all, the inadequacy of her stress safety valves have all contributed to her burnout depression.

Feeling down is a common response when some aspect of work seems intolerable. You can't quit, you can't fight it, you can't make it go away. "My wife goes through cycles of feeling depressed about her job almost every week," one man told us. "She loves the work, but her boss is totally disorganized and that's a constant frustration." This woman feels that the only chance for relief from stress would come if her boss resigned. But that seems so remote she feels trapped and depressed.

Dr. Brodsky of the University of California Medical School in San Francisco discovered that the hopeless feeling about job frustrations often begins with some significant event. For one prison guard it started after a riot. He knew that he would walk into the prison at the start of his shift; but he also thought he couldn't be sure he would ever walk out again. For a high-school teacher nearing retirement, it started after her school was integrated. New students threatened to tear off the wig that covered her thinning gray hair. The stress of these situations brought anxiety that slowly turned into depression.[20]

In these first three stages of job burnout, people not only have different symptoms, but they travel through these stages in different ways. Some move rapidly; others slowly. Some remain in one stage for years, then move quickly through the others.

In our interviews with people suffering from job burnout we found a certain number who are *repeaters*. They burn out over and over again. They race through the honeymoon stage, deplete their energy in the fuel shortage stage, and then move quickly into the chronic symptoms stage. The repeater often attacks the problem, develops new safety valves, and recovers quickly. In a matter of months, repeaters often find themselves back at an earlier stage feeling much better, only to begin again the downward slide. It can almost become a way of life.

Jeanette Nicholson, whom we discussed earlier in this chapter, was a repeater. She felt emotionally drained after the second year of teaching at the University of Indiana. "It was my first teaching job; we had two preschool children; babysitters were a hassle; and I had a running battle with Dr. Norwood in my department." Chronic fatigue engulfed her; she withdrew emotionally from students, cutting back on office hours, avoiding the graduate-student lounge. "When school ended in June I wondered if I ever wanted to teach again." But that summer Jeanette played tennis, took her kids to the beach, lay in the sun hours on end, and redecorated the living room. "I didn't read a single book all summer or even think about school; when September came I couldn't wait to get back into the classroom." A new honeymoon stage had begun. But three years later Jeanette had come full circle to the third stage of burnout.

Sometimes the repeater cycle coincides with job changes. An administrative clerk in an accounting and payroll department at Dow Chemical said, "First, I'm excited about my job; then it gets boring. Then the problems increase, making the problems at home more severe. They feed into each other and more tension develops. I get headaches and feel depressed, then I resent work and finally quit to find another job. It's become a cycle." Like many people, this repeater had developed a single major strategy for dealing with unrelieved stress: *run for it*. By diminishing the power of all the risk factors, she might have stopped job burnout from making her career decisions.

Carter Nicholson, on the other hand, has marched through each stage in an almost deliberate manner. When emotional fatigue, irregular heartbeats, and depression signaled the third stage of job burnout, he tried some remedies, but none became the miracle cure he had hoped for. He made the common mistake of underestimating the length of time it takes to reverse job burnout once it has progressed to the third stage.

Stage Four: Crisis

You may find just enough relief from stress to remain in the third stage for years, without recovering or moving on. But if you have several high risk factors going at the same time, they can push you directly into a burnout crisis. Four significant changes mark the gateway to this stage:

1. Your symptoms become critical.
2. You become obsessed with your frustrations.
3. You become pessimistic; self-doubts permeate your thinking.
4. You develop an "escape mentality."

Let's look at each of these changes.

Burnout symptoms become critical when they intensify or increase in number. The chronic acid stomach becomes a bleeding peptic ulcer. The tension headaches are joined by chronic backache, high blood pressure, and difficulty in sleeping. The creative ideas you need at work dry up altogether and your job discontent becomes deep disillusionment.

For Carter Nicholson, the crisis stage hit one day before he flew to New York to present a workshop on executive stress. He had cleared his appointment calendar to spend the day preparing three lectures. The morning brought unexpected family pressures. Jeanette left early for her eight o'clock class; as usual, Carter prepared breakfast for Debbie and Carter, jr., then got them ready to go to the day-care center. As they were hurrying to the car so Carter could get to the office sooner, Debbie fell and cut a deep gash in her leg. The drive to the doctor's was chaotic; Debbie screamed all the way while Carter tried to drive and hold a diaper on her leg. He paced the waiting room impatiently while the doctor took six stitches to repair the injury. He rushed into his office at ten-thirty, already two hours behind schedule.

"Don't take any calls," he told his secretary. He pinned a *"Do Not Disturb"* sign on his door and went to work. The first lecture came easy; he had started on the second by lunchtime. He wolfed down a sandwich and his fifth cup of coffee at his desk and continued working on the second lecture. He worried most about the third one because the unfamiliar subject would require a search through books and journals he couldn't take on the plane.

Deep in concentration, his phone rang and he picked it up, irritated. "The vice-president just called and wants you in his office for an emergency meeting at two o'clock," his secretary said timidly. "God damn his emergencies!" Carter said to himself as he hung up the phone. But twenty minutes later the elevator took him to the sixteenth floor. The meeting dragged on for an hour and a half; the "emergency" turned out to be still another discussion about how to deal with an incompetent department head. Carter returned to his office at 3:30, fuming. He threw himself furiously into gathering ideas for the third lecture.

Then, without warning, his heart began beating so fast he felt short of breath. Leaning back in his chair he checked his pulse. The flutter of rapid beats had climbed to more than two hundred a minute, well over twice his normal pulse. Dizziness swept over him; he tried to calm himself but his heart refused to slow down. Ten minutes later, heart racing faster than ever, white faced and anxious, Carter lay on a bed in the company physician's office.

"Yes, it's over two hundred beats a minute," the doctor said. "You're having a tachycardia attack. It may stop by itself, but I'll give you some Valium to relax you; that may help. You should rest here until it goes back to normal." Two hours later the rapid heartbeats stopped as suddenly as they had begun. "They're brought on by too much coffee and too much pressure," the doctor told Carter. "You'll have to watch both."

Drained and exhausted by the experience, Carter took a few books home, worked some that evening, and muddled through his lectures.

In the weeks that followed, almost any deadline pressure could bring on the tachycardia. Carter worried constantly about having a heart attack. He had reached the crisis stage of burnout.

It took Ken Adams twenty-two years to reach a crisis. As president of his own construction company in Miami, he lived with the pressures of bidding on jobs, hiring personnel, meeting payrolls, and watching his company expand. Several times on the verge of bankruptcy, he always managed to pull through. He'd had trouble sleeping for years, but with the crisis stage the symptoms intensified.

"If I could only get a good night's sleep I'd feel a lot better. But no matter how many Sominex I take, I still find myself tossing and turning. It's one hundred percent more stressful lying there at night and thinking about my problems than during the day. And then sometimes I do get to sleep but dream about the company. Two nights ago I dreamt about my banker foreclosing on my place. I sometimes think I'm going nuts and I guess . . . partly, I am."

When burnout symptoms reach an acute phase, most individuals will become obsessed with their problems. Dramatic evidence of this is seen in a study undertaken by Dr. Carroll Brodsky, a physician at the University of California Medical School in San Francisco, who studied burned-out teachers and prison guards. The subjects had very few waking moments when their thoughts weren't back on the job. They thought about work while driving home at night. Watching television in the evening, their work problems lay heavily in the back of their minds. Falling asleep became difficult because of the preoccupation, going over and over the argument with the principal, the trapped feelings, the fear of prisoners' threats, the responsibilities that lay ahead. There came an increasing awareness that "this job is bad for me; the problem isn't going to go away."[21]

The husband of a woman in the crisis stage of burnout described how the obsession had invaded their family life. "That's all we talk about anymore: her boss, the conflict with the office manager, the frustrations of her schedule. Every day she comes home and work is everything. She's obsessed with it. She has nightmares almost every night. It's the first thing she talks about in the morning. The sad part is that I can't help her. I don't know if anything can."

Sometimes the obsession turns people into moody, withdrawn individuals. The wife of a young attorney who had failed his bar exam for the third time said, "Ron has really changed; he's so down I can't even get him to talk about it. He hasn't told anyone at the office that he failed the exam. It's like nothing has happened on the outside, but underneath, that's all he thinks about. Now some of the younger guys just out of law school have begun to pass the bar exam and Ron knows it but won't admit to anyone what's going on."

Like Ron, many people in the crisis stage find that obsession with their unrelieved stress breeds self-doubt and deep pessimism. When Ken Adams talks in his flat, monotone voice, you can readily hear the lack of confidence that plagues his every waking moment. "The unknown is the worst part. I wonder whether I'm making the right decisions. The other day I bid four hundred fifty thousand dollars on a job for the city. I learned through the grapevine that every other bid came in at over five hundred thousand dollars. Now I'm really sweating it out. Maybe those guys know it can't be done for four hundred fifty thousand. If they're right and I'm wrong, it will wipe me out."

When Bill Hansen, the Methodist minister we discussed in the first chapter, went into the fourth stage of burnout, he quickly started to doubt his ability to preach good sermons. One Sunday evening he told his wife, "I looked at every face in the congregation and wondered what in the world I could possibly say that would help any of them. I wanted to walk right off the platform."

During the crisis stage of burnout, the feelings of discontent become so intense that sufferers often look for an escape hatch. If you have stayed in the battle with unrelieved stress for months or years, immense pressures will build to follow the "flight response." Burned-out people in the crisis stage often comment, "I want to get the hell out of my job, my family, my whole way of life." Ken Adams put it this way: "I needed to get out of my problems so bad that bankruptcy didn't seem like such a bad option. In fact there were some nights when I considered everything from suicide to hospitalization to packin' off to a foreign country." Mr. Hansen thought about cashing in his pension fund, putting it in a bank, and trying to live off the interest until he could find another job. One woman told us she thought about "getting pregnant so I wouldn't have to work anymore." Unfortunately, in searching for a quick exit, you will burn up more energy and further deplete your inner resources.

We can see a clear progression during the first four stages of burnout. Satisfaction with work and even exhilaration mark the honeymoon stage. The first stirrings of job dissatisfaction creep in during the fuel shortage stage; other early warning signals appear. If the safety valves fail to work adequately, job burnout symptoms become chronic; individuals begin to talk about their frustrations, and their discontent usually focuses on some aspect of job or career. With the crisis stage, self-doubt and even despair blanket their perceptions. Wishing for a convenient escape hatch and finding none, the individual feels like a trapped animal.

Stage Five:
Hitting the Wall

Running a marathon is a grueling test of endurance and training. Dr. George Sheehan says that the marathon really begins at the twenty-mile mark with six miles yet to go. That's where many runners "hit the wall," an experience so devastating it can knock them completely out of the race. In the contest with stress you can also "hit the wall" and find yourself unable to continue working, even disqualified for years to come.

What happens when long-distance runners hit the wall? The working muscles draw their fuel from glycogen stored in the muscles; when that runs out, it takes time to restore it from fatty tissue or new intake of carbohydrates. At the point where your glycogen is all used up, the body becomes dehydrated, your temperature rises to 106 or 107 degrees, and there is a loss of blood volume. Muscle paralysis can occur; dizziness, fainting, and complete collapse can sometimes follow.

In our research we discovered people who had reached stage five of burnout, hitting the wall. Their adaptation energy depleted like a runner's glycogen, they lost control of their lives, and for some it ended their working careers forever.

We first met Ed Crichton on skid row in Seattle.[22] He was caught in the revolving door of drunkenness and arrest, swept into jail for a few weeks at a time, then released to find another bottle in a bar back on skid row. Ed had spent the last five years as a tramp drifting from the apple harvest in Spokane to the bars along First Avenue in Seattle, to the flophouses of skid row in Portland. A casual appraisal of Ed and you'd never suspect how far he had come. Slowly the story came out.

An editor for a newspaper in a northern California city, Ed had lived with the intense daily pressures of his occupation for seventeen years. His work stress had been compounded by family pressures. Burnout progressed slowly, but Ed had learned few strategies for reducing stress. He began drinking heavily after a tense day at work; his wife had grown up with an alcoholic father and created a scene every time she found him drinking. The risk factors climbed higher as Ed went into the crisis stage of job burnout. The unbearable pain increased and one day he hit the wall. He walked off the job, left his wife and kids, and headed for skid row for a marathon drunk. He never returned. "I keep telling myself I oughtta go back," he says wistfully when sober. But as the years pass, the likelihood of that happening has dwindled. Ed Crichton will probably live out the rest of his days in the last stage of job burnout on skid row.

When you hit the wall, it means that burnout has become so entwined with other problems like alcoholism, drug abuse, heart disease, and mental illness, that it can't be untangled from these other maladies.

George Loring took a job as vice-president in a large aerospace corporation. As head of research and development, eighteen different departments reported to him, each staffed by engineers, physicists, chemists, and other PhD scientists. Independent, highly creative, and highly paid, the research-and-development staff were a law unto themselves. One department had become completely unproductive; individuals throughout the division held irregular hours, came and went as they pleased, and refused to institute the new evaluation system developed by the personnel department.

George Loring came to his job with a mandate: Clean up the division. "Tighten up the ship," a senior vice-president had told him. "Cut that department; get those scientists off their asses." Already in the third stage of burnout from his previous job, George wasted no time in meeting the resistance head on. By the end of his first year every department head had dug in his heels; George had developed a new symptom, chronic backache.

By the end of the second year, everyone was talking about George. "I only know three people in all of research and development who would support the guy on anything!" said one department head. Passive resistance to the new evaluation system infuriated George, but he never showed it. In fact, no matter how heated the arguments he had with his staff, George never got ruffled, and people said, "He sure takes the heat well." But George had reached the crisis stage of burnout. He couldn't sleep well; he walked around stooped with pain. His mind wandered during conferences with the staff. He couldn't make decisions, or quickly reversed ones he did make. The senior vice-president asked for an executive evaluation and some said George knew the axe was about to fall.

George hit the wall one morning. His wife dropped him off at the office on a Saturday so he could catch up on some extra work. The guard let him in. Several hours later a janitor found him in his office. George had slashed his wrists and bled to death.

It's possible, but improbable, to hit the wall and recover. Bill Hansen must be counted as one of the lucky few. He hit the wall one Sunday morning in the pulpit of Treemont Methodist Church. Filled with increasing self-doubt, anxious about his sermons, he went to the pulpit, announced the text, and collapsed. Gasping for breath and tormented by wrenching pains in his chest, he was rushed to the hospital cardiac intensive-care unit. A battery of electrocardiograms revealed no damage to his heart; Bill Hansen had not suffered a heart attack. "It must be anxiety," the doctor said, and recommended a long rest. After several months away from the church, George returned, rested, eager to resume his duties. Shortly before he was to preach his first sermon in months, Bill Hansen felt short of breath and couldn't stand up. The church leaders met and decided to invite guest preachers for several more months. Slowly Bill Hansen recovered, anxious to return to the pulpit, and before the year was out had taken a church in eastern Montana, a thousand miles from Treemont Methodist.

Recovery in the last stage of burnout will elude some; others may regain their equilibrium in the battle with stress, but it will take time and understanding from those around them.

It is not inevitable that we go through the stages of burnout. Modern society presents us all with complex and unrelieved stress. But we can also learn to cope, to prevent the process, and to recover when burnout does occur. Knowing which stage we're in is one of the first steps in dealing with job burnout

Part Two
The Treatment
of Job Burnout:
Personal Strategies

Chapter Four
Taking Control
of Job Burnout

When suffering from job burnout, it's not uncommon to feel utterly helpless, as if invisible forces have begun to dismantle your life piece by piece. But such feelings do not come from wild paranoia. Invisible forces *have* taken control of your life. When job burnout sets in, it signals the fact that you have become powerless over many different aspects of your work and your life. You've lost control over determining the nature of your work. Revolutionary changes in the last fifty years have robbed millions of people of their power to determine the way work is structured, how fast they must complete tasks, the amount of work they will do, the way work hours are scheduled, the chance to use their minds, and the opportunity to learn new things. Many people have never developed the ability to recognize easily those work stresses that lead to job burnout. Your stress response goes off automatically: without your consent, your body reacts with the chemical and physical changes that lead to so many problems.

Effective treatment of job burnout must proceed along two avenues at the same time. First, you will need to develop *personal strategies* to regain control. Second, you will have to learn how to manage stressful jobs by employing *organizational strategies*. In our research we found many people who had developed the ability to cope with stress in their personal lives. They thrived on jobs that would burn out most of us, yet they did not succumb to job burnout. We had the feeling they could probably survive on almost any stressful job. In many cases, they also tried to change the nature of their work to reduce the stress factor. They changed scheduling, rearranged tasks, made suggestions to their boss, and joined with other workers to redesign their jobs. Although personal and organizational strategies to take control of job burnout often overlap, we will consider them separately. For the remainder of part 2, we will show you how to build up your own immunity to job burnout. The strategies we'll outline can lead to recovery if you're suffering from job-burnout symptoms; they can prevent a recurrence of the malady. Then, in part 3, "The Treatment of Job Burnout: Organizational Strategies," we will consider the job itself and how to get control of specific kinds of work stress.

Let's begin our analysis of personal strategies for treating job burnout by considering the case of Phil Korbeski, who holds a job as a directory-assistance operator.[1] At twenty-nine, Phil has been on the job for more than five years. He feels he can easily live with the stress of emergency calls for police or medical assistance, a night or two of overtime, and even a fight with his supervisor. They represent short-term stress; none happens frequently and they quickly pass. But three features of his job have turned into chronic stress for Phil: *time pressure, too much supervision,* and *little hope for promotion.* These stress conditions have robbed him of his control at work, brought on physiological reactions he can't control, and given him symptoms of job burnout that he has little power to deal with.

Each day Phil arrives at the office, picks up his headset, and takes a position at one of the fifteen "quads" in the directory-assistance room. Four operators sit at each quad, headsets plugged into a small console with eighteen buttons for accepting and routing calls. Then the eight-hour routine begins.

"Directory assistance. This is Phil. May I help you?" Most calls come from people wanting the telephone number of a friend, Dayton's Department Store, their bank, the Varsity Theater ticket office, or their favorite restaurant. Now and then someone wants to know the score of the Minnesota Vikings football game, the weather forecast, or something else besides a telephone number. Although repetitious, Phil's job, along with the fifty-nine other operators', doesn't appear particularly stressful—until you look more closely at the way the company has designed the work.

From the instant Phil pushes the "Trunk One" button to take a call, the computer in the teletype room begins to time how long he takes. "Every time I take a call I know I'm being watched by that damn computer. If I fall behind an average of thirty-five seconds per call, I know I'm in big trouble." The computer punches out Phil's AWT (Average Work Time) once a day, and at any time his supervisor wants to see it. At periodic evaluation meetings, the supervisor will put the pressure on Phil to increase his time. The computer also reports an Average Work Time for all sixty directory-assistance operators. This is posted every half hour to motivate operators to go faster.

As if the computer were not enough, Phil's supervisor, or S.A. (Service Assistant), will "take remotes," company talk for eavesdropping. Without his knowledge, at any time during the day or night, someone will listen to how he handles calls. And for each mistake ("irregularity"), he will lose points off his "work index." What constitutes a mistake? Well, during the thirty seconds he has to answer a call, Phil must follow a strict routine that can be divided into thirteen discrete steps. Failure to follow this lock-step procedure knocks off points. Phil knows he can lose one point if he fails to "acknowledge" the caller. He will lose two points if he doesn't ask for the spelling of a name. And so on. He starts with 100 points, and if he doesn't keep his index in the nineties, he will hear about it at his next evaluation.

Phil's supervisor also watches his behavior. If he takes too long on a break, if he must go to the bathroom too often or for too long, he's bound to hear about it. "I was really irritated with one customer, and so after I hung up, I was swearing quietly to myself before taking the next call. Lo and behold, my S.A. tapped me on the shoulder—she was standing there listening the whole time!"

In addition to time pressure and too much supervision, Phil feels trapped in a dead-end job. He has two kids to support, so he can't think of quitting. But he also knows his chances for promotion are slim. Together, these three frustrations eat away at him, creating stress that he takes home every day after he punches out. "It's not just the routine that gives me a headache almost every day, but the lack of freedom. It's knowing I'm being watched, timed, and supervised every damn second of the day. It's as if they're trying to make me into a machine!"

Because the long-term stress in Phil's job comes in small doses, he cannot easily follow his fight-or-flight impulse. How do you fight the computer or your supervisor who keeps the pressure on for faster calls? How do you attack a bureaucracy that offers little chance for upward mobility? How do you fight a work system that supervises your every move? Because work stress seldom reaches the boiling point, Phil doesn't consider quitting. The alarm reaction, with its call to fight or flight, goes off many times a day, but Phil has come to accept the "tensions and pressures" as part of the job. Over the long haul, though, it has begun to take its deadly toll, sapping Phil's adaptation energy and leaving him burned out.

It would be possible for Phil to attack the problem of job burnout at the organizational level, trying to change the sources of stress. In fact, Phil knows about efforts along this route and has participated in them. On 15 June 1979, members of the Communication Workers of America, Local 7200 in Minneapolis, attacked work stress by bringing it to public attention. "WE ARE PEOPLE, NOT MACHINES!" read the sign one man carried at the peaceful demonstration in front of Northwestern Bell Telephone's downtown office in Minneapolis. "NO MORE TIMED POTTY BREAKS!" read another carried by a young directory-assistance operator. Other members milled around, passed out leaflets to the noonday crowd, or released balloons "to show we need relief from job pressures."[2]

In dozens of other cities around the United States similar demonstrations marked this first "National Job Pressures Day." It was one of the first times that a major AFL-CIO union had left behind the more traditional issues of job security and pay increases and turned to work stress—things like compulsory overtime, arbitrary absenteeism controls, and computerized scheduling and evaluation of workers—the kinds of pressures Phil Korbeski experienced in his job. Their protest was aimed particularly at dehumanizing jobs. And they plan to continue putting the pressure on corporate policymakers who have the power to redesign jobs in ways that reduce the stress that leads to burnout.

But Phil could also attack the problem of job burnout with personal strategies that could bring some immediate relief. The gnawing sense of helplessness that only adds to his stress would disappear quickly. The rest of this chapter will cover five basic principles for taking control of job burnout.

Understand the Nature of Job Burnout

As in most cases of job burnout, Phil Korbeski's lack of control stems from almost total ignorance of the work-stress connection. Although he sometimes vaguely senses that his symptoms and his job are connected, he has yet to comprehend the full significance of this connection. Nor has he come to understand that he has the potential to change the situation.

The most important first step in taking control of job burnout is understanding how it works. Simply knowing the nature of stress, the power of work stress, the way our bodies have been constructed to respond to stress, and how unrelieved stress can bring on job burnout symptoms will let you start taking the reins of your job and your life. Knowing the symptoms of job burnout and the stages it goes through will help you make an accurate diagnosis of your own situation. But there's much more to understand, including all the various treatment strategies we will present. If you're willing to read and study these ideas, you will find your helpless feelings wane and your sense of control return.

If you have a thorough grasp of how the five job burnout risk factors discussed in chapter 2 work together, then you can begin to treat job burnout by attacking any of the five. Those who successfully deal with burnout tend to work on all risks simultaneously. They seek to reduce family pressures; they change what they find frustrating at work; they look for ways to circumvent environmental demands; they work to change their perceptions of stress; they take steps to improve their faulty stress safety valves and add more useful ones to their repertoire. Every personal strategy for treatment has a single objective: *lower the risk of living with unrelieved stress.*

Raise Your Consciousness of Work Stress

The second strategy is to increase your awareness of the stresses you face. Because we are almost continuously under stress, we develop routines for dealing with it that slip into the less conscious recesses of our minds. Phil Korbeski has lived with his job pressures so long that he takes them for granted. He has trouble pinpointing exactly what features of his job bring him the most trouble. Our analysis of the major frustrations related to Phil's job burnout were not things he had carefully analyzed.

Many people seem hardly conscious of the stress events most responsible for damaging their health. Yet those who do cope with job burnout have raised their consciousness of work stress, often without realizing it. A young housewife said, "Housework doesn't bother me, that I know. But two things do: being cooped up in the house day after day, and being tied to the kids. Pretty soon I'm really climbing the walls and feeling a tremendous need to talk with some adults for a change. So, I take a 'mental-health break' one afternoon each week. I call in a baby-sitter and go to lunch with a friend, shop, see a movie, or do something else. At first I felt guilty for spending the money; now I know it's what I owe myself if I want to survive."

A busy writer and consultant told us, "I used to just plow into my work without much thought. It didn't occur to me that some things might be more stressful than others. Then I began analyzing it with my wife and discovered something I hadn't realized. My major stress came from bringing work home every night, thinking I may work if I feel up to it or maybe I won't. But at least it will be there if I decide to work. But here's what happens. On those nights I decide to work, I have trouble sleeping and the work I do isn't very good. But here's the real catch: if I don't work, I feel guilty all evening and I still have trouble sleeping!" Once his consciousness had been raised about this conflict, he decided to schedule two nights a week for work at home and take the others off. This brought just enough relief to bring his life back on an even keel. His leisure evenings became more enjoyable, his work evenings more productive.

One way to start raising your consciousness about work stress is to write down all the things you complain about in a typical week. You may complain to colleagues at work, your spouse, or only quietly to yourself. Keep a list for a week and see if you can add to it by writing down what other people complain about. This exercise might not reveal all the causes of your own job burnout, but it will sensitize you to the prevalence of stress factors in the workplace.

Raising your consciousness of work stress has an extremely important function. You will recall that nature has given us effective equipment for dealing with life-threatening stress situations by our fight-or-flight response. This tends to place most of our dealings with stress outside our consciousness. We become trapped by patterns, both learned and inherited, that have little correspondence to the realities of the workplace. In order to take control of job burnout, you will need to become conscious of how you see and respond to stress.

Listen to Your Body

Because your stress response is an involuntary process largely regulated by the autonomic nervous system, you have slight awareness of the mobilization and energy consumption phases of this response. However, the autonomic nervous system and the central nervous system do not run on completely separate tracks. With practice, most people can become much more conscious of what's happening to their bodies under stress. You can listen to your body. It has a reliable warning system even though many people don't seem to hear the sirens go off. Again and again in our research we found people in the late stages of burnout who refused to listen to their bodies. This was especially true of people who enjoyed their work, worked long hours, and were productive and creative. They simply turned off the early warning system, disconnected the alarm, and pushed on in spite of aches and pains or more serious illness.

Brad McCone sat staring at the scoreboard during a Boston Red Sox–New York Yankees baseball game. As the third inning dragged by, Brad could no longer sit still. "Why did I waste five bucks on this game?" he asked himself angrily. Driving home, he realized how tense he felt. His back muscles were tight and sore. His eyes burned from the exhaust of the freeway traffic. He pulled into the driveway and slammed on the brakes in order to avoid driving over his daughter's bicycle. Angrily he pushed it into the bushes.

After checking the bills that arrived in the afternoon mail, he poured himself two jiggers of Johnny Walker Red Label. His eyes swept the front page of the newspaper before tossing it to the floor. "God-damned inflation is going to get us all," he mumbled. He went into the family room and switched on the television set. Three hours later he pulled himself up the stairs and into bed.

Brad's psychological and biological alarm clocks were going off. If he had listened, his body would have told him what was going on. Your body can tell you when your brain needs a rest and when your muscles need to relax. It can tell you when you need to go for a walk and when you need to go to bed. It can tell you when you're working too hard or not hard enough. It can even tell you about your level of irritation and about potential problems with your spouse, your kids, or the boss.

In order to tune up our internal systems, eliminate corrosive tensions, and regenerate depleted energy supplies, we must look at and listen to what our bodies are telling us. Brad McCone finally heard the message one evening when he ran up the stairs at home, reached the last step, and felt as if he was going to faint. He sat on the bed and realized he was totally winded. He recalled how sluggish he had felt after a big evening meal. His energy level was so low that he could barely bring himself to cut the grass. He knew he had to do something.

Listen to your body! Chronic tiredness may mean the load is too heavy or you have nothing in your job that requires much energy. If your muscles are tense, your body may be crying out for activity. If you feel depressed and lethargic, it may be saying, "I feel trapped." If you keep reaching for the Bufferin or Valium, you know your system is overloaded. It's time to take off the pressure, to alleviate the stress. The very act of listening can be a step in the right direction.

Brad McCone made his decision sitting there on his bed trying to catch his breath. The next day he bought a pair of hiking boots and started walking around the high school football field a mile from his home. Gradually he built up his endurance so that he could hike four to six miles. His favorite place to hike was along a river about an hour's drive from his house.

Six months passed and one Sunday afternoon on a hike Brad found himself listening to his body again. He felt a deep sense of contentment. The air felt refreshingly cool, the leaves on the trees had begun to change color. "I even saw a deer standing perfectly still, sniffing the wind," he recalled. He helped a young boy stalled in his boat, fishing line entangled in the motor. As Brad drove home he realized how good he felt. He found himself chuckling as he thought about how many times as a kid he had gotten his own fishing line tangled on everything but a fish. His back and legs ached, but this kind of soreness was exhilarating—he was in tune with his body again. More important, he had broken the stranglehold that the continuous demands of a high-pressure sales job had brought into his life.

Your body can inform you about your general condition, as Brad's informed him, or if you listen carefully, you can monitor specific changes that occur when you're under stress. It's one thing to read about how job pressures can alter your physiological processes; it's quite another to actually observe the change. You don't have to hook up to a biofeedback machine to find out. "I knew staff meetings made me angry," said one woman. "But it wasn't until I started taking my pulse and it shot up from seventy to eighty-five that I knew it was doing something to me." An engineer said, "I knew I smoked a lot more under stress. So I started to pay attention to my body every time I reached for another cigarette. I could actually feel the tension starting to build right under my diaphragm. Then I started noticing my breathing rate had increased."

Many people can easily distinguish between those days on the job when pressures seem unmanageable and the low stress days. But they easily miss the physiological correlates of these differences. We recommend a simple way to listen to your body more systematically: *keep a stress-response diary*. Simply note down, perhaps on a scale of one to five, the level of stress in your job for that day. Then describe any physical changes that have occurred. After a month you can clearly see the patterns. "It only takes two or three days of high pressure to finish a manuscript," said one writer, "and I have a stiff neck that sends shooting pain right up to the top of my head. It can take weeks for it to go away, but then a couple stressful days and I'm hardly turning my head." One woman in the public-relations office of a large university said, "Once I started watching my stressful days, I noticed that my eyes became like sandpaper, all the moisture seemed to dry up. I'd been to the doctor and he didn't know what could cause it—said to rinse them in Murine. Now I know that when stress lifts, my eyes go back to normal."

One effective way to monitor your stress response is to take your pulse. Find the blood vessel on the inside of your wrist and count the beats for one minute. If you write it down in your stress-response diary, taking your pulse several times each day, you can observe fluctuations that occur with changes in your stress level. Your heart offers an easily accessible listening post to find out how your body is doing. Some long-distance runners take a count of their resting pulse every morning. On those days their pulse rate has become five or ten beats a minute faster, they see it as a sign of overall stress and take a day off or engage in less vigorous training. By monitoring your pulse rate over a period of weeks, you can note the kinds of work stress that cause it to race even a few beats faster. "It's the best clue I know for finding out when I'm under pressures at work," said one department head in a large manufacturing firm. "I found that days when I rushed from one meeting to another my pulse rate would go from its normal seventy-five beats a minute to eighty. And it stayed there for a day or two even if the stress went down. I didn't think much about it until one day I ran a few numbers on my calculator and realized that meant my heart had to do nearly two million beats of overtime a year. That made me really start to do something to deal with those pressures."

As with this man, listening to your body and raising your consciousness of work stress often go together. We believe that people who want to live lives free from job burnout are well advised to make these strategies part of their everyday life, as routine as brushing their teeth.

Take Control of
Your Stress
Perceptions

Becoming aware of work stress and your body's response will not bring job burnout under control. Indeed, we found some people in our research who were keenly aware of both: they complained loudly about the various pressures on their job and how bad they felt almost every day. But they never took the next important step of gaining control over their perceptions of stress. Many of us can't phase out the stress components of our job, but we can change our perceptions.

Although some stress events, such as being mugged or having a loved one die, profoundly affect nearly everyone, the power of most stress events varies from one person to another. This comes from the fact that we learn to perceive stress in different ways. Consider the following example: Jerry Albert and his wife Nina live three miles from the Buffalo airport, directly under the flight path where 747s, DC 10s, and other smaller jets land daily. When these planes skim the Alberts' rooftop, their windows shake, the television screen dances in wild patterns, and the Albert family conversations come to a halt. Some evenings, the noise of as many as ten or fifteen jets bombards their otherwise quiet neighborhood.

Both Jerry and Nina dislike these planes. But you won't find much similarity in their attitudes toward the noisy jets. Jerry fumes with anger. "Those damned planes are driving me crazy!" he has shouted above the deafening noise on many nights. "Someday one is going to crash right in our neighborhood and then they'll move that airport to the country where it belongs." With each new vibration and high-pitched roar of engines, Jerry's pulse races; his blood pressure rises; adrenalin and other hormones pour into his bloodstream preparing him for fight or flight. But he can do little except seethe with frustration.

Nina dislikes the noise, but not enough to trigger the stress response. She says philosophically, "I just figure it isn't worth getting upset about. We bought this house. We like the area and we don't have any money to move. Anyway, there could be worse things, like living next to the Love Canal with all those chemicals coming up through the ground to give you cancer."

It's almost as if Jerry and Nina Albert each had different "stress antennae." Jerry picks up the weakest signal of an approaching airplane and his picture of stress comes in loud and clear. Nina's antenna, on the other hand, only brings in a faint picture of the stress event. Even when planes have shaken the house all evening she has been known to say, "I hardly noticed them."

Jerry and Nina obviously took different courses in stress perception; from early childhood they had different teachers who instructed them to look at this type of frustration in different ways. By precept and example, these teachers taught Nina to ignore and minimize the stress of noise and intrusions into her privacy. Jerry's teachers instructed him in the fine art of blowing these same frustrations all out of proportion. Like all of us, they acquired these perceptual skills informally, as they grew up, and now they seem God given and permanent. But such is not the case. We can all discard old ways of perceiving stress and learn new ones.

We hasten to point out that Nina has no more control over her stress-perceiving process than Jerry does over his. Like most of us, their perceptual screens both work in a reflexive fashion. With other stress events, their reactions take them in opposite directions. For instance, Jenny, their nineteen-year-old daughter, recently moved in with her boyfriend. This violation of family morals and their Baptist religious convictions has brought intense, unrelieved stress to Nina, who says, "My daughter is living in sin and I just can't accept it." Jerry doesn't approve and feels bothered, but has an easier time, saying, "Well, it's her life and she has to make her own decisions." Nina's stress response goes into high gear over her daughter's behavior; Jerry's goes out of control when the jets fly overhead. They have not learned to take control of their stress perceptions.

The first step in taking control is to give up the popular myth that says, "Something outside of myself is completely responsible for the stress I feel." If Jerry continues to blame low-flying aircraft for upsetting him, the stress will continue to control his life. If Nina continues to blame her daughter's living arrangement, she will go on feeling stress until that changes. If, instead, they accept the fact that their own perceptions of these situations partly create the stress they feel, relief becomes possible.

Probably the most stressful aspect of Phil Korbeski's job as a directory-assistance operator comes from having too much supervision. He intensely dislikes the feeling that his S.A. knows exactly how fast he has performed on any day or at any hour of the year. He resents the monthly evaluation conferences. "Why can't they just trust us to do our job?" Phil complains. "It's like you're back in the third grade where the teacher walks up and down the rows making sure everyone is reading *Dick and Jane!*" If you talked only to Phil Korbeski, you would come away with the impression that this kind of supervision is an inescapable stress for directory-assistance operators. However, both the nature and intensity of the stress for Phil depends to a great extent on how he has learned to *perceive* job supervision.

Mary Watkins has worked as a directory-assistance operator in the same office with Phil for three and a half years. At first she resented the supervision practices, but not with Phil's intensity. They often talked while on break or had lunch together and discussed their mutual dislike of the S.A. "Pretty soon I began to resent being checked on so much it was making me miserable," said Mary. "The more I listened to Phil complain, the more I thought about how unjust it was for them to treat us like kids, and the more I found myself complaining to others. Pretty soon, just seeing the S.A. walk around the quads or write our time up on the board made me upset." Without her realizing it, Mary's *perception* of this work stress had begun to change.

But Mary had learned to take control of her stress perceptions. When she realized what was happening, she took action, something she had done often in the past. "I suddenly saw myself turning into a bitch, complaining about things that hadn't bothered me before. 'I'm making myself miserable,' I thought. 'This has got to stop.' First, I avoided talking with Phil about the supervisors. Then I started making mental lists of all the things I *did* enjoy about my job. I tried to talk to my S.A. on our coffee break, just to see her as a human being, somebody who was just doing her job. Then I began to think of it as a big game. We were all playing a game and my S.A. had her part to play and I had mine and it didn't matter that much how fast I went or how many mistakes I made. Wow! In a few days I was even surprised at how quickly the cloud over my job had lifted and, you know, at my next evaluation I had the best score I'd ever made."

As Mary discovered, mere acceptance of the fact that your perceptions help determine the stress you feel does not change those perceptions. You have to stop laying the entire blame on external work stress, but you also need to consider seriously *other possible definitions of the situation.* Too much supervision had become a stress for Mary when she unwittingly came to accept a definition of her job as something like this: "The biggest and worst part of this job is continuously being checked, graded, and criticized by stupid supervisors." She began to change this definition by considering all of the following alternative definitions:

1. It's not the biggest part of my job, there's lots of things I enjoy. (Making a list expanded this definition.)
2. My supervisor is not a stupid, critical person, but another human being trying to earn a living by doing her job.

3. This job isn't the most serious undertaking in my life, but only a game I play to earn a living.
4. It doesn't matter how fast I go or how many mistakes I make.

The fact that these new definitions are not necessarily *true* does not, in this case, make them any less effective in changing Mary's perception of stress. Obviously, that's not always the case. You cannot stand in front of an oncoming locomotive and say, "It's not important whether I'm hit by this train; it's only a game; it really can't injure me." Furthermore, although Mary easily revised her definition of the situation, Phil may find this extremely difficult. In fact, it may prove almost as stressful for him to try and change his perception of too much supervision as to endure the pressure of the supervisory practices themselves. We do not believe that people can take complete control of their perceptions of stress and thereby render every form of work stress powerless. For millions of people, the best, perhaps the only option, is to change the stress itself. However, we believe that most people can make significant changes in their perceptual practices. We can consider other possible definitions of the situation. And, if successful, it can give us dramatic and lasting relief from work stress.

Here is a simple but effective exercise to help bring your perceptions under control. Imagine that in the darkroom of your mind there is a piece of photographic equipment that can *enlarge* and *reduce* the mental picture you have taken of some stress event. Begin by "developing" the mental picture you normally operate with; take out a sheet of paper and briefly describe the way you think about too much supervision, the boredom of the assembly line, the lack of challenging work, or any other frustration in your job. Phil Korbeski might develop his picture of his dead-end job as follows:

This job has no future. I could go another five years before I get promoted into another job—or it might be fifteen. The yearly salary increments don't keep pace with the cost of living. I feel trapped in this dead-end job.

Observe that this mental picture states facts, impressions, and feelings. Don't worry about making an objective description; simply record what you think and feel on most days about the particular work stress.

Now you're ready to begin the *enlarging* process. Imagine that you have adjusted the photographic equipment to "enlarge" the frustrations you feel about the situation. Write a brief description of this mental picture. For example:

> This directory-assistance-operator job is a complete dead end. This company is out to screw every employee and I'll never move up to a better job. My life is being wasted and I feel like a caged animal.

Now, mentally adjust the equipment and see if you can enlarge the picture again, this time to its largest size, to the point where you would quit your job, move your family, go on welfare, or take some other drastic action to escape the stress. Phil Korbeski might describe such a mental picture as follows:

> I've had it. This job is the pits. It blocks completely my need for job satisfaction. It has no future whatsoever and each day grinds me down even more until I'm becoming a robot. I can't stand it a minute more. I'm going to take my headset and walk up to my supervisor and tell her in no un-certain terms what she can do with this job! I don't care if I have to go on welfare for the rest of my life; that would be better than suffering in this dead-end job for five more minutes.

Once you reach this upper limit, take a few minutes to see what it does to your stress response. Read it over slowly; mull over the in-justices you perceive, the anger you feel. Let yourself get really in-volved in perceiving this situation as a high-level stress. You'll probably feel your stomach tighten up, your breathing become more rapid, and your heart begin to pound. All to the good! Now you have not only become aware of work stress, how your body responds, but *how your mental perceptions can influence these processes.* You may come away with the feeling, "I made this happen! I imagined this as an awful stress and made my body respond as it did. Maybe I have some control over things after all."

Once you reach the upper limit for perceiving something as stressful, return to your first mental picture, your usual definition of the situation, and start to "reduce" the picture in size. Here's Phil Korbeski's job again, which he feels has little future, reduced in two steps:

1. This job has no future. At least that's the way it seems right now. But something might come along; I should check the personnel bulletin board. And, anyway, these are hard times and I can stay on the job for now even if it has little future. I do get a pretty good salary even if it doesn't keep up with inflation.

2. This is a directory-assistance-operator job, right? And no one ever said it was the first step to becoming president of Ma Bell! The future doesn't look great, but who knows, that might change. And anyway, I want to keep this job until my wife finishes nursing school. I'm not sure my hopes for the future will ever be in a job anyway, but in my family and my hobby of collecting antiques. And furthermore, not only are there lots of other jobs that would be much worse, I could be out of work altogether in this recession. I'm really thankful I have this job for now.

After you reduce your perceptual picture of the stress to its smallest size, test your feelings against what you see. Then read slowly over the list, from the least frustrating stress picture to the largest, most upsetting one. Read slowly, trying to sense what happens to your stress response as you shift from one potential way of viewing your situation to another. This simple act of mentally shifting up and down this perceptual scale will increase your ability to control your perceptions.

We call this simple mental exercise "Darkroom Therapy." It is based on techniques developed by professional psychologists who use cognitive-behavior therapy to help people gain greater control of their lives.[3] You can practice this darkroom therapy at any time or any place. When you have identified the range of ways to perceive a stress event, you will have to decide which perception you want to make your own. For those situations you find impossible to change or escape (such as the airplanes that fly over Jerry Albert's house), realistic acceptance is the best route to preventing more stress and possible burnout. Other stress events call for less acceptance in order to maintain your own efforts to bring about change. Dr. Albert Ellis, a noted cognitive behavioral psychologist, has summarized this perspective on dealing with stress:

> This attitude—as epitomized in the writings of Marcus Aurelius, St. Francis, Reinhold Niebuhr and others—says: "I feel determined to strive to use whatever power I have to change the unpleasant stresses of life that I can change, to dislike but realistically accept those that I cannot change, and to have the wisdom to know the difference between the two." This kind of a philosophy will not eliminate all stress or our overreactions to it. But it will significantly help![4]

Lower Your Expectations

Now we turn to a closely related, but distinctly personal, strategy for taking control of job burnout: lowering our achievement expectations. Consider the following three cases.

"How can I be a mother, wife, den mother, church organist, and work forty hours besides? I guess I must be nuts to do all of this!" Mary Conklin felt exhausted and irritated. She had just arrived home from a hard day at the office. Her daughter's first words were: "Why don't I have any clean underwear?"

Mary Conklin put a casserole into the microwave and then surveyed the house. Newspapers lay strewn over the living-room floor. Muddy boots lined the entryway. Coats and sweaters hung over the backs of chairs. Dust lay on the dining-room table. Wherever she looked, Mary saw things she ought to do. She slumped into a chair. "I just can't keep up anymore."

John "Brack" Brackenfield almost killed himself through his unrealistic expectations. He bragged that he could drive longer and farther than any other truck driver at the Bristow Trucking Company. Last year he logged in over two hundred thousand miles. A young driver began to challenge his claim. He was logging in almost twenty thousand miles a month. Day after day Brack tried to squeeze in an extra fifty miles. One night at 2:00 A.M. he fell asleep at the wheel. He not only didn't meet his mileage expectations, he almost lost his life.

Chuck Hammel had a personal goal of having his firm sell 10,000 tires in a single year. He drove the salesmen hard. He often would work an extra shift himself in order to reach his goal. In early December it became obvious that the firm would, at best, sell 9,500 units. Chuck felt depressed and angry. It didn't help that his company was in the black. He called a sales meeting and unloaded his frustrations on the sales staff. Two of them promptly quit. On December 31 the total was in: sales for the year amounted to 8,910 units.

The personal histories of Mary Conklin, Brack Brackenfield, and Chuck Hammel are different yet similar. Each had high expectations. Mary Conklin was trying to do triple duty in the home, community, and on the job. Brack Brackenfield wanted to be known as the superman driver of the truck company. Chuck Hammel wanted to be named salesman of the year by the Chamber of Commerce.

Why do we push ourselves so hard? Why do we burden ourselves with unrealistic deadlines? Why do so many of our work expectations continue to go up and up and up? At a very early age we learn we should accomplish a lot in a short period of time. "Idle hands are the devil's workshop." As we grow older we encounter bosses who tell us that "time is money." In addition to doing well in our jobs, we live with high expectations in our roles as mother, father, husband, wife, friend, neighbor, civic contributor, church member, and so forth. We live in a society that emphasizes doing and doing fast. When 2,252 workers were asked if they commonly felt rushed, just to do things they had to do, 25 percent said they *always felt rushed;* less than 15 percent said they never felt rushed.[5] Under these conditions, you can either increase stress by speeding up to get more done, or lower your expectations about what you *have to achieve,* and thereby lower your stress.

Mary Conklin realized that something had to give. She resigned as den mother and told the principal that she could not serve another term as vice-president of the Parent-Teachers Association. She assigned household duties to each member of the family. Although a bit reluctant, everyone started to pitch in. Mary Conklin began to take control of her life by lowering her expectations.

Brack Brackenfield and Chuck Hammel had difficulty in lowering their expectations. As soon as Brack recovered from his accident, he put in even longer hours behind the wheel. "Have a lot of catching up to do." Two months later a second major accident demolished the truck and over $100,000 worth of expensive equipment. Two weeks later the company fired him.

Chuck Hammel not only chewed out the salesmen for not meeting the sales targets, but he set even higher ones for the next year. He drove the salesmen harder, raising their stress levels. Morale eroded. Their sickness rate shot up. Absenteeism and job turnover increased. One year later, tire sales had dropped by twenty-five percent and Hammel had to sell the business.

Don't set yourself up for failure by setting unattainable career goals. Hitching your wagon to a star can cause enormous stress if it is a million light-years beyond our galaxy. Dr. Matti K. Gershenfeld, a psychologist, notes: "We tell kids that everybody can be President or chairman of the board. The reality is that a lot can't and there's no real confrontation of why they can't—because they never accept reality. They force themselves to perform to reach a goal they have no chance of reaching."[6]

Learn to lower your goals. If you never become vice-president of your firm, principal of the school, or foreman on your shift, it doesn't mean you've failed. In fact, you may live a much richer life in the type of position that you now have.

People with unrealistic career goals usually respond in one of two ways, each one an expression of burnout. Some become passive, give up on their goals, believing they aren't worth anything. They often retire on the job or in some cases drop out of the work force and become beachcombers. They have caught what one physician calls the "Peggy Lee Syndrome," named for her song, "Is That All There Is?" Other individuals become aggressive. As Dr. Gershenfeld says, "You keep bombing away, keep screaming. Everything that goes wrong is somebody else's fault."[7]

A better response is to say, "I'm going to do the best I can at what I'm doing. But I'm not going to kill myself. I'm going to take all that energy expended in worry over not meeting my goals and put it into activities that bring some rewards." Once you lower career goals and high expectations you've placed on yourself, you might take up sailing, tennis, the stock market, jogging, antiques, Big Brothers, politics, stamp collecting, or some other hobby. Many people have discovered that when they quit worrying about where they would be five years from now, they became more relaxed and enjoyed life again. Ironically, those characteristics might be the key to landing a better job.

It helps to lower expectations by setting realistic goals during each working day. Marty Kimble was determined to have all the dictation off the belt by 4:30 P.M. each day. A laudable goal, but not always realistic. On days that she couldn't complete her typing because of various interruptions, she found her stomach in knots. At three-thirty, with two more hours of transcribing to do, she became anxious and irritable. Marty would be better off if she did what could reasonably be accomplished and then continue typing the next day.

Sometimes workers need to lower their high expectations of other people. Randy Altman finished a degree in sociology and took a job as director of a shelter home for abused adolescents. The court placed the kids in the shelter home until permanent homes could be found. Within months Randy's frustration level had skyrocketed. "These kids don't appreciate anything you do for them. You turn your back and they steal you blind. They're sneaking off to smoke dope and fights break out almost every day."

A probation-officer friend noticed Randy's anger. "You're going to burn out quick if you don't change your attitude," he said. "You've got to remember where these kids are coming from." A month later, a much calmer Randy Altman confided to his friend, "That really helped. I've really lowered my expectations. I don't expect them to be everyday teenagers. When they aren't, I'm not surprised. And now the kids are starting to trust me a lot more."

When we lower our expectations, we detach ourselves emotionally from a stressful job. The more pressures we feel, no matter what kind of work we do, the more distance we need from that job. Most of us invest our lives in work. We want it to mean something. We believe in what we're doing and wouldn't have it any other way. Although basically satisfied, we still may need to use our minds to gain a healthy distance from our work. We have seen this kind of action not only help control job burnout but also improve the quality of work.

When we first talked to George Feldman, a high-school math teacher, he was burning out. "I just can't leave my work at school, I'd never finish. I love teaching, but it's wearing me down. I just can't get those kids off my mind at night." About a year later when we asked George how his job was going, he answered enthusiastically, "Great! It's Fred's Factory now and that has made all the difference."

We could immediately sense that George had a new emotional detachment from work, but his answer puzzled us. He explained, "Last summer, my oldest son, Fred, took a job in a food-processing factory where he worked on a slow assembly line. He had to pack these bags of beans into cartons. He had a great time! He didn't take the work very seriously and devised all sorts of ways to escape on the job. He'd rearrange bean bags, throw them, try new procedures for packing, pack with his eyes closed, all the time thinking about other things. I began to realize I needed to see my job like Fred's Factory." When we asked if he now treated his students like so many bean bags, George laughed and said, "Well, not exactly. Actually, I'm probably treating them better now that I am a bit more detached from the job."

The best way to begin treating job burnout is by taking control of this debilitating condition. This can help you lower your stress, raise your hopes, and start you on the road to recovery. Taking control doesn't always come easily, especially not after years of chronic burnout. But you can do it by systematically applying the personal strategies of understanding the nature of job burnout, raising your consciousness of work stress, listening to your body, taking control of your perceptions of stress, and lowering your expectations.

Chapter Five
Stress Safety Valves

If you live in a northern climate you've probably watched someone try to move a stalled car out of a snowdrift. Some drivers impatiently step on the accelerator in a futile attempt to plow forward, spinning their wheels frantically as the rut grows deeper and deeper. Some rock back and forth, hoping to gain enough momentum to move ahead. Others flag down a passerby and ask for help or even call a tow truck. A minority of drivers get out of the car, analyze the situation, plot their strategy, shovel the snow, put down a little sand, straighten the wheels, and give the car just enough gas to move ahead slowly.

People respond in similar ways to job burnout. Some curse their situation and take drastic but futile action. They quit their job, leave their town, end their marriage, or switch careers without ever having learned to take control of the problem. In 1977, a nationwide survey that found the highest levels of worker discontent in decades asked people if they would make an effort to find a new job in the next year. An astounding one in three workers said they did plan to look for a new job.[1] A minority of job burnouts stand back from their job and family, study the nature of job burnout, then plot their strategy and take corrective action.

In chapter 2 we identified *faulty stress safety valves* as a major job-burnout risk factor. We now want to consider how to improve defective safety valves and increase their number and variety. We like to think that stress safety valves serve at least two important functions. First, they enable you to escape the direct pressure of work stress. Your instinctive stress response mobilizes you for a single escape strategy: vigorous physical flight. If you can develop effective stress safety valves, it's as if you are taking conscious control of this flight response. Sometimes it will involve carefully planned physical escape, but just as often psychological escape. In either case, you will find that these safety valves relieve the stress.

The second function of stress safety valves is to counteract the bio-chemical and psychological changes that occur when our bodies mobilize to deal with stress. You may or may not be aware of this buildup, but it occurs nevertheless. It manifests itself in muscle tension. It shows up in changes in body chemistry we can sometimes feel, as with a burning stomach, itchy eyes and skin, or dry mouth. We can become aware of it through changes in physiological processes such as heart rate, respiration rate, and even nausea from digestive-tract changes. An increasingly large body of scientific studies has shown that this mobilization buildup includes biochemical changes associated with chronic disease. These manifestations, such as elevated cholesterol levels in the blood, are outside our awareness but can be detected in the laboratory.

Sometimes the stress safety valves relieve stress and mobilization buildup through rest, relaxation, and sleep. But many times, these safety valves work on the *stress substitution principle:* relieving one type of stress by substituting a different form of stress. For example, if you're emotionally drained from a job that requires intense mental concentration, relief can come if you play a physically exhausting game of racquetball. If you suffer from a job that doesn't challenge your mind, you can relieve stress by doing something that requires concentration. The substitution of one form of stress for another appears to give our bodies the chance to restore our immediately available adaptation energy. Job burnout follows the depletion of energy reserves when the same type of stress goes on day after day, week after week, with no relief.

As you read about the stress safety valves in this chapter or discover new ones from other sources, keep this stress substitution principle in mind. If you're suffering from the boredom of an unchallenging job, you may need a safety-valve activity that offers competition and achievement. If you work in a heavily controlled job environment, as Phil Korbeski does in his job as a directory-assistance operator, you may need the freedom of hiking alone in the woods. If you've been passed over for promotion, and a sense of failure eats away at you day after day, find a safety valve that brings the satisfaction of success. If you must deal with demanding clients all day, a couple of nights a week at a garden club might prove the best safety valve. By the same token, if your life at home and at work involve the stress of inter-personal conflict, engaging in highly competitive sports might not serve as the best safety valve, but only increase your overall level of stress.

The following safety valves are ones that have worked for hundreds of people. Not all will fit your needs, nor does this list exhaust the possibilities. But if you can find even a few that become part of your daily experience, you can prevent the pressure of stress and the tension of your body's mobilization efforts from leading to job burnout.

Change Gears

Changing gears involves shifting *from* work *to* something else. If nothing else exists for you, you may remain stuck in the work gear. In order to change gears, try to find activities that capture your interest. Psychologists call such pursuits "intrinsic motivators." They give you a feeling of well-being. The more burned out you've become, the longer it may take you to find some intrinsic motivators that will help you leave the job behind both mentally and physically.

Frank Hassenberg, the president of a small firm that produces computer software, was exhausted. His company was being squeezed out by the computer giants. His products had piled up in the warehouse even though he pumped more resources into the advertising budget. Nothing seemed to help.

Each evening Frank would sit in his overstuffed chair staring at the wall. He tried to read novels but couldn't get interested. He began to doubt his own administrative ability. His feelings of discontent began to spill over into his personal life. He gave up two season tickets to the San Diego Chargers football games. "Just don't have time for that anymore." When his wife talked to him, his mind kept going over problems back at the office. He seldom had time for the children and his teenage son in turn felt that "Dad lives in another world."

Four months prior to the onset of Frank's financial difficulties, a small event happened that later paid unexpected psychological dividends. It taught Frank how to change gears. It started when he bought a dog for his son.

Rolfe was a handsome Norwegian elkhound. Frank had made a bargain with his wife, who argued against the purchase. "I'll go along with it," she said, "if you'll promise to take it to obedience school." Frank agreed without realizing what it would require. When Rolfe outgrew his puppy stage and the classes began, Frank debated about whether to enroll. "How can I waste an evening training a dog when my world is falling apart at work?" he asked. "I'm not going to do it," his wife announced firmly, "and you made a promise."

The first evening at class Frank was amazed at what he saw. Dogs everywhere! He visited with other dog owners and the diversity of people surprised him—an attorney with a poodle, a physician with a Great Dane, a railroad repairman with a Saint Bernard, a nurse with a beagle, housewives with German shepherds and Doberman pinschers, and other people with every conceivable breed.

The first night, Rolfe seemed uncontrollable and Frank only managed to keep him at his left side by brute force. "Now, you will each have to spend at least twenty minutes a day teaching your dog to heel this week," the trainer said as class ended. Every evening after work, Frank took Rolfe out for twenty minutes of training. At first he resented the time, but soon it grew to thirty and then forty minutes.

While Rolfe was learning to heel, Frank was learning to change gears. He had never done anything like this before and he loved it. Once or twice a week he found himself taking Rolfe out again after dinner for a free run in a large, open field. Rolfe caught on quickly; by the third week he would "stay," even off leash, and by the fourth week he would lie down and sit. At the last class every owner had to show what his dog had learned. Rolfe's performance was flawless. Even Frank couldn't believe how obedient his dog had become. After his last command and Rolfe's instant obedience, everyone applauded and Frank received the top award for the evening.

Driving home that night he thought about the dog and his problems at work. "It was about the only activity I did where I didn't mull over the problems back at the office," he recalled. "And I found myself going to work the next morning with one hell of a better attitude."

Changing gears not only removes your attention from the pressures of work; it helps drain off the pent-up tensions. You may find the pursuit of almost any nonwork project or hobby can reduce stress. A business executive who frequently came home seething with frustration had trouble changing gears. "I found myself working just because there wasn't anything else I wanted to do. Then I decided to remodel my basement. It really helped, partly 'cause it was such a different type of activity. Every nail I pounded seemed like some client who had let me down!"

Leonard Randolph works in the printing and duplicating shop at a small college in Salt Lake City. His one consuming passion was fishing, but when the winter would roll around, he'd put away his gear and wait impatiently for spring. The winter months often brought more work pressure, with faculty and staff wanting course outlines and reports duplicated. "I'd come home exhausted, too tired to do much but watch TV. One night I decided to check out my fishing gear. I started taking reels apart and sharpening hooks on all my plugs. Pretty soon I was visiting a sporting goods store a couple nights a week, checking out new lures. That cleaning job stretched out for several months. I'd find myself thinking about it during the day, and now you couldn't get me to stay after five o'clock."

The things you can do to change gears are unlimited. A housewife said, "I always wanted to learn to play the Hammond organ. At forty-seven I thought that if I didn't start now, I'd never learn. I forgot many of the problems I was having with my mother."

As we said earlier, it probably helps to pick something that contrasts with what you do all day. If you work with people, you may want an individual pursuit to change gears. If you work alone, you may need to join a class. An assistant hospital administrator found a renewing contrast: "One day I got so sick of listening to all the bull in a staff meeting that I decided I had to get my mind off of it. I took a course at the vocational school. I'm a total klutz when it comes to cars but pretty soon I could adjust a carburetor and even time the engine. It was good therapy. You get awful tired of all that committee-work nonsense."

Don't overlook the fact that changing gears can involve the entire family. You might help reduce the stress others are facing by a little creative planning together. The Dick Bardsley family agreed they would spend every Saturday afternoon during the summer months together. One member of the family would plan the activity for a given Saturday with an important ground rule: everyone had to go along with whatever that person decided.

When Chip, a twelve-year-old, planned the Saturday outing they invariably went to a movie. It proved to be a cool way to spend many a hot Saturday afternoon. Mrs. Bardsley used her Saturday afternoons to tour some of the local points of interest they had neglected. At the end of the summer the family had visited the assembly line of a truck company, a brewery, and the state capital. Dick Bardsley invariably chose a sporting event for the family to attend. They saw two professional baseball games, a preseason Pittsburgh Steeler football game, and even went fishing at a nearby lake. By the time school started, everyone agreed the outings had made their summer. Dick realized that he hadn't spent a single Saturday at the office. Monday mornings he felt both calm and excited about his work. Changing gears had lowered their family stress level.

Cut Back on Excessive Hours

For many people, burnout and overtime go hand in hand. But how much work does it take before the pressure reaches the critical point?

You will have to answer that question for yourself. For some people it takes more than sixty hours a week to bring on unrelieved stress; for others even forty hours may create problems. Although we can't say exactly when you should cut back, we do know two important things about the hours required by many jobs.

First, the predictions of shorter work weeks have not come true for most Americans. Even the forty-hour week is a myth for many people. In 1969, 39 percent of all workers put in more than forty hours a week. By 1977 that figure had climbed to 42 percent. Thousands of workers rush off to second jobs in their efforts to make ends meet in a time of double-digit inflation. (The 14.3 percent who had second jobs in 1977 represented a 5 percent increase from 1969.) If you consider all the hours of work Americans put in, whether they have one or two jobs, by 1977 nearly half (47 percent) worked more than forty hours a week; 27 percent grind out more than fifty hours a week, and 13 percent are trapped in jobs that require more than sixty hours a week. That means twelve hours a day if you want to take the weekends off or putting in seven full days a week! No wonder some people argue that we are a workaholic nation.[2]

The second thing we know about excessive hours has to do with stress. The more hours you work, the more likely you are to burn out. In a national study conducted by the Survey Research Center at the University of Michigan, 33 percent of all workers reported they often had to work overtime. Only a tiny fraction (13 percent) reported they never put in overtime. This study also measured job-related tension and discovered a significant relationship: the more overtime people worked, the higher their levels of tension.[3]

If you suffer from any job-burnout symptom and feel like Fred Blake, the Los Angeles mechanic, who said, "If I only worked a forty-hour week it would be like a holiday!" you may need to cut back on excessive hours.

It was 4:30 on a hot, humid Friday afternoon. At the end of a horrendous week, Catherine Ispler's desk was still stacked high with unfilled orders. The telephone never seemed to stop ringing as irate salesmen demanded to know why she had not processed their orders.

Five minutes before Catherine left work, an inch-thick report from her boss arrived with the following message: "Catherine: Read before Monday morning. Important."

Catherine tossed the report and the unprocessed orders into her briefcase. Exhausted, she headed for the elevators. "Just aren't enough hours in a week!" she mumbled to the janitor as the doors slid open. When someone in the car pool asked Catherine about her weekend plans she replied, "Oh, nothing special." For the past year her weekends seemed almost nonexistent. It was always something—a new report, catching up on orders, or analyzing the budget.

For many workers, if they could create an eighth day in the week, they would work that day also. Catherine Ispler, for example, usually worked all day Saturday trying to catch up on things she didn't get done during the week. Brad Crikey, a high-school civics teacher, works every Sunday on next week's lesson plans. If he has tests or papers to read, Saturday goes down the work drain as well. Kip Konners, a taxi-cab driver, spends Saturdays repairing his cab or working an extra shift.

Why do American workers put in so many hours? The self-employed often find themselves trapped by a belief that no one else can do the work. The fourteen-hour days Ruth Rogers works at her own laundromat-cleaning business add up to more than eighty hours a week. But she can't see any alternative. "If I close up at six o'clock, I'm gonna lose a lot of business. If I hire someone else, it would cost me a lot and they wouldn't know what my customers wanted." If the truth were known, Ruth could stand the loss of income but not the loss of feeling indispensable.

Some wage and salary employees can't avoid working overtime. However, that problem isn't as widespread as many think. In a national survey, less than 20 percent said they could *not* refuse overtime without some penalty. That leaves 80 percent who choose to work the extra hours, and since one out of five do not even get paid for overtime work, something besides money keeps them on the job.[4] One thing that contributes to this phenomenon is what we call the *burnout work cycle.* It serves as a ball and chain to keep workers locked in to long hours.

Bonnie Mercheson represents a typical case. A few years out of nurses' training, Bonnie took a job as staff nurse on a pediatrics ward of Eastside Hospital in Little Rock, Arkansas. Like many hospitals, Eastside was understaffed and Bonnie's eight-hour shifts often seemed like a marathon. "I'd ask someone to bring me back a sandwich from the hospital cafeteria and I'd eat between checking IV's and taking temperatures." But the stress of too much work couldn't compare with the heartbreak that came from seeing the children who filled her workday.

"When you see a microcephalic baby . . . or one without arms and legs, it really gets to you. And the little two-year-olds, like Johnny, who I'm taking care of now, with leukemia. He has to have chemotherapy every day and it makes him sick. He cries for his mommy and doesn't know why we keep sticking him with needles. It really pulls me apart. I come off an eight-hour shift just drained emotionally. I get home and break into tears for no reason."

As job burnout set in, Bonnie found herself sticking around after her shift, "just to make sure things were going OK." Knowing how rushed the day shift had been, she wanted to make it just a little easier for those kids. The hospital policy allowed no overtime, so Bonnie would punch out, then go back on the ward to finish up things she had begun. She started doing this once or twice a week; then she found herself working an extra hour or two almost every night. And the burnout work cycle that kept her tied to the ward only increased her depression and fatigue. Without realizing it, she was working nearly fifty hours a week.

Cutting back on overtime can require you to tell your boss no, a sometimes difficult assignment. Jack Hammond, a copywriter in the promotion department at Peterson Publishing Company, felt coerced into working late several nights a week. "We're a deadline business and everything is due two weeks ago. The head copywriter is single and that job is her life, so she kept asking me to stay and finish up something so it could go on to keylining the next day. I felt like I couldn't turn her down, but finally I just told her that all this overtime was affecting my family life. I couldn't keep it up. She took it real well and now only asks if it's really a major crisis, and then I don't mind staying."

Catherine Ispler, the secretary we introduced earlier in this section, muddled along in a state of fatigue and frustration until her husband exploded one day. "You're married to that goddamned job! You put in forty hours at the office and another forty at home." Shaken by his outburst, Catherine started by making a clear distinction between work time and overtime. She kept track of her overtime hours and it shocked her to discover how much work had invaded her evenings and weekends. She began to plan other activities after work and to leave her briefcase at the office. "I'm sorry, I have a prior commitment tonight that I can't break," she would tell her boss when he asked her to stay late. She didn't think it necessary to explain that the "prior commitment" was to her family.

Many people want to work fewer hours. In a national survey conducted for the U.S. Department of Labor by Robert Quinn, 950 workers were asked, "Would you like to spend less time working so that you could spend more time with your family, even if it meant having less money?" Of these workers, 42 percent said yes in spite of significant reductions in buying power brought on by inflation.[5]

Why, then, do so many people find it difficult to cut back on the extra hours of work that lead to job burnout? We believe that the burnout work cycle works in several ways. With people like Bonnie Mercheson, the nurse working with children, as she grows more fatigued, her ability to achieve a healthy detachment from patients declines. Exhausted from work stress, she gives in more easily to the tug at her emotions by helpless, suffering children, which leads to longer hours of work, and more exposure to work stress. This downward cycle makes her especially vulnerable to moving rapidly through the stages of job burnout.

For other people, the burnout work cycle operates in a slightly different way. They can manage high-stress jobs as long as their safety valves are in good working order. Then along comes something that pulls them into working overtime: the boss requests it, guilt makes it seem necessary, a personal deadline demands it. The extra hours of work *prevent* them from engaging in the safety-valve activity that was a shield against too much stress. "I can pinpoint when I started down the road to job burnout," said one woman. "I had to put in a couple weeks of overtime at the office; I had to give up swimming four evenings a week, which I really enjoy. At the end of those two weeks I felt emotionally drained, and then I started staying late for no good reason, just to catch up." Six months later she woke up to the fact that job burnout had taken control of her life. For many people, it's difficult to say no to overtime; job burnout makes it even harder.

Finally, the job-burnout cycle keeps some people glued to their jobs through inefficiency. Some kind of work stress starts the cycle of energy consumption and consequent fatigue. Then they lose their efficiency at work and have to stay late more and more frequently to finish up. But this overtime only speeds up the process, for it adds an additional work stress. Often, as the burnout victim falls farther behind, he or she can lose self-confidence and work even harder and longer to make up for the sense of inadequacy. It's a self-destructive cycle that speeds up the job-burnout process.

Exercise

Because burnout almost always comes from excessive mental and emotional stress, physical exercise offers one of the best safety valves. Dr. George Williams, Director of the Institute of Health Research in San Francisco, believes that exercise is one of the most effective ways to counteract work stress. He suggests that it works as a stress innoculation, not only relieving the pressure at the end of a hectic day, but making it possible for you to deal more effectively with stress the next day.[6]

Jim Jackson's youth director job meant ongoing conflict with the minister at Memorial Presbyterian Church. Jim found that a couple of games of handball dissipated his anger: "Sometimes I'd find myself really slamming the ball and even muttering to myself about what was going on at work. But I felt a lot better after the game."

Regular exercise is one of the best antidotes for the fatigue of burnout. Scientists studied a group of workers at Exxon's physical-fitness lab in New York and found that after only six months of exercise, these workers had a significantly increased capacity for work. Most reported they felt less tired at the end of a workday.[7]

Exercise does not have to be strenuous or competitive. Walking offers many benefits and can put you into excellent cardiovascular condition, as well as reduce stress. Whatever form of physical activity you take up, start slowly and work up to higher levels of exertion. If you can build your endurance until you jog, walk, swim, or bicycle for thirty minutes, several times each week, you will maintain an excellent level of fitness.

Dr. John Greist of the University of Wisconsin tested the value of jogging as a treatment for depression, one of the major symptoms of burnout. He divided depressed patients into two groups. One underwent psychotherapy, the other began jogging. At the end of ten weeks, those who exercised showed more improvement than those undergoing psychotherapy.[8]

Increasingly, business corporations have recognized that exercise can prevent burnout. Company gymnasiums and time off for exercise have become commonplace in many organizations. A Soviet factory introduced a running program for all its employees, and absenteeism due to sickness dropped dramatically. Days lost went from 436 per year to 42.[9]

If you must live with a job that fills your day with pressure, gnaws away at your satisfaction, or leaves you feeling unfulfilled, set aside time for exercise. Your experience may be similar to George Sanders's, a department head in a large engineering firm. "I was really burned out, tired all the time, restless, eating too much. I started jogging and walking for thirty minutes, three or four times a week. At first I couldn't run more than two blocks without feeling my lungs were going to collapse! But in a month I could go a mile, then two. Soon I was addicted because I felt so much better! I began looking forward to a run before dinner rather than a nap. My fatigue disappeared and I felt in control of my job again. I wouldn't stop running for anything. It cured me of job burnout, and more than anything I do it prevents me from burning out again."

We believe that exercise probably releases the tension caused by the body's mobilization for fight or flight better than any other stress safety valve. The very fact that your body mobilizes to meet stress by vigorous muscular activity should tell you something about the value of exercise. Your blood pressure goes up to prepare you for physical exertion; your pulse rate increases to get you ready for running or fighting; your blood chemistry changes for the specific purpose of muscular activity. We interviewed a number of people who could feel the buildup of tension from their own stress response, and the healthy dissipation of that tension with exercise.

An accountant who worked in his office at home seemed to thrive on stress. He thoroughly enjoyed the work he had chosen, but was not unaware that he had to stay in control and keep his safety valves working. "Because I work alone," he said, "I find it hard to take breaks. My work is like solving a big puzzle. I sit at my desk working at a very intense pace, hour after hour. On many days I can feel my body churning away: my back and arms and legs get tense; my pulse will go up; I can even get to feeling dizzy. At times it's quite exhilarating. I get a real high from seeing the pieces to the puzzle fall into place. But I know when I need a break, so I'll go out for a five-mile run. With each mile I can feel the poisons begin to go out of my system and I come back feeling fresh and ready to tackle a new problem."

Two British physicians, Dr. Peter Taggart and Dr. Malcolm Carruthers, used several new techniques to study occupational stress reactions. While the drivers were under the stress of race driving, the doctors took blood samples from them and found a marked rise in noradrenaline, a common biochemical response to stress. This substance mobilizes free fatty acids from the body's tissue stores in preparation for vigorous muscular activity. However, one hour after the race, they discovered that the rise in free fatty acids in the blood had been succeeded by a rise in *triglyceride* levels, a substance associated with coronary artery disease. This, they thought, was "due to lack of utilization of the free fatty acids under the mentally active and physically inert conditions of the race."[10] They found that changes in blood chemistry occurred in other stress situations as well. Presumably, some kind of vigorous exercise after a stressful period would use the free fatty acids and block the rise in triglyceride levels. We expect that future research may well show many similar connections between stress and the value of exercise as a stress safety valve.

Pamper Yourself

Most of us know how to pamper *other people* when they experience a life crisis. We send flowers to a friend in the hospital, shovel snow from the walk of a neighbor who recently lost his wife, or take a friend to lunch who has lost her job. Such special attention helps people cope with stress. Pampering yourself can have the same effect. If you're overloaded with work, frustrated by cantankerous customers, or burned out from dealing with other people's problems, you deserve some reward. You've been in a combat zone! Be good to yourself. Don't forget how the U.S. Army discovered that "pampering" soldiers in Vietnam almost eliminated combat fatigue.

Bill and Joyce Cromwell discovered that it didn't cost a great deal to pamper themselves. Bill, a car salesman, found his job at Countryside Ford especially depressing in the wintertime when the snow piled up. To make matters worse, his monthly commission always hit the year's low point in January. Joyce felt trapped at home without a car and with two preschool kids. Vaguely aware that each was under stress, they spontaneously hit upon a plan to pamper themselves.

They had sent their tax return in early. They desperately needed the $598.60 refund to make February payments on bills run up over Christmas. The check from the IRS came on a Saturday morning. When Bill opened the envelope, his eyes met Joyce's and they smiled at the same moment. "Just think of all the fun we could have with this check!" he said, reading her thoughts.

Reality quickly overcame their fantasies as they recounted their outstanding financial obligations. Caught by the pressure of unpaid bills, they both felt themselves slipping into a "down" mood from the pressure of belt tightening. Then they made one small but important decision to help them over a low point in the winter. They decided to put $500.00 toward the mountain of bills, then take $30.00 for a "great night on the town," and each would have $34.30 to spend in whatever manner they pleased. The following Friday evening they went to the Café de Norvèlle, a fancy restaurant they had wanted to try. Years later they still remembered that beautiful and relaxing evening.

The next morning a babysitter stayed with the kids, and Bill and Joyce each took $34.30 and went on separate shopping trips. They met at a little corner café for lunch, both excited. Joyce, an avid gardener, went to several different flower shops and bought some exotic bulbs to plant in April, and a spider plant for the kitchen. Bill had found two bookshelf stereo speakers on sale at $33.00. "I've got a dollar left over and I am going to pamper myself with that too!"

That night, after the stereo was working, they sat down in front of a roaring fire and talked. It had been a special day. They felt renewed.

There are many ways to pamper yourself. The harassed assembly-line worker might plan a series of minivacations instead of taking all two weeks in a single block of time. The salesman who feels a need to take a break from the daily run might enroll in an evening-school course at a community college. The housewife might arrange a trip to visit an old friend or plan an evening out—without the kids! The businessman who is tired of the eight-to-five grind might purchase a new putter, a new pipe, or perhaps a new suit.

The key objective in pampering yourself is to break the routine. Sometimes pampering someone else can help you and them cope with work stress. Dorris Keanyon will never forget the night that her husband left work early in order to get home before she did. The steaks were already cooking on the outside grill, the wine was being chilled, and some fresh-cut flowers filled a vase on the table. It was just the lift they both needed in order to get through a difficult week.

Get Involved

A boring job can lead to burnout as easily as a challenging one with too much pressure. If your work does not use your skills, if it leaves you thinking that "even a chimp could do this," you may need to *get involved.*

Gloria Ronson, a rather private person, always avoided involvement. She passed up civic activities and dreaded school and church committees. Her home was her life. Married to a successful pediatrician, Gloria accepted matter-of-factly the many evenings alone with the children. "I didn't mind," she recalled. "In fact, keeping up the home front was my job and I loved it."

Then the kids started leaving. Billy went to the University of Colorado and two years later Jennifer went east to Smith College. John, the youngest, hardly seemed a member of the family he was so busy with his high-school friends. Gloria became progressively more withdrawn and moody. Her husband began writing Valium prescriptions.

When John pulled away in his 1968 Chevrolet and headed for the University of Texas at Arlington, Gloria cried uncontrollably. Nothing could make the cloud lift from her unfulfilled and empty days. She took a painting class, a vacation in San Francisco, then a trip to see her sister. She still felt depressed.

Gloria's work as a housewife no longer held challenge and meaning. She straightened the house each day, shopped, supervised the weekly cleaning lady, and did her best to create projects around the house. As never before, time hung heavily on her hands. The stress became even more unbearable because her husband and friends couldn't understand her discontent. Gloria had come to share with them the myth that burnout only strikes people who work too hard. But, like Gloria, thousands of people in hundreds of different jobs face the same problem. In late 1978, the Survey Research Center at the University of Michigan released a nationwide study that asked workers to evaluate the quality of their jobs. The study found that 39 percent suffered from the feeling that time drags at work. Another 35 percent reported that their skills were underutilized on the job; and 32 percent felt they were overeducated for the work they did each day.[11] In another 1978 study by the National Commission on Working Women, two out of five women surveyed complained that their jobs were boring.[12]

Gloria became involved almost by accident, but it went a long way toward alleviating her stress. One day, on a visit to her neighbor's, she learned that a private developer had purchased ten acres of vacant woods immediately behind her home. Her neighbor told her, "They're going to clear out all the trees and put in townhouses or condominiums." Gloria returned home feeling angry. She loved those woods. Her kids had built forts and treehouses there. They had spent endless hours fishing for bullheads in a small pond near the middle of the woods. She could already see a bulldozer plowing under the big oaks that gracefully sheltered the area.

When she told her husband about the rumors, he agreed it was too bad, but added, "Well, development is the American way of doing business."

"Over my dead body!" Gloria replied.

The next day she invited some of the neighborhood women in for coffee to talk about the problem. It was the same story: their husbands had little time to become upset. A few phone calls revealed that the proposed development scheme was on the agenda for the next city council meeting. The women decided to attend and listen to the debate.

They sat near the back of a half-full hearing room. After some preliminaries, the developer announced his intention to have the property rezoned and subleased to one of the biggest automobile dealerships in the city. Gloria couldn't believe it. She felt flushed and angry; her heart was racing. When the city council asked for comments, she jumped up impulsively and in angry tones told them about all the hours her kids had spent in those woods. The council made no decision that evening, but after the meeting one member said to her privately, "Look, lady, no one gives a damn about all the good times your kids may have had. That's taxable land." Gloria left boiling with indignation.

The next day she called a neighborhood meeting. They designed a strategy. Gloria decided to pull out of her savings account $2,000 to hire an attorney. A few others contributed lesser amounts.

The attorney immediately called for an environmental impact statement. The council agreed. That set the project back four months and Gloria Ronson got to work. She put an ad in the paper requesting that interested residents come to a meeting about the "wooded section of property between Fairmont and Oak streets." Over 150 people responded. Gloria spoke of her concerns. Everyone applauded her comments and they agreed that the land should be left in its natural state. That night they drafted a petition.

With help from a close friend, Gloria organized canvass teams that started going door to door. In one month they had over 4,000 signatures from a suburban community of 5,200 residents.

The showdown came on a Monday night meeting of the council when the developer again presented his ambitious plans. Gloria's attorney persuasively argued against the proposal and then Gloria presented to the council a stack of petitions containing the 4,000 signatures. The crowd at the meeting roared their approval as the council voted by a four-to-one margin to leave the land as a nature preserve.

After the meeting, in the midst of congratulations, someone asked Gloria, "Have you ever thought of running for the council?" Four months later when the kids came home from college, they found their mother in the middle of an election campaign.

Not everyone can become as involved as Gloria Ronson. But even a small investment of time can pay dividends by erasing the fatigue that comes from boredom and unchallenging work. One woman who worked in a shirt factory volunteered to help coach the Babe Ruth League. "They thought I was nuts, but I helped them out a lot. I knew more about baseball than any of those kids."

Daniel Klein found himself caught in the routine of selling insurance. "I always dreamed of getting a promotion and becoming vice-president or something," he said. "You know, having a secretary and a fancy desk. When I got to be fifty I just knew it would never happen. I almost cracked up when they passed me up for the fourth time. I talked it over with my minister and he asked me what I did in my spare time. I told him that all I did was sell insurance."

"Would you be willing to supervise a group of church kids on a backpacking trip?" he asked me.

"Did we have fun! I really liked those kids and pretty soon they were calling me and asking advice about their personal problems." Daniel now spends at least two nights a week involved with the church youth group. He has become like a second father to many of them. "I still wish I was vice-president," he said with a relaxed smile. "But being one of those big shots wouldn't let me spend so much time with those kids."

Warm Up Slowly

You can often get control of a tense, pressured workday if you change the way it begins. The basketball player warms up before the buzzer sounds to start the game. The deep-sea diver descends in a gradual and deliberate manner. Sports trainers know that warm-up exercises prevent dangerous muscle pulls, hyperventilation, and fatigue. They prepare the body for the stress of the battle about to commence. If your day begins with a sudden rush of activity or a mad scramble on some crowded subway, it will add to your stress.

The most important two-hour period in your day is prior to starting work. During that period you set the tone for the day. That's when you enter your own compression chamber.

Jack Carlson always began his hectic days in a hurry. He jumped out of bed, gulped a cup of coffee, hit the freeway, fought for a parking place, crowded into an elevator, and arrived at the office tense as a watchspring. Sometimes his headache began before nine o'clock, almost always by noon.

One winter morning Jack woke at 5:45 A.M. Wide-awake, he lay in bed thinking how good scrambled eggs, bacon, and hashbrowns would taste. At 6:15 A.M. he pulled onto an almost deserted freeway heading for work. He set the cruise control at fifty miles per hour and whisked toward a little restaurant not too far from the office. He ordered a "ranch breakfast," purchased a paper, and sipped a steaming cup of coffee. It dawned on him that this was the first time in months that he had read a sports page.

After breakfast he walked to the office. The lights were out. No one was around. For the next half hour Jack thought through what he wanted to accomplish during the day. He went over his appointment schedule. He organized the piles of papers on his desk. When other employees came charging into the office, Jack leaned back in his chair and smiled. He had found a way to get control of a busy day. That night driving home he could still feel the calming effects of his slow warm-up. In the months that followed, Jack found other ways at home, at restaurants, and at the office to get control before the day began.

Joyce Haffner hated freeway traffic as much as Jack Carlson. But she had to put her two kids on the school bus and that prevented her from escaping the clogged freeways. Joyce got up with the children, helped them get dressed, ate a hurried bowl of cereal, put the kids on the bus, and finally raced off to work. Usually she made it with two or three minutes to spare.

Joyce made several simple changes in her early morning routine. She set her alarm clock one hour before she needed to awaken the children. That one hour of solitude became very important. She took more time to fix her hair, read the morning paper, sipped an extra cup of coffee, and sometimes sat quietly and listened to the stillness. "It made such a change in my day at work that I started thinking about the frustration of fighting the freeway traffic." She decided to buy a tape deck for her car. "I really love being escorted to work by John Denver, Diana Ross, or Neil Diamond!"

The little things you do in the morning can prepare you for the tensions you encounter during the day. Brad Hartoff, a consulting engineer, avoids telephone calls during the first hour of work and sets his objectives for the day. Judy Loutter, a secretary, parks her car four blocks away from the office and enjoys a leisurely early-morning walk. Bruce Conford, president of a grain company in Minneapolis, spends the first thirty minutes reading the *Wall Street Journal.* "Any crises can wait thirty minutes," he tells his secretary.

Release Pressures
on the Job

The people who burn out are often the best workers. They take their jobs seriously, work faster and harder than others, and never shirk responsibility. This very commitment makes them more susceptible to work stress. The pressures build up and they don't find it as easy to open the safety valves, goof off, or escape for a few minutes. There are scores of ways to release the pressure during the workday. While some workers complain they feel trapped in their jobs, others turn every bit of on-the-job freedom they have to their own advantage.

Denny Keptler, an assembly-line worker, felt frustrated by the daily episodes of "down time" on the line. The day seemed to stretch out forever until he started bringing car magazines to work. Now, whenever there is a breather, he keeps abreast of the latest developments and gets ideas for rebuilding the car he works on at night. "I used to get pissed off whenever the line stopped; now I look forward to it!"

Scott Lamatto drives a cement truck for Midwest Portland Cement Company. One day he asked his boss if he couldn't have a run near his house. Now he stops and has lunch with Grace, his wife, a couple of noons each week.

Marla Bruster, a record custodian for the government, never eats lunch, but she can't work through the noon hour and go home early. Reading on her lunch hour doesn't help; it's too much like the work she does. Then Marla started jogging on her lunch hour. Not only does she enjoy the exercise, it relieves many of the tensions that build up by noon.

Buddy Capronie works in a liquor store. He has a continuous game of chess going with the janitor. They always play at noon and sometimes during their coffee breaks. When things get a little slow in the store, Buddy thinks about his next move.

Gilbert Stanek, a farmer in Iowa, finds that the harvest season in late summer adds to his stress. "At the point where I can't keep my eyes open I take a quick nap in or under the combine. I wake up in ten or fifteen minutes and feel like I've had a night's sleep."

Judy Clifford, a telephone receptionist, uses the time between telephone calls to study for an evening class. Time used to drag; now the days fly by. Dan Sage works the night shift in a Popsicle company, cleaning up after the day crew. The sweeping, mopping, and washing down of machines won't allow him to study his textbooks for classes at the university. But he hit on an idea: he wrote chemical formulas and history dates on small three-by-five cards that he carries in his shirt pocket. Now the long hours each night of lonely work go by faster and Dan has raised his grades in every course.

Kate Malone teaches twenty-seven sixth-grade students. By noon she feels tired and on edge. She secured permission from the principal to have the music teacher instruct her students from 1:00 to 2:00 P.M. Since a teacher's aide watches the kids over the lunch hour, she now has almost a two-hour block of time to herself.

Bill Tildon, an insurance executive, has meetings crammed on his appointment calendar each day from eight to five. One day he crossed out all appointments on subsequent Thursday and Friday afternoons and labeled them "Long-range Planning." "I really do whatever I damn well please on those afternoons," Bill said with a grin. "It makes me a much better boss and I've cut out a lot of unnecessary meetings."

Burned-out workers often overlook their on-the-job freedom. Tom Triston, a stockman in a large supermarket, had few good things to say about his job. "All I do is load the shelves day after day. It never stops." In truth, Tom does spend the entire forty-hour week unloading trucks and stacking shelves. The routine does not vary. One day Tom asked another stockman, "How do you stand this place? You're the first one here in the morning. Sometimes you stay after your shift is over. You actually seem to like it here!" "Oh, I do," said the stockman emphatically. "Hell, I feel good. My friends are all down here. Next year the union contract calls for five weeks' vacation. Can you imagine —*five* weeks? I got to figure out what I am going to do with all that time. Furthermore, nobody hassles me. I do my job, go home, and play with the kids. But you gotta learn how to work this job. I do the worst jobs when I'm fresh and save the easy ones for the end of the day."

This stockman has the right idea. One of the best ways of releasing the pressure on the job is to rearrange your schedule. Gerald Fisher, a management consultant, suggests that one way to deal with stress is to confront difficult tasks when you are fresh. If you find that mornings are your best times, take on the tasks that cause you the most strain then. When you become tired, the pressure can hit you harder. Tom Triston took the advice of the other stockman. He now unloads the heavy boxes in the morning. By noon he knows that the day's major work is over. "That simple change made me feel one hell of a lot better."

Remember, no one controls your mind, your lunch breaks, what you do with your vacation, and how you organize yourself to get the job done. Whether you make three bucks an hour or thirty-three, your time is precious. Do the job competently and efficiently, but use on-the-job freedom to your advantage.

Practice Relaxation Techniques

You will recall from chapter 2 that the stress response goes through four processes: mobilization, increase in energy consumption, muscular action involved in fight or flight, and then a return to equilibrium. This last state is when the body relaxes naturally and restores itself. Our adaptation energy is renewed. Engaging in vigorous exercise or some of the other safety-valve activities we have described allows the body to discharge tension and return to a state of equilibrium. You can aid that process by learning to switch off the stress response and switch on the relaxation response.

Dr. Eugene C. Walker, a psychologist, describes a simple exercise you can do several times each day:

> First sit in a comfortable chair or lie on a couch or bed. Then say something like the following to yourself: "I am going to relax completely. First I will relax my forehead

and scalp. I will let all the muscles on my forehead and scalp relax and become completely at rest. All of the wrinkles will smooth out of my forehead and that part of my body will relax completely. Now I will relax the muscles on my face. I will just let them relax and go limp. There will be no tension in my jaw. Next, I will relax my neck muscles. Just let them become tranquil and allow all the pressure to leave them. My neck muscles are relaxing completely. Now I will relax the muscles of my shoulders. That relaxation will spread down my arms to the elbows, down the forearm to my hands and fingers. My arms will just dangle from the frame of my body. I will take a deep breath and relax, letting all of the tightness and tenseness leave. My breathing will now be normal and relaxed, and I will relax the muscles of my stomach. Now I will relax all the muscles up and down both sides of my spine; now the waist, buttocks, and thighs down to my knees. Now the relaxation will spread to the calves of my legs, my ankles, feet, and toes. I will just lie here and continue to let all of my muscles go completely limp. I will become completely relaxed from the top of my head to the tip of my toes.[13]

You will find this entire exercise useful at the end of the day to counter the tension buildup from a stress-filled job. Parts of it can enable you to relax at various periods throughout the day. We know many people who use this safety valve while sitting at their desks, lying on their office floor, or riding the bus home at night. Although it can reduce tension the first time you employ this method, it often takes months of practice before you will achieve the full benefits for coping with job stress.

Chapter Six
Burnout
Blind Alleys

If job burnout had uncomplicated symptoms, a simple cause, and a single cure, this book would be unnecessary, and so would many of the commercials and advertisements for sleep aids, painkillers, tension reducers, and indigestion relievers. Valium, the most widely prescribed medicine in the world today, would probably disappear from millions of medicine cabinets. Absenteeism would decline in hundreds of workplaces; productivity would increase.

But we cannot reduce job burnout to a simple, uniform condition with a single personal treatment strategy. Consider these facts:

- —Unrelieved stress comes in packages of every conceivable shape and size.
- —The risk factors can combine in a variety of ways to bring on job burnout.
- —Each individual has a unique job-burnout threshold. Some people can take much larger doses of unrelieved stress than others before they burn out.
- —The symptoms of burnout will vary from one person to the next.

—Each individual has learned to perceive stress in a unique way.

—The severity of job burnout changes as it goes through each of the stages.

—Each individual has learned a different combination of stress safety valves to cope with job burnout and will need a unique combination to recover.

All this adds up to a pretty complex picture. It means that the road to recovery, unlike the single ribbon of highway that cuts across a desert, will seem more like a maze of streets and alleys. We can give you a road map, but you will have to study it carefully and pick your own treatment strategies. Although the goal is clear—to take control of job burnout and live free from *unrelieved* stress—many paths can lead to this destination. And among them you will find dozens of *blind alleys* that can take you for miles in the wrong direction, finally coming to an abrupt end.

In our research we discovered that most people make some *attempt* to take control of job burnout. As suffering from this debilitating condition increases, some form of fight-or-flight behavior occurs. But all too often the actions taken lead down a blind alley. They seem to offer a solution to your present problems. They invite you to find the "real reason" for how you feel. And when caught in the flames of job burnout, finding reasons and taking action become top priority. It is precisely because these blind alleys look like solutions that they become so dangerous. Instead of leading to a cure, they only contribute to unrelieved stress and drain off valuable adaptation energy. The most common blind alleys that we discuss in this chapter are (1) The Ostrich Response, (2) The Scapegoat Reaction, (3) The Workaholic Trap, and (4) The Guilt Trip. But we will do more than merely describe these common detours on the road to recovery from job burnout. We will show you additional personal strategies for self-treatment, strategies that lead you out of these alleys and bring relief from damaging work stress.

The Ostrich
Response

The ostrich belongs to one of the swiftest, largest, and most powerful species of birds, yet it has amused generations of observers as it sticks its head into the sand in the midst of a troubling and potentially dangerous situation.

The human animal can respond in a similar way. The early warning signals of burnout may be going off like Fourth of July rockets, yet some individuals will disregard the fireworks that pose a real threat to their well-being.

The ostrich response to job burnout simply ignores the symptoms. Tiredness, lack of enthusiasm, headaches, high blood pressure, or excessive drinking are dismissed as unrelated to a stressful lifestyle. This approach often takes the form of "Yes, but . . ." "I'm under stress, *but* . . ." The list of excuses can range from heredity to astrology. "Sure, I'm under pressure," says a policeman on the L.A. force, "but my uncle had a bad skin problem all his life. It runs in the family." Inherited tendencies may explain why he broke out with red patches of eczema on his hands and arms instead of suffering from ulcers or depression, but it doesn't get at the underlying cause. Family history influences the "target organ" that first breaks down under unrelieved stress. Hypertension does run in families; so does heart disease. But the ostrich response uses these facts to completely rule out unrelieved stress as the culprit.

Why do people put their heads in the sand when burnout symptoms erode their happiness and productivity? Some have learned to live with the pain and discomfort of their symptoms. The president of a church-related college told us: "Sure, I am always tired. But that's the cross I have to bear if I want this job." A probation officer said, "Yeah, I got an ulcer, but so would you if you had someone whippin' a game on you all the time."

Such comments represent one of the most potentially dangerous aspects of the ostrich response to burnout. If you keep your head in the sand long enough, you can begin to believe your symptoms are "normal." Unfortunately, like an adding machine, "the body totals up the insults," as Dr. Robert Rose, a psychiatrist, says.[1] Although it may take years, the continued attacks from stress take their toll.

Some ignore the early warning signals by taking the advice of well-meaning and trusted individuals. Spouses, often the best source of encouragement, may inadvertently contribute to the belief that we can continue as normal. Bosses are notorious for the way they encourage workers to ignore burnout symptoms. Geri Christoff, a buyer of women's fashions, felt run-down and plagued by recurrent headaches. She contemplated quitting her job in order to take a break from her fast-paced environment. Her boss dismissed her problems as insignificant. "You seem pretty energetic to me, and look at the fringe benefits you get here. Your future is bright in this company. What's more, you are laying a financial base for your family that would be tough to beat anywhere." Geri continued in her job, ignoring the symptoms of unrelieved stress.

Even physicians can encourage an ostrich approach. Most physicians have received little training in the destructive power that stress can have in one's life. Paula Wayland, a writer, consultant, housewife, and lecturer, raced through life at top speed, thriving on the challenge of creative projects. She often worked seven days a week, and family vacations found Paula lugging along her briefcase filled with projects, "just in case there's some time to catch up." The family organized their activities around Paula's enterprises.

It took six years for Paula's burnout to come to the surface. First came early-morning headaches, waking her at five o'clock with pounding, ferocious pain. Aspirin, and later Valium, helped the throbbing to subside. A chronic backache soon began to bother her and Paula increased the Valium and added prescription painkillers. On a routine checkup her doctor discovered high blood pressure. Paula momentarily recalled the way her family and friends said, "You're putting yourself under too much pressure," or "Don't you think you need to take some time off?" What worried her most was not the physical pain, or now the rise in blood pressure, but the growing sense that her creative ideas for writing had almost dried up. Only under intense pressure of a deadline could she come up with the ideas she needed, but that seemed un-related to her physical symptoms.

As the doctor removed the blood-pressure cuff from her arm, Paula asked, "Can that be caused by the stress of my work?"

"I don't think that's the problem," he said. "You're suffering from a disease known as hypertension. We can easily control it with medications but you'll have to take them regularly."

"Would it help if I slowed down?" she asked, pressing the doctor further.

"No, probably not," he replied. "In fact, if you're a hard-driving person, trying to slow down might make things worse. If you're enjoying what you're doing, I'd stay with it." Paula breathed a sigh of relief. Not only could she continue her demanding pace, but she now had new ammunition for her husband, who would surely nag her again to slow down.

Paula didn't need to "slow down." But she did need to take control of job burnout and adopt personal treatment strategies to bring periodic relief from the stress she enjoyed and that gave meaning to her life. As Dr. Selye says in *Stress Without Distress,* "Often a voluntary change of activity is as good or even better than rest. . . . For example, when either fatigue or enforced interruptions prevent us from finishing a mathematical problem, it is better to go for a swim than simply to sit around. Substituting demands on our musculature for those previously made on the intellect not only gives our brain a rest but helps us avoid worrying about the frustrating interruption. Stress on one system helps to relax another."[2] Paula Wayland needed to learn this stress substitution principle.

Still other individuals take an ostrich approach to their burnout symptoms because they feel that it is a sign of weakness to admit that they need help. This is particularly true of individuals who see themselves as strong and self-reliant and can't bring themselves to talk about their weaknesses.

Several studies have confirmed the fact that police officers are under a great deal of stress. A recent study of an urban police department revealed numerous stress-related problems; 76 percent of the policemen were anxious or impatient on their jobs.[3] One in three men on the force had developed a drinking problem. Rotating shifts disrupted homelife. The policemen often took out their frustrations on members of the family and many admitted that they were too hard on their children. They came home sullen and irritable, making communication difficult between themselves and their wives.

Unfortunately, the policemen would try to ignore even acute burnout symptoms. As the investigators noted: "They have the attitude that mental-health problems are worse than cancer. So they deny and they deny and they deny, until they end up shooting themselves or somebody else."

As with these police officers, when people employ the ostrich response during the first three stages of job burnout, they often fail to pull their heads out of the sand when they reach the crisis stage. Because no "quick fix" can bring a cure when you experience a job-burnout crisis, it becomes even more tempting to deny the power of unrelieved stress. That way you don't have to make the difficult changes in your life-style that the crisis stage requires in order for you to take control of job burnout.

How do you cope with job burnout in this crucial fourth stage? How does someone like Carter Nicholson, the industrial psychologist we met in chapter 3, treat his burnout crisis with its symptoms of tachycardia, shortness of breath, emotional exhaustion, depression, and anxiety about having a heart attack? At this stage, a simple readjustment of faulty safety valves will probably not suffice. He will need to take more drastic action. Yet he *can recover* even after his symptoms have reached a crisis.

We suggest three "job-burnout-crisis rules" for anyone caught in the crisis stage. Even though you can expect some immediate relief by following them, these rules won't bring an instantaneous miracle cure even though that may be what you've hoped for. Follow these rules, then the principles for taking control of job burnout and improving faulty safety valves, and you will gradually regain control of your life.

Rule One: Accept the fact you are in the midst of a dangerous crisis. Don't allow yourself to deny, avoid, and remain trapped. A crisis is upsetting. So get upset! No more business as usual. No more blaming your job, your boss, or your spouse. Something has gone haywire. A demon is on the loose and it has devastating potential for you and those you love. The demon is unrelieved stress. It can become as vicious and lethal as anything you will ever experience.

If you once acknowledge—in your gut—that your burnout has reached a crisis, you can begin the journey toward health and sanity. But to repeat: first you have to recognize that a state of crisis exists.

A fascinating study done by Dr. Gerald Caplan of the Harvard Medical School demonstrated the importance of this first rule. Dr. Caplan set out to determine why some people survive the stress of crises better than others. He and his coworkers studied 100 parents who had a child born prematurely. In the days after the birth of the infant, extreme stress engulfed the parents. The infant's life often hung in the balance. No one knew whether the child would be handicapped for the rest of its life. The researchers followed each family for two months after the birth and made a surprising discovery. Those who acted as if the birth had been almost normal still had not come to terms with stress. On the other hand, those parents who recognized the potential catastrophe, who treated it as a crisis and became extremely upset, had quickly recovered. By recognizing they were in the midst of a crisis, they were able to accept help and better overcome the stress.[4]

The beginning of the journey out of the burned-out wilderness begins with the admission that you are in trouble. As members of Alcoholics Anonymous say, "You get well after you hit bottom." Hitting the bottom can become the first sign of hope.

Rule Two: Find someone to give you assistance.   When in a state of crisis, you simply cannot view your situation accurately. It's as if you have lost your way on a country road late at night. You come to an intersection without a clue as to whether the nearest town lies to the left, the right, or straight ahead. You need a signpost to help you regain your bearings and point you in the right direction.

A relative or friend, a minister or priest, a psychologist or counselor can give you a new perspective, steer you down the right road. Don't beat around the bush. Explain exactly how you feel and the frustrations that brought about the crisis. The very act of talking will release pressure. Soon new signposts will appear, often from your counselor, but many from yourself. Gradually you will sense the direction you need to take.

Rule Three: Don't feel guilty about retreating from danger. The crisis stage is hardly the time to merely tune up your safety valves. You will probably need to find the best way to escape from the powerful enemy of unrelieved stress. If a mugger followed you down a dark street, you wouldn't hesitate to run. If a truck leaped the curb and headed straight for you, the fastest exit would make the best defense. If your house caught on fire, you would rush to the fire escape. At this stage of burnout, the forces that have done you in constitute an equally real danger to your health and safety.

Does running from the enemy mean quitting your job? Many people at this stage find they must take that route. But we recommend that you begin by looking for the easiest, most accessible fire escape. One head nurse, caught in the stress of dealing with autocratic physicians and a high employee-turnover rate, felt burned out. "I didn't know what to do, but I was given a project for about a year that took me away from my nursing unit completely. I had a chance to be independent while working on that project. I returned to my unit feeling refreshed in mind and body." Some people in crisis take a vacation; others go on a leave of absence or take all their sick leave. However you retreat, don't look back and feel guilty. Retreat can sometimes become the best strategy for winning the war.

Carter Nicholson recovered from burnout. His wife became the major source of assistance. "You've got to get out of that job," she said, a new tone of seriousness in her voice. "It's going to destroy you, our marriage, and our family. It's not worth it." Carter slowly redefined his situation. "We can get along without your $30,000 a year until something else opens up," his wife said. "I'd rather be poor than a widow." With a firm decision to resign, the cloud lifted. Several opportunities to go into business as a free-lance consultant opened up. It took months after his last day on the job for Carter to recover fully from burnout.

Today, after a six-mile run around a lake near his home, he smiles and says, "It wasn't worth it. I'd never go through that kind of hell again for anything."

The Scapegoat
Reaction

Andy Cooper lives with the constant work stress of a dangerous job. A high-voltage man with Pacific Gas and Electric, Andy has no trouble working with "heat" (live wires) all around him. But what makes a day especially tense is when the foreman assigns him to work with someone he doesn't trust high up on a pole. "Like there was this guy we all called 'Jerky' and he was really somethin'. You never knew what he was gonna do up there. You have all this heat around you and here is this guy swinging around like a monkey. Nobody wants to work with him. Whenever you found out he was your partner, somebody would always say, 'Watch the soles of his feet.' If you can see the soles of his feet, then you're on the ground and he's up in the wires."

Andy tried not to fight with his partner; instead, after a tense day, someone at home became a scapegoat. Andy would walk in the door, tense from a day on the poles with Jerky, and shout, "Get that god-damned noisemaker off!" to his teenage son playing the stereo in the living room.

Most of us, on occasion, kick the dog, slam the door, get angry with someone not responsible for our problems. But when fighting those around you at work or home becomes a regular occurrence, it may mean the burnout process has driven you into a blind alley. When unrelieved stress builds, the scapegoat reaction can mean constant complaining about someone, saying to yourself, "I'll get the bastard someday," direct verbal attacks, or even physical assault.

If burnout pressure builds and scapegoating becomes a habit, it may lead to unpremeditated violence. During the early months of 1979, Chicago experienced its worst winter on record. Mountains of snow clogged the streets; snowplow drivers lived with incredible stress of long hours, parked and locked "snowbirds" that sometimes blocked narrow streets, and angry pedestrians and drivers. Under weeks of this pressure one snowplow driver went berserk and drove his plow into several cars, killing one person.

Attacking and blaming other people when you're burned out can take many forms. Some people will threaten to quit and, in the process, blame others for their problems. Such was the resignation of Denver Nuggets basketball coach Larry Brown as reported in *Sports Illustrated:*

> ... On Feb. 1, when the team was 28-24 and 3½ games behind Kansas City, Brown acted on a threat that players and management had grown tired of hearing. At a tearful press conference, he announced that he was resigning immediately; he was in the first year of a lucrative five-year contract.
>
> Brown talked of pains in his chest and his side, and mentioned that his father had died of a heart attack at 43. That very day Brown had been pronounced fit by a doctor and had run seven miles. His "poor health" story got little credence. "I've got coaches' disease," he admitted. While that malady is not to be found in medical texts, it is truly a disease of the heart, particularly for an emotional 38-year-old who knows of no greater job than coaching.

Donnie Walsh, former assistant coach and Brown's best friend, who took over the team, said, "I think Larry just burned out. He'd been doing the same thing for six straight years without once forgetting basketball—in the summer, at home, in restaurants. His problem was that he intensified everything so, particularly the negative things. He was upset with the fans; he wanted more from the players than they were willing to give."

In the months that preceded his resignation, *Sports Illustrated* said that "Brown would usually begin his comments to the press by saying, "I don't want to sound like I'm blaming David [a player], but . . ."[5]

For some job burnouts, the scapegoat reaction follows the rule of "Don't get mad, get even." They fight back through a subtle but energy-draining form of manipulation. They often enjoy the game of intrigue that surrounds most intraorganizational wars. They fight from behind the scenes to keep their adversary off-balance, sometimes choosing an obvious scapegoat instead of the person directly responsible for their frustrations.

Cameron Hostler had given twenty-six of his best working years to Douglas Manufacturing Company. He worked his way from stock boy to sales manager, and prided himself that "I don't even have a college degree." Without much knowledge of formal management theory, Cam had developed an intuitive skill at managing and he had recruited what many felt was the finest group of young, aggressive salesmen in the industry. With each promotion that moved Cam up the ladder, his trust in and respect for the company president grew. When the number-two position in the firm became vacant, Cam thought he was a shoo-in for the job.

At the time of the annual stockholders' meeting, the president announced that Cam's young assistant, Bruce Bartow, would be promoted to the executive vice-president's chair. Stunned and angry, Cam's feelings turned to deep resentment when he learned through the grapevine that the president told the chairman of the board that "Cam is a damn good manager, but he doesn't have the polish for that job. We need someone who can work with all those Harvard types in the East."

As the months passed, the unrelieved stress of being passed over for a promotion that "should have been mine" began to drain Cam of energy and affect his sleep at night, finally bringing him to the verge of resignation. Slowly he was edged into the blind alley of developing a full-fledged scapegoat reaction. He vowed to himself that he "would get the kid." He didn't know when or where, "but by God, I'm going to get him."

The next week Cam went into Bruce's office, supposedly on other business, and casually and belatedly congratulated him. Then he began six months of reconnaissance work, watching how the new executive vice-president was doing and plotting to do him in. His chance finally came. Working behind the scenes, he filed a routine report he knew Bruce would overlook, with vital information needed before a critical stockholders' meeting. At the meeting, Cam watched the drama unfold;

finally a stockholder stood to ask a crucial question that required the information only Cam had access to. Bruce fumbled, hesitated, finally admitted ignorance, only to have Cam rise slowly to his feet and adroitly give a concise, accurate answer. Storming into Cam's office the next day, Bruce demanded, "Why didn't that information reach my office before the stockholders' meeting?"

"It did!" said Cam, looking innocent and surprised. "It's in that report that you probably forgot to read. I sent it to you two weeks ago!"

Although Cam believed he had won the battle, he was rapidly losing the war. Each personal attack or small "victory" in the war against a scapegoat usually results in additional frustration. Soon the word got around the Douglas Manufacturing Company that Cam was out to get his former assistant. Sensing that Bruce wasn't being given a fair shake, the employees began to voice their concerns to the president. Six months later Cam was demoted.

One of the more disturbing characteristics of scapegoaters is that they impute negative motivations to others. When they criticize, they send forth their wrath like God Almighty. Dr. Herbert Freudenberger, a psychiatrist who studied burnout in human-service agencies, aptly describes the self-righteousness of the scapegoater: ". . . a suspicious attitude, a paranoia may evolve. The burnout victim begins to feel that everyone is out to screw him and this includes his fellow staff members. This paranoid-like state may be heightened by feelings of omnipotence. The [burned-out] victim feels that he or she knows it all, has been through it all, has experienced every kind of rap, every kind of con man or woman around, and has handled it all before. The person is more than a little irritated by the stupids, the novices, the incompetents, and the ingrates, both on the staff and among those who come for help— in short, anyone who does not accept his advice."[6]

Blaming others, trying to get even, and imputing evil motives to others often leaves one feeling guilty and remorseful. Instead of using energy in creative ways to relieve anger, scapegoating compounds your frustrations. Whenever you make friends, colleagues, and loved ones your personal whipping boys, it's a clear danger sign. It means you've lost your way in a blind alley. But recognition of that fact can become the first step toward dealing with the underlying problem of unrelieved stress. Otherwise, you can develop into a chronic fighter, changing scapegoats but never winning the battle over job burnout.

The Workaholic Trap

When the major source of unrelieved stress comes from your job, working harder can become a blind alley that looks like a thoroughfare to recovery. The workaholic trap can lead you into burnout; it can also become a self-defeating strategy that develops after burnout has closed in on you. With some people, addiction to their job works both ways.

Workaholics value themselves according to how much they accomplish. If they fail to meet a self-imposed goal, they redouble their efforts to achieve success. If the boss utters a harsh word, they fortify themselves for the next round by arriving at work earlier, staying later, taking more projects home. When denied a promotion, the workaholic steps on the accelerator so that "the next time, by God, I'll get it." Even the awarding of that longed-for promotion brings little solace. The next round of promotions is only a year away.

Without realizing it, the workaholic has bought—hook, line, and sinker—the philosophy of John Calvin, an influential nineteenth-century theologian. Max Weber, the pioneer German sociologist, called it the "Protestant Ethic," but it affects Catholic, Jew, and Protestant alike. Indeed, the Protestant Ethic has so permeated our culture that many people call it the American Work Ethic. John Calvin believed that eternal salvation came as a free gift to those God selected. You couldn't buy it, work for it, or influence a sovereign God to make you one of the chosen.

How, then, could you know if God had selected you for eternal salvation? How could you know if you would escape the eternal damnation of hellfire? The proof that you were one of the chosen came when God bestowed spiritual and material blessings on you. God took care of his own; he made them prosper. Most important, *he made their efforts productive.* Thus, by hard work you might prove to yourself (and everyone else) that God had selected you for his kingdom. Hard work could not earn your salvation, but it could demonstrate your worth in the eyes of God. As this belief seeped into the stream of Western culture, *hard work became synonymous with personal worth.* Work became holy. Work became noble. Work became the surest way to everlasting life. The old Gospel hymn couldn't express it more clearly: "Work, for the night is coming!"

The work ethic no longer brings eternal salvation to millions of people, but it still promises the good life. It has become translated into a thousand rules of conduct. "Work hard and you will get ahead." "Work hard and you can become President of the United States." "Work hard and you can become rich." "Work hard and you can solve any problem that comes your way." Because we learn these premises early, even when they fail to work we seldom abandon them. The net result is that many individuals develop a neurotic relationship with their jobs.

Most workaholics work sixty-, seventy-, and even eighty-hour weeks because of what Christopher J. Hegarty calls a "massive fear of failure."[7] Consequently they drive their subordinates, push papers, write memos, call staff meetings, and spend most of their time putting out organizational fires. Unfortunately, workaholics confuse productivity with busyness, and leisure with wasting time. It's no accident that 85 percent of all executives in this country can't fully enjoy their leisure. As Hegarty notes, the worst day of the week for the workaholic is Sunday. "He can't stand it—no phone ringing continually, no paperwork to shuffle, no meetings to call. The whole game's closed for the day."[8]

The workaholic's life-style erodes the health of the organization in which he or she is employed. The workaholic is not fun to be around. He seldom talks about anything personal nor is he interested in the nonwork lives of his colleagues. He tries to do two or three things at once, whether answering the phone in the middle of a conference or clipping his nails. Because he seldom takes time to recharge his batteries, his thinking becomes dull and uninspired.

When the fires of burnout burst into flame and ravage our lives, it becomes all too easy to fall back on the tacit assumption that hard work can solve this problem also. Many latent workaholics turn up this blind alley first in a futile effort to cope with their burnout. Take the Reverend Carl Westerberg, a minister who knows all about the Protestant Work Ethic, yet can't free himself from its shackles. In seminary, Carl Westerberg proved to himself that hard work pays off. He graduated summa cum laude and his classmates voted him the seminarian most likely to succeed. He took a small, forty-member congregation in a rural setting in South Dakota. Hard work and long hours saw the membership double in the first two years, at a time when most rural churches were losing members. The invitations to serve larger congregations began to roll across his desk as the word spread about his accomplishments.

Each succeeding church was larger, with a bigger budget and a more impressive physical plant. Mr. Westerberg did not consider himself a workaholic, though he "recognized [he] could fall into that trap [himself] " when he preached about keeping a balanced perspective between work, play, social life, and spiritual concerns. At the age of fifty, he received a call to the tenth-largest church in the denomination.

He started this new job at a time when stage two of burnout had also begun. He didn't realize that his fuel reserves had become depleted. But within months a new and debilitating stress emerged, one he had never experienced in any of his other churches. He announced to the board of trustees that he wanted to begin a new church-wide Bible study program, one developed outside the denomination. The board, composed of powerful community leaders, businessmen, and university professors, grilled him with penetrating questions and advised him to wait until they could review the new program.

A few weeks later, after a Sunday morning sermon, a college professor left him speechless by mumbling, "Pretty shallow theology, Reverend." That same night a college youth group took him to task for some of the comments he had made in the morning service. Then, several weeks later, he was taken aside by two different leaders in the church. One said that he knew of several people on the verge of leaving the church because his theology was so conservative; the other told him that two families had threatened to leave because they didn't think he was "born again." By the end of his first year, Mr. Westerberg was plagued by insomnia and emotional fatigue.

As criticism of his leadership became more open, he decided to send out "feelers" to some other churches without ministers. When word came back that they considered him "too old," he was dumbfounded. In addition, news of the problems at his current church seemed to precede his inquiries.

The downward slide gathered momentum. A prominent family transferred their membership to another church and everyone knew it was "because of Reverend Westerberg." Then the Christian Education director, a woman liked and respected by the Sunday school teachers, took a job in another city. "I need a better working environment," she confided to the Christian Education board. Finally, the Council on Church Ministries, which was responsible for the Sunday morning worship service, told Mr. Westerberg they would like the young associate minister to preach at least half the time.

Devastated, confused, and exhausted by his loss of control, Carl Westerberg took a two-week vacation with his family. During the first couple of days he could not relax, even felt angry that his family had pulled him away from the church at a crucial time. He tried fishing but just stared at the float in the water. "What has gone wrong?" he kept asking himself. By the end of the first week he began to talk with his wife about his feelings of failure. Although sympathetic, she also had her own hostilities, which had been building for months. She unloaded on her husband about his lack of interest in the family and about the unfair load she had to carry—managing the family budget, taking care of all the teenage problems brought home by the kids, even making repairs on the parsonage.

The next few days Carl tried to spend time with the two youngest boys; they hiked in the woods and he felt renewed. For the first time in months he felt physically tired that night when he went to bed. By the end of the second week of vacation he felt as if he had a new lease on life and he told his wife what he planned to do about the church problems.

"Rather than working too hard," he told her, "I haven't been working hard enough on the things that really matter." He showed her the plans he had sketched in order to "get on top of the situation." "I remember once in seminary," he said, "when at midterm my grades fell to a C+ and for weeks I studied day and night to bring them up. It worked." He had written out an hour-by-hour schedule for each day of the week, pinpointing church responsibilities and family tasks. The way he figured it, "I have been just like that fishing float, bobbing aimlessly and reacting to every little wave that comes along." He only needed to "take the bull by the horns," schedule his time so he could write better sermons, have more frequent staff meetings, and reserve two nights a week for the family. Salvation would come through hard work.

Carl Westerberg's solutions are fairly typical for anyone who gets caught in the workaholic trap. The fundamental value of hard work, learned in childhood, applied through high school, college, and early work years, seems like a life raft to the person burning out. Job problems have always dissolved when you applied the extra effort, set aside more time, became better organized. Unfortunately, what may work when your adaptation energy reserves are high will only complicate problems when you've begun to burn out. Like all blind alleys, this one only increases the constant stress you're under.

Carl Westerberg had suddenly raised his expectations rather than lowered them. His new, regimented schedule allowed less time for alternating the emotional pressures of his job with physical exertion. He had not redefined the way he perceived stress; he had not improved his defective stress safety valves; he had not even gained a comprehension of his true problem, job burnout.

Instead, he had merely put new pressures on himself. Instead of fifty hours a week he now began to average sixty. Instead of taking time to cultivate and enjoy relationships with members of the church, he locked himself in his office working hard on Sunday morning sermons. When the students from the university asked why he never came to the student union to have coffee with them anymore, he said he still wanted to see them but they would have to make an appointment with his secretary. When a parent called with an urgent need to talk about problems with her children, he told her he would see her on the day he did his counseling. Her name went down on the waiting list, since the one day per week scheduled for counseling had filled up.

Mr. Westerberg couldn't keep up with his self-imposed schedule. The workaholic blind alley came to an unexpected dead end: the church board fired him six months later.

The Guilt Trip

One of the most insidious blind alleys that burnouts consistently take is the guilt trip. "I'm to blame," they say over and over to themselves. "Something is wrong with me for feeling exhausted, for getting sick, for having headaches, for not keeping up at work, for failing to handle the conflicts." The litany goes on and on, but the chorus is always the same: *I am the one at fault for all the problems.*

When you take a guilt trip, you have turned your anger inward, against yourself. You have become your own scapegoat. Dr. Christina Maslach, a psychologist at the University of California, studied several hundred burned-out people in the helping professions, from psychiatrists to cops. She found this guilt reaction very common and pointed to the ways it is expressed and reinforced by others. "By turning the heat on themselves, helping professionals begin to make more self-deprecatory remarks, to question their suitability for this line of work, and in general to lose those qualities which are essential for a helping professional, namely self-confidence, sense of humor, and a balanced perspective. The alleged personal flaws of helping professionals do not go unnoticed by critics who are willing to argue whether the matter involves a lack of ability, a motivation deficit, or a character defect. 'He's a cold fish,' 'She hasn't got a brain in her head,' 'You have to be crazy to be a psychiatrist,' 'What can you expect from cops, since they are all sadistic types to begin with'—so goes the diagnostic analysis."[9]

When you feel guilty and blame yourself, it can paralyze any constructive activity toward burnout recovery. Guilt handcuffs you. It makes it difficult, if not impossible, to change your perception of long-term stress. It hampers every effort to reduce the stress of family life, work, or environmental demands. Guilt blocks the development of new safety valves. All your energy flows into self-deprecation. "I'm no good" is the sign posted all along this blind alley. As Dr. Herbert Adler, associate professor of psychiatry at Hahnemann Medical College in Philadelphia, says about guilt, "When it runs amok inside, it can— quite literally—paralyze us, making us totally unable to function as human beings."[10]

Juanita MacIver has reached the third stage of burnout. She suffers from chronic fatigue, one cold after another, and feeling down more often than not. It has taken more than five years of pressure from working full time and managing four children, but the chronic stress finally used up most of her reserves. She has few safety valves. "All I ever do is work, at the department store or at home."

Richard and Juanita MacIver live in a lower-middle-class community. Richard drives a bus for the Municipal Transit Company; Juanita works behind the jewelry counter at Roberts Department Store. While they struggle to meet their monthly bills, most of their hopes in life center on their four children. They strive to make certain their children go to mass every week, have adequate medical and dental care, and enjoy a close family life. "I wouldn't think of working until all the kids are in school," she said for years. When Billy, aged eleven, started first grade five years ago, she began the clerk's job. She still does all the cooking and shopping, but Richard and the older children help out with cleaning. "It's a grind," she says, "but we couldn't make ends meet any other way." Then, several years ago, the stress of teenage children speeded up the burnout process and Juanita began to slip into a guilt trip.

Currently, Nancy, the nineteen-year-old, is living with her boyfriend. Sixteen-year-old Greg hangs around with a group of boys the MacIvers feel are "young hoodlums." And Janet, at thirteen, has begun to smoke, sneaking a joint or two of marijuana after school. She has had frequent run-ins with her teachers. Only Billy, the eleven-year-old, seems to reciprocate the love his parents have showered on their children.

Juanita's guilt has focused on her failure as a mother. "Maybe I should never have gone to work," she says. "Then I would have been here when the kids came home from school." Despite numerous studies to the contrary, Juanita shares this belief with thousands of people. When asked in a national survey, "Do you feel that a mother who works outside the home can have just as good a relationship with her children as a mother who does not work?" more than 40 percent of those interviewed believed the working mother's relationship to her children suffered.[11]

Juanita believes that in spite of all she has done, her children have betrayed her. When she talks to her best friend she often refers to the "mess the kids are in." But despite her deep anger toward them (Nancy has "lost all her marbles and her morals"; Greg is "self-centered and disrespectful"; Janet's behavior is "totally beyond my understanding"), her feelings more often focus on her own shortcomings. At night, when everyone has gone to bed, Juanita fixes herself a cup of hot tea. She usually sits at the kitchen table, alone with her thoughts. She engages in a self-defeating game called "What if . . .": "What if I hadn't worked?" "What if I had made them come home every night at ten o'clock?" "What if we had forced them to go to church more often?" "Maybe they shouldn't have been allowed to date at such an early age." In her most reflective moments she wonders what things would have been like if she had been more conciliatory and understanding. The anguish of such thoughts are almost more than she can bear.

Let's take another case. At thirty-nine, Brian Simpson has the security of a tenured full professorship at Brandon College in Ohio. When he first joined the college history department ten years ago, he spent as much time with students outside of class as he did sitting around seminar tables. "This is a great place to teach!" he used to say frequently to his fellow historians. But all that has changed.

Brian's burnout showed up first in deep job dissatisfaction and anger at those around him. Brian is angry at the dean of the college, who asked him to teach a large introductory course. Brian is angry at his colleagues, "who write more articles because they aren't carrying their share of teaching." Brian is angry at his students. "They are pampered and lazy, just looking for an easy grade." He often wishes for the good old days when they protested the War just so he would know "that these kids are capable of thinking about something besides themselves."

He is even angry at his wife, who doesn't understand the reasons for his discontent. Sometimes he wakes up in the middle of the night thinking about some nameless student, such as the one who wrote "what a waste!" across the bottom of a course evaluation form the previous semester.

But most of all Brian is angry with himself. Unfortunately, he feels powerless to do anything about it. While he often rants and raves about the shortcomings of those around him, in his honest reflective moments he feels that he has let everyone down.

Ever since the dean required him to teach large courses, his confidence in his teaching ability went into a prolonged slump. Preparing lectures for large classes took extra time he had previously devoted to writing scholarly articles. He is the only member of the department who has gone for five years without a single publication. He rationalized his lack of research by saying, "Well, I put in a lot of time on the city council." In reality, his election to that office has not cured the nagging doubts about whether he can really compete with his fellow historians. Brian also feels guilty about his family life. More and more of his evenings have been taken up with school work, city-council meetings, and "feeling too tired when [he's] home to do anything with the kids."

Brian's tendency to blame himself is similar to the attitudes of many people who outwardly live successful lives but inwardly feel a sense of alienation from themselves. Such persons often have high expectations of themselves, are conscientious, but believe somehow they have failed. The energy needed to attack the source of their burnout problems gets used up attacking themselves.

Why does job burnout lead to guilt in so many cases? Why do we often blame ourselves for the symptoms of burnout, for not being able to handle the pressures at work? Why is stumbling into the blind alley of guilt so widespread? "The feeling that 'I have become a bad person,' 'something is wrong with me,' or 'I am too weak or incompetent to handle this job,' was fairly pervasive," reported Dr. Christina Maslach after studying burned-out people in the helping professions. "Even when they recognized the special situational stresses of their work, people were still prone to lay blame on some flaw within themselves ('I should have been able to handle it'). Consequently, they experienced a sense of failure and a loss of self-esteem, and a state of depression would often set in."[12]

We believe there are four major reasons for the widespread guilt reaction to burning out. These factors all work together to "blame the victim" of job burnout.

The first guilt-producing factor is the superman/superwoman complex in Western culture. Every culture has its heroes. Held up in myths, stories, books, films, and other media, these heroes embody the ideals of a culture. As children we learn the exploits of the mythical heroes and strive to pattern ourselves after them. Each person's conscience is formed, in part, as we learn the "good" and "bad" portrayed by these cultural heroes.

The type of mythical hero varies from one culture to the next. Among the Salish Indians who live along the northwest coast of North America, stories about individuals who acquired supernatural power in a "vision quest" portrayed the culture hero. Among the Comanche of the plains, the warrior who could invade an enemy camp with great stealth, and kill, plunder, and "count coups" was the mythical hero. Among some American Indian groups the mythical hero was Coyote, a trickster who managed to achieve greatness by his cunning and skill.

In American culture, the most important mythical heroes are endowed with amazing physical power and strength. Superman, Superwoman, the Bionic Man, the Bionic Woman, Spiderman, Batman, and hundreds more pour out of the television screen, motion-picture theaters, and comic strips. To adults, these personages become translated into the business tycoon, the sports star, and the person who achieves against all odds by his personal strength and effort.

Burnout, by its very nature, contradicts everything in the superman/superwoman complex. Our strength gives out. We fail to achieve. Our abilities falter. Our endurance collapses. How do we cope with the conflict between the ideals of the mythical heroes and the realities of our burned-out condition? We do not discard the myth. We blame ourselves instead.

The superman/superwoman complex finds its way into many job descriptions without our realizing it. One perceptive secretary said, "My boss wants me to be a supermomma! In fact, most secretaries are expected to be pleasant, cheerful, kind, self-sacrificing, generous, impartial, tireless, modest, quiet, uncomplaining, and nurturant. It's like they want some kind of ultimate mother model. It hardly reflects the whole person coping over time. It punishes reasonable anger, fatigue, and bias."

A family physician who burned out ran directly into the superhuman expectations most people place on the medical profession. "I didn't know when to say no and I was unable to cope with the continuous pressure and my general feeling of inadequacy." A counselor in a substance-abuse clinic, faced with treating addicts whose odds of recovery are slim, burned out, in part from "extremely high expectations of staff involvement." Sometimes the superhuman demands can come from too many bosses: a woman suffering from burnout who finally quit her job said, "I was exhausted from working for two attorneys of polar-opposite behaviors simultaneously. My coworkers wouldn't help when I was overloaded with work. I had to take a nap every evening after work and then had no energy all evening."

A number of national surveys have shown how the superman/superwoman complex invades the workplace. In 1977, a large sample of workers was interviewed and 22 percent said they had too much work to do everything well; 42 percent said they never seemed to have enough time to get everything done on their jobs.[13] Imbued with the deep feeling that they ought to strive to be superhuman, such workers can easily fall prey to guilt, blaming themselves instead of the stress of the job.

The second guilt-producing factor comes from the type of stress that leads to burnout. When a tornado destroys your home, a flood brings a catastrophe to your life, or some other *acute* stress occurs, you can easily see the reason for feeling the way you do. But the long-term stress that contributes to job burnout is seldom dramatic. If you search for the cause of your plight, the only apparent change is *yourself.* That makes it easy to blame yourself and feel guilty. Brian Simpson felt the strain of job burnout. He felt he was losing control at work. But nothing much had changed; even the new teaching responsibility had come nearly three years ago. Like most people, he had adapted outwardly to the long-term stress of his job and family, so that when the burnout occurred, he felt it was most logical to blame *his own weakness.*[14]

A third factor that can produce paralyzing guilt comes from what we called job burnout isolation in chapter 1: the feeling that you alone are suffering from burnout. In her research, Dr. Christina Maslach also made this discovery: "Our observations uncovered a tendency to deny or to avoid revealing any personal thoughts or feelings that would be considered unprofessional, and to behave instead as if one were in control of the job and doing well. When everyone puts on this facade of 'I'm all right, Jack,' and fails to share [his or her] true reactions with each other, then any one of them is liable to make the erroneous assumption that he or she is the only one experiencing such problems."[15]

A growing body of research suggests that job burnout has a far greater incidence than imagined. Look around you—there are people where you work who are burning out, but will never reveal it. They may look angry, they may be using the ostrich response, they may be working harder, or merely feeling guilty. But one thing is for sure: they seldom announce to their colleagues, "I'm burning out!" And so burnout victims continue to feel alone; if no one else is burning out, the reason for this malady is clear: *they are to blame.* And the vicious cycle of the guilt trip speeds up.

Finally, many supervisors on the job reinforce the belief that the individual is at fault. When things go wrong, we don't look at the structure of the work or the work environment, but to *people.* Every work organization has its own legends, handed down from one generation of employees to the next, about people who "couldn't take the heat," lazy and inefficient employees, workers who didn't fit in, all justifiably fired by the boss. Jobs don't get terminated when workers suffer from burnout symptoms; *people get terminated.* When it happens in any company, the rumors spread like wildfire, leaving a trail of anxiety in their wake. "Did you hear about Sally? The vice-president called her in last week and told her to start looking for another job." The lesson becomes engraved on the hearts and minds of all who remain: the worker failed, not the work organization. We say, "The worker couldn't take it," not, "The job was designed in a manner that created unrelieved stress." Blame the victim, not the cause. And so when job burnout sets in for any of us, we become anxious about our ability to handle the job and guilt grows.

Even our analysis of job burnout can appear to speed you on your way along the guilt trip. If you filter everything we have said thus far through the unquestioned assumption that workers are responsible for their failure to cope with work stress, it may sound like this: *"If you're suffering from job burnout, you're to blame. You've been too stupid to recognize and cope with work stress."* But the message of this book has a radically different theme. If you're suffering from job burnout, you've been exposed to occupational hazards you didn't know about. These hazards permeate the atmosphere of your job in the form of work stress. Furthermore, millions of years of human evolution have given you an obsolete involuntary stress response. These two forces, working together, have victimized you. The personal treatment strategies we have discussed can help you *cope* with these twin causes of job burnout. But they only take you part of the way. In the next section, we turn to the treatment strategies aimed at work stress itself. We believe it's possible to "humanize the workplace"; that means designing jobs to better match our Stone Age physiology and biochemistry. As we examine organizational treatment strategies, ways to manage stressful jobs, we will see how nature's original game plan of "fight or flight" can be adapted to eliminating the hazards of work stress in millions of jobs.

Part Three
The Treatment of Job Burnout: Organizational Strategies

Chapter Seven
Managing
Stressful Jobs

The most effective treatment of job burnout goes to the root of the problem: work stress itself. Such treatment goes beyond the *personal strategies* discussed earlier—taking control of job burnout, improving stress safety valves, avoiding burnout blind alleys. It adds to these certain *organizational strategies,* which focus on the structure and content of the job.

Each worker faces a dual challenge in any job. First, he or she has to carry out assigned tasks. The minister must visit the sick, counsel parishioners, prepare and deliver sermons. The assembly-line worker in a Popsicle factory has to package the fudge bars as they come down the line. The magazine editor has to select articles, edit them for style, prepare copy for the compositor, and correspond with authors. All jobs have such required tasks; they make up the work you do.

The other challenge of every job is not so obvious. Each worker must deal with the secondary demands that arise from the content and structure of required tasks. Take the job of packaging fudge bars on an assembly line, for example. The worker must pick up the bars, place them in groups of twelve in a cardboard container, seal the container, and place it in a larger box for shipment to the freezer. At first, it is these primary demands that concern the worker. But the structure of these tasks, the fact that they are linked to a larger assembly-line procedure, creates secondary demands. The worker has to come to terms with repetition, monotony, machine-paced pressure, and restricted physical movement. If the same tasks were carried out by small work groups responsible for the entire production process, this alternative structure would change the secondary demands. The minister has to cope with unexpected interruptions; he must deal with his own emotions evoked by exposure to the dying. The magazine editor has to cope with juggling numerous responsibilities, angry authors, and delays in production schedules. All workers, then, must do their primary tasks as well as manage these secondary demands.

How do workers cope with the secondary demands of their jobs? On the surface it appears that everyone deals with work in her own unique manner. We shared that assumption as we began our research. If we have more than 30,000 kinds of jobs, we reasoned, and millions of workers, surely people will cope in an infinite variety of ways. But as our investigation of job burnout continued, we discovered five dominant styles of coping with jobs and the stress they produced. Most workers adopt one of these patterns or a combination of several. The most frequent coping styles we call the *loyal servant,* the *angry prisoner,* the *stress fugitive,* the *job reformer,* and the *stress manager.* We were especially interested in the stress manager; our study of people who adopted this coping style revealed important organizational strategies for managing stressful jobs. After briefly describing these five styles, we will discuss the five principles used by stress managers to deal success-fully with work stress.

Loyal servants deal with the vicissitudes of their jobs by passive compliance. Managers and bosses design the structure and content of their job; they follow orders and do their work as assigned. "I'm just a hired hand around here," said one social worker. "You take the cases assigned and do everything by the book." Loyal servants act as if their job, with whatever stress it creates for them, has been chiseled in stone. Because work organizations often reward loyal servants, this style may become the only alternative for many workers. "If you try to change things in this company or go about your work in a new way, you're labeled a troublemaker," said one accountant in a large engineering firm.

When work stress piles up, loyal servants try to relieve the pressure by using on-the-job safety valves. A staff nurse told us, "We bitch at lunch, bitch at coffee, bitch whenever we can. And we joke about the really difficult patients. After a hard day we all go out and party. We take every chance we can to celebrate a birthday or anniversary. It's the only way we can survive." Instead of getting control of the stressful job, the loyal servant tries to escape or control his or her stress response. Some manage this successfully, avoiding job burnout or postponing it for years. But many other workers, because they are limited to a few personal strategies for coping, experience chronic symptoms of job burnout.

Angry prisoners cope with their jobs by passive resistance. They come to feel that their work organization is like the state penitentiary: unchanging and inescapable. Work stress comes automatically with a life sentence you serve on the installment plan—eight hours a day. A teacher in an urban school described this feeling: "It's like I'm serving time in this school. My classroom has become a cell and I'm scared stiff to walk up and down the halls." Those who adopt a prisoner stance toward their jobs think they have no power to control their jobs. This same teacher said, "The parents have their ideas and control the school board; the administration's afraid to do anything; and the students have all the rights and freedom."

When your job becomes a prison, the risk of burnout sharply increases. Even so, some who adopt this style of coping seem able to "do easy time" by keeping their anger under control and remaining passive. "Don't fight it, that's the only way to keep your sanity on this job," said one worker. "Those who fight the system only do hard time."

Stress fugitives cope with their jobs by running from work stress. When the head nurse offers the staff a choice of patients, the fugitive type quickly selects the ones that seem to need the least care. Within the limits of the job, the stress fugitive tries to escape stressful tasks. Avoidance, procrastination, and outright neglect of responsibilities all characterize the stress fugitive.

When it becomes impossible to avoid work stress, the stress fugitive runs to a new job. Without realizing it, the fugitive has become captive to the idea that there just has to be a perfect job. A public health nutritionist who had worked in four different agencies in three years told us, "I kept thinking sometime I would find an agency where there wouldn't be office politics." The frustrations and strains in the present job appear overwhelming to the stress fugitive; the problems in a new job seem minimal. But it becomes only a matter of time until the need arises for another escape route.

Stress fugitives run a high risk of job burnout for two reasons. First, they never learn to manage the stresses of their job and so the pressures build. Second, they seem limited to a single personal strategy for coping: escape. But each escape involves a job change and this brings the added stress of learning and adjustment, draining their adaptation energy even further.

Job reformers deal with work stress by focusing all their energy on a crusade for change. They seldom make effective use of personal strategies for dealing with stress. Instead, they lay all the blame on the conditions of work. They see the organizational sources of work stress more clearly than anyone else. And they dedicate themselves to changing the organization. Job reformers make little distinction between changing an organization to reduce work stress and changing an organization to fit their image of the ideal corporate entity.

Although job reformers often include work stress in their frontal attack, the changes they seek go far beyond merely reducing stress. They spearhead a zealous campaign—complaining, organizing, and urging others to join their cause. When they meet with resistance from other workers or management, they fight harder, then grow discouraged. Work organizations such as hospitals and colleges with a large number of professionals often encourage job reformers. The administration appoints committees and solicits ideas for change; this gives the appearance of shared power. Change appears possible. Yet, in the final analysis, the job reformer wields little actual power for change. Job reformers tend to go through cycles of job burnout and recovery. They crusade for change, meet hidden resistance, continue fighting the system until they reach the brink of job burnout crisis. Then they withdraw, perhaps for months or years, and this can bring recovery. Sooner or later, many job reformers are drawn into the fray again.

Stress managers cope with their jobs by identifying and controlling work stress. These people manage their own stress responses by using many different personal strategies. However, they also use organizational strategies to change the structure and content of jobs to bring relief to themselves and others.

We found stress managers in every occupational group we studied. These individuals, adept at managing work stress, were not supermen and superwomen blessed with a God-given talent for managing stressful jobs. Rather, we found workers who knew their limitations, who periodically came home frustrated and tired, yet often exhilarated by their work. Among the effective stress managers were nurses who cried when one of their patients died, salesmen who became discouraged over the impact of the recession on their quarterly reports, teachers who had misgivings about whether they had entered the right profession, and high-salaried executives who silently wondered whether their careers had hit a plateau. In other words, effective stress managers do not have an immunity to feeling the consequences of work stress.

We also found that many stress managers did not consciously realize how they managed their stressful jobs. They often attributed it to "working for a great boss," or "being lucky to find this job." In fact, as we listened to them talk at length about their work, we found they all employed certain basic principles for managing stressful jobs. In the remainder of this chapter we present five principles that stress managers followed most faithfully. We believe that you can learn to apply them to your job situation, thereby treating the very root cause of job burnout.

Keep Your
Stress-Management
Objective Clear

All of us have many different work-related goals. You may want to get a promotion, increase your productivity, get a year-end bonus, organize a baseball team, or transfer to an outside job. Most people seek to perform their jobs well; they want to get along with coworkers. These and other goals add meaning to work. But all too often, workers who burn out hardly give a passing thought to another objective: managing the work stress inherent in the job.

Effective stress managers were all people who had a healthy respect for the power of work stress. They knew it could become a deadly hazard to their health. Their highest priority was to control their job rather than let the job control them. They wanted to lower work stress just enough to avoid job burnout, not so much that the challenge disappeared from the job. The job reformer has a much more ambitious goal—to bring about drastic changes in the work situation. Although the stress manager may have highly idealistic notions about changing the organization, these remain secondary to the more important but limited objective of managing stress.

We encountered stress managers who held supervisory positions. They not only wanted to control the stress that affected them personally, but made this a clear objective for those they supervised. "I try to observe everyone on my staff, and when I sense someone is under stress, I call him or her in and we talk about it," said one executive. "'There's one thing more important than doing your job,' I tell them, 'and that's staying on top of your job, managing the pressures.'"

Most people want to manage stress, but at best it's a vague goal. Keeping this objective clearly in focus may require daily reminders. Some stress managers reinforced their commitment to stress control by attending frequent workshops, others read books on the subject. One busy consultant told us, "I drew a small target on a card and wrote work stress in the bull's-eye. I keep that on my desk as a daily reminder that if I don't manage the stress in my work, no one else will." Whatever means you use, taking control of your job begins by keeping this objective clearly in mind.

Develop a Detached
View of Your Job

Most employees want workers willing to make a commitment to a particular job. After interviewing five people for a sales position, the district manager for a tire company hired the one "who showed the most enthusiasm and commitment to the job." Promotions within an organization usually follow the same logic: look for the person who is dedicated. When new recruits are hired by the New York Fire Department, they go through an intensive training period. As in most organizations, these training programs teach the recruits more than how to fight fires. They build a sense of involvement and dedication to the job. "I had doubts about being a firefighter," said one recruit. "But after fire school I knew it was for me. I came to love the work and really *felt* like a firefighter." The long years of schooling required by physicians, astronomers, accountants, university professors, and other professionals function in a similar manner. Most of us come to identify closely with our jobs.

A strong emotional attachment to a job develops also as a result of work stress. Our stress response always includes an emotional component. When job pressures build, we *feel* anger, fear, insecurity, frustration, challenge, or elation. When pressures go on month after month, we develop strong negative and positive attachments to the job. These often lie outside our awareness but influence our behavior nonetheless.

In order to identify work stress, assess its impact, and manage it, you must first achieve a detachment from your job. But the pressures for attachment and commitment are often so strong, you become locked in an emotional closeness that keeps you blinded to the problems that surround you. The job reformer, for example, crusades for reform out of a deep sense of injustice. This belief that things must change for the better prevents the reformer from developing a detached, objective view of his or her circumstances. The loyal servant has a strong sense of commitment and loyalty that doesn't allow standing back to look at the work situation. The angry prisoner cannot treat the job in a detached manner because of his hostility. Other workers feel guilty about taking a detached view of their work, as if they are being irresponsible.

The stress managers we studied had an uncanny ability to stand back and look at themselves and their jobs in a detached manner. One hospital administrator said, "Sitting in staff meetings I sometimes feel like I'm a visitor from outer space watching these earthlings hassle over their tiny problems." Sometimes the detachment comes with a sense of humor. A college professor told us, "I sit in our faculty meetings listening to the angry debates about requirements and grading policy and I suddenly imagine a group of chimpanzees in serious debate, or I imagine all those dignified professors wearing bathing suits. What others take in utmost seriousness, I can't help but see in a humorous light." Others developed a detached view by talking at great length with a spouse or friend about their job. The outsider, free from emotional involvement in the job, helped the stress manager maintain a sense of detachment.

We believe that this detached perspective, so common in effective stress managers, gives this kind of worker the ability to see work stress in a way that others miss. Without the detached view, you will find it difficult, if not impossible, to follow the other principles of stress management, such as analyzing the hidden structure of your job or taking a stress inventory. Here are several things you can do to increase your ability to take a detached view of your job:

1. *Imagine someone else is doing your job.* Stop for a few moments during a busy day and imagine another person sitting at your desk, giving your lecture, taking care of the patient, selling the product, or sitting at the board meeting. Give that person a name. Think of yourself as standing nearby watching and listening from an invisible observation post. What do you see and hear? Can you achieve a *feeling* of detachment?

2. *Think of your job as a one-act play.* As Shakespeare said, "All the world's a stage." By adopting that perspective, you can transform your office, classroom, hospital ward,

or executive suite into a stage. Think of yourself and others as actors on that stage. Think of their actions as directed by a script, their words as lines in the play. Now, think of yourself in the audience watching this play. If you feel like a spectator even for a moment, you have achieved a certain degree of valuable detachment.

3. *Write down on-the-spot observations.* Writing down a description of what goes on around you makes you an observer and recorder. It will separate you for a moment from being an actor at the center of the stage. Take five minutes and write down everything you see going on around you—people walking about, phones ringing, desks piled high with papers—whatever you see. Describe the atmosphere you sense, the temperature of the air, the color and arrangement of furniture. Writing down a description of what you and others are actually doing helps to separate yourself from those actions.

4. *Describe your job to an outsider.* Find a friend, someone who knows little about your job, and tell that person what you do. Describe a typical day, the kinds of people you work with, the way your job is organized. The more often you talk to outsiders about your job, the easier you will find it to take a detached view of it.

Developing a detached *view* of your job doesn't mean becoming detached and unconcerned. Far from it. Stress managers consistently assumed a detached perspective because they were concerned. They wanted to create a healthy work environment and manage the hazards of work stress. Their detached *view* was a stepping-stone to that objective.

Analyze the Hidden Structure of Your Job

This strategy for managing a stressful job involves a way of thinking about your job. It requires you to use your mind to analyze the hidden structure of your work and the organization that employs you.[1]

All of us develop habitual ways of thinking about our jobs. In our research, as we listened to hundreds of people talk about their jobs, it became clear that stress managers were *analytic thinkers.* They saw their job in its total context, yet constantly dissected it into its smaller elements. When we asked someone to describe his job, a stress manager seldom summarized or told us the major activity; instead he dissected and divided his work into many smaller parts. A fireman-paramedic, instead of saying, "I make fire runs and medic runs," would become quite explicit: "I make eight different kinds of fire runs and more than twenty medic runs, like psych runs, O.B. runs, diabetic runs, ten forty-five runs, overdose runs, and turkey runs." If we asked, "What do you do on a fire run," a stress manager would not summarize by saying, "We just go to the fire and put it out." Instead, his answer revealed an analytic-thinking process: "Well, it's a pretty complex procedure with more than a dozen steps—things like putting on gear, sizing up, ventilating, putting out the fire, ventilating again, and so on."

This tendency of stress managers to break down their jobs into many smaller tasks extended beyond their own immediate job to their work environment. A cocktail waitress, for example, who managed her stressful job well, easily identified more than twenty different tasks she performed each night. These included such things as taking orders, giving extra service, carding, running errands, giving last call, and keeping busy. But she also divided the range of customers into eight types: regulars, real regulars, loners, couples, businessmen, drunks, women, and people off the street. When we asked about the bar, she quickly drew a map and marked off male territories, female territories, waitress stations, and places where fights took place. She described not only the work she did, but the kinds of people she served, the dimensions of the bar, the way people talked, and many other aspects of her work environment.[2] Stress managers in other occupations engaged in similar types of analysis. Most were hardly aware of this tendency; it had become second nature to them.

Workers skilled at coping with work stress went one step further to identify the *hidden structure* of their jobs. They had a deep appreciation for the fact that every organization has both a formal and an informal structure. No one writes the informal structure into our job descriptions; we learn it by a kind of social osmosis from other workers. Some people never recognize the existence of this hidden, informal structure; for this reason they sometimes seem like misfits. Still others hear the informal rules and follow them carefully, but cannot articulate what's going on. They seem to have an intuitive sense of the hidden structure. They know how to do their jobs, get things done, and get along with others, but never think much about the informal rules. Stress managers, on the other hand, have a keen awareness of this hidden structure; they analyze it, talk about it, and devise ways to deal with it.

Jill Renton, a senior executive secretary who supervises six other secretaries at Metropolitan Enterprises, a computer software company, offers a good example of someone who was aware of the hidden structure of her job. We asked Jill to tell us about her work. "First there's my job description," she said, as if it were important. "I hire staff secretaries, delegate work fairly, conduct performance reviews, and make appointments for my boss. But it took me a while to learn what I was *really* supposed to do. My real job is to keep Roberta happy—she's my boss. No one really cares about whether I'm delegating things fairly to my staff or whether I hire according to affirmative-action policies, or whether I'm nailing incompetent loafers. What really matters is what Roberta thinks about me. Coffee has to be served within five minutes of her arrival. I have to screen out unnecessary appointments—and knowing which ones depends on Roberta's mood on any particular day. And, oh yes—always make certain her pencils are sharpened." Jill Renton continued to elaborate on the informal structure of her job. But she had not only learned these hidden rules, something most competent workers do, but she constantly analyzed this structure, expanding it to other features of her work environment. She knew that the vital information traveled informally over the office grapevine, not through office memos or bulletin-board notices. She knew that the formal rewards of a pay raise or promotion were foreshadowed by numerous informal rewards. Like other effective stress managers we interviewed, Jill Renton made it her practice to know the hidden structure of her job.

How does the ability to analyze the hidden work structure contribute to effective stress management? It comes from the fact that work stress can pervade both the formal and informal structure of your job. At the formal level, you can easily identify work stress and do something about it. But when the pressure and frustration of your job come from the hidden informal structure, it's impossible to deal with them unless you have become *aware* of that structure. Stress managers make it a habit, though often without conscious effort, to analyze the hidden structure of their work environment. In doing so they can easily identify forms of work stress that others do not see.

Consider another example. Jack Bogardus took a position as counselor in a residential treatment program for children. At the first staff meeting he learned the rules for "complete openness and honesty" among the staff. Each of the sixteen persons, ranging from the psychiatrist-director to the new counselors, were expected to reveal their feelings about the job, about the children, and about other staff members. An atmosphere of complete acceptance of those feelings pervaded the meetings. "At first I felt a little uneasy," said Jack, "but pretty soon I was opening up like all the others."

But within a few months Jack had run headlong into a series of hidden rules, ones that caused him great stress. "The first thing that happened was that the director asked me if I thought children had a good chance of improvement in this program. I told him I had serious doubts and told him why. Well, the two assistant directors immediately began to comment on my attitude. I became the center of discussion for two staff meetings and finally the director said he thought I needed to be in therapy myself. I'd learned the first unwritten rule: express all feelings except those that criticize the director or the program." In the weeks that followed Jack withdrew from exposing his feelings so openly. Other staff members then began to ask him what he was "hiding." So Jack volunteered several positive feelings about his work and the children he supervised. This led to a long inquisition that probed for his "true feelings." "I realized that another unwritten rule said you could talk about your negative feelings, but not your positive ones. And either way, they could use what you said as proof that you had some deep-seated psychological problem. Then I saw the most important hidden rule of all. Nearly everyone on the staff had tacitly agreed to use their whole psychological framework of treating the disturbed children to control the staff! Once I saw that, I also could work out strategies for coping with it."

Analyzing the hidden structure of your job begins with an awareness that it exists. Then you can go on to sensitize yourself to how it operates. We believe it is useful to think of your workplace as a small "tribal society," one with its own rituals and traditions. Consider yourself an observer from another culture (that important detached view), and try to figure out what's going on around you, what most people take for granted. What are the hidden values and rules that people accept without realizing it? What kinds of rewards and punishments are given out? How does the communication system work? What language do people speak? Is there a hidden power structure? What alliances have people formed and for what purposes? Do hidden conflicts exist? Analyzing the hidden structure of your job is not a once-and-for-all task, but an ongoing process, a way of thinking. It's an organizational strategy that will take you a long way down the road to taking control of work stress.

Take a Stress Inventory

In order to manage a stressful job, you need to know the specific kinds of work stress you face. We were often surprised to find people suffering from advanced cases of job burnout who had great difficulty identifying the work stress they encountered. After years on a job, they accepted demands as "part of the job," hesitant to admit that those pressures caused their problems.

Good stress managers have learned to take frequent stress inventories.

They often do so without realizing it, taking immediate action to attack the problem identified. If you want to deal with the sources of stress within your job and work organization, we suggest taking a systematic stress inventory.

Begin by taking the widest view of your life situation. Divide a sheet of paper into three columns, one for each of the major types of stress we identified in chapter 2 as burnout risk factors. List the major frustrations you feel in the course of a week, dividing them into the categories of family pressures, work problems, and environmental demands. Let's look at some examples. In an earlier chapter we examined how Jerry Albert and his wife, Nina, perceived several stresses and how they could take control of their perceptions. Now let's look at Jerry Albert's stress inventory. Jerry, an assistant manager of a supermarket, identified the following stresses he thought came from the wider environment beyond his family and his job:

1. Noisy airplanes flying low over my home (I live three miles from the airport).
2. My 1974 Plymouth has 85,000 miles on it and something seems to break down every week.
3. Inflation: my salary doesn't seem to stretch far enough.
4. The long, cold winters in Buffalo; huge amounts of snow.
5. The Planned Parenthood abortion clinic that opened last fall six blocks from my house.

Each of these things causes Jerry to get upset and angry, often demanding hours of time to wait for his car to come out of the shop or shovel snow from his walks.

Under "family pressures" Jerry made the following list:

1. Teenage kids coming in at all hours of the night disturb my sleep.
2. Elderly mother living in Rochester has trouble taking care of herself but won't move to a nursing home; must visit her nearly every weekend.
3. Eldest daughter who had graduated from college now

lives with her boyfriend; it's against our wishes and all
we taught her.
4. Wife's health has not been good; with all the kids busy
she has little to do and gets depressed during the day.
Afraid to find a job; anxious about going back to school.

Jerry enjoys his job at the supermarket and at first couldn't identify
things he thought were "really stressful." After sixteen years as assistant manager, he said, "I've got it down to a routine," but then began
recognizing some of his frustrations. Three kinds of work stress stood
out as most important:

1. My boss has kind of "retired on the job" and I end up
doing a lot of his work. I really ought to be manager.
2. Working some nights and weekends. I don't mind too
much, but it would be nice to have an eight-to-five job.
3. Firing inefficient checkers and stock boys. The boss
leaves that up to me and I hate to do it.

Once you've written down those stresses that come quickly to mind,
you can focus on your job frustrations. Because of the importance of
work stress in causing job burnout, we recommend that you spend
more time on this part of the stress inventory. Take a second sheet of
paper and write "Work-Stress Inventory" across the top. Divide it into
three columns and write the major features of most jobs across the
top: *activities, people,* and *work conditions.* Then, beneath each, try to
identify as many of each in your job, regardless of whether you find
them stressful or frustrating. If you have developed a habit of analyzing the hidden structure of your job, this part of the inventory will
come easily. But take a few minutes to probe your memory for informal rules and work conditions that are easily taken for granted.
We studied the work stresses encountered by cocktail waitresses at a
small college bar, which can serve as an example.[3] These women identified the activities of a typical night of work, the people they worked
with, and their job conditions. The work-stress inventory sheet on the
next page shows these three features of their job.

WORK-STRESS INVENTORY
(for a group of cocktail waitresses)

Activities	People	Work Conditions
going to work	managers	noisy
getting ready	customers	crowded
keeping busy	female customers	hassles with cus-
waiting on tables	drunks	tomers
taking orders	people off the	nighttime
serving orders	street	joking
making change	couples	on your feet
taking a break	loners	boring
giving extra service	businessmen	repetitious
rechecking tables	regulars	family atmosphere
carding	real regulars	hustled by men
running errands	waitresses	dealing with drunks
picking up tips	bouncers	meeting new guys
giving last call	bartenders	
clearing tables		
turning in money		
punching out		

With a list similar to this one for your own job, you can easily circle the items you think are related to stress. Look it over carefully and ask: which things on my list are frustrating? boring? make me angry? nervous? tense? Which ones would make this a better job if I could eliminate them?

Most jobs create more than one kind of frustration. In a recent U.S.

Labor Department survey, 69 percent of a national sample of workers reported two or more sources of dissatisfaction and stress. Some reported as many as fourteen such problems.[4] The waitresses we studied, for example, all found customer hassles, crowded conditions, and giving extra service stressful. Most disliked "carding," having to check identification of underage patrons. Female customers and drunks usually created the most hassles.

Even a simplified inventory list such as the one for cocktail waitresses can lead directly to changing the structure of your job, thereby relieving work stress. One cocktail waitress told us that she felt a strong responsibility to deal with drunks and not call for help. Yet this type of customer came out high on her stress inventory. "When I finally realized how upset I could get over dealing with a slobbering drunk, I thought to myself, 'Why should I feel it's my duty to put up with drunks?' I decided that was one responsibility I could shift to someone else. Now, at the first sign of trouble, instead of trying to deal with the drunk, I just call the bouncer or the bartender. That one change made a significant difference in my job."

In order to assist you in taking a stress inventory, we have prepared a work-stress checklist. Every item on this list has been found stressful to some workers. Read the list carefully, checking the appropriate space as to whether each particular work stress is *present* or *absent* in your job.

WORK-STRESS CHECKLIST		
Present	Absent	Work Stress
		Threats to Health and Security
———	———	1. Physical danger
———	———	2. Unhealthy working conditions
———	———	3. Too many heavy physical tasks
———	———	4. Threat of violence from others

Present	Absent	Work Stress
		The Stress of Work Overload
____	____	5. The work is never done
____	____	6. Unrealistic deadlines
____	____	7. Must take work home to finish it
____	____	8. Responsibility for too many people
____	____	9. Inadequate help to do the work
____	____	10. Inefficient subordinates
		Threats to Job Security
____	____	11. Threat of being laid off or fired
____	____	12. Inadequate health insurance
____	____	13. Inadequate pension plan
____	____	14. Inadequate financial rewards
		Time Pressures
____	____	15. Have to work too fast
____	____	16. Pace of work is machine-controlled
____	____	17. Shift work and/or rotating shifts
____	____	18. No time for coffee or lunch breaks
____	____	19. No time off for personal affairs
____	____	20. No variation in the pace of work
____	____	21. Have to work too slowly
____	____	22. No flexibility in starting and quitting
		The Stress of Work Underload
____	____	23. Not enough work to do
____	____	24. Required to look busy
____	____	25. Not enough responsibility
____	____	26. Mind, skills, and abilities not used
____	____	27. Overqualified for the job
____	____	28. No chance for personal growth

Present	Absent	Work Stress
		Stressful Social Relationships
____	____	29. Unfriendly fellow workers
____	____	30. Demands too much teamwork and cooperation
____	____	31. No support from the work group
____	____	32. No one shows personal interest in you
____	____	33. Too much red tape
		Dead-End-Job Stresses
____	____	34. No hope for advancement
____	____	35. No hope for increased earnings
____	____	36. No hope for learning new things
____	____	37. No hope for more freedom on the job
____	____	38. Sex, age, and/or racial discrimination
____	____	39. Need "pull" to get ahead
____	____	40. No chance for transfer in the organization
____	____	41. Lack authority to carry out your job
____	____	42. Can't do what you do best
____	____	43. Inadequate recognition for your work
____	____	44. The work has little meaning to you
		Boredom Stress
____	____	45. Narrowly specialized and repetitious tasks
____	____	46. Never learn anything new
____	____	47. Requires little or no skill
____	____	48. Can't see end product of your work
____	____	49. Monotonous work

Present	Absent	Work Stress
		Threats from the Boss
____	____	50. Boss gives you little or no feedback
____	____	51. Too many bosses
____	____	52. Boss supervises too closely
____	____	53. Overcritical boss
____	____	54. Boss has retired on the job
____	____	55. Incompetent boss
____	____	56. Can't communicate with the boss
____	____	57. Conflicting and unclear job description
		Threats to Your Rights as a Human Being
____	____	58. No right to refuse dangerous tasks
____	____	59. Can't refuse overtime work
____	____	60. Excluded from decision-making process
____	____	61. Cannot communicate in your native language
____	____	62. Can be fired without chance of peer review
____	____	63. Can't refuse unethical work assignments
____	____	64. Can't blow the whistle on illegal or unethical activities
____	____	65. Have no say in how work is done

Look back over each work-stress item that is present in your job. Try to evaluate which ones are most serious. This checklist as well as the stress inventory sheet presented earlier are only suggested approaches to taking a stress inventory. You may want to design your own. But whatever strategy you employ, the goal remains the same: to achieve a detached view of your job, analyze the hidden structure of your job, and then identify the sources of work stress that can lead to job burnout.

If most of your stress comes from people you serve, you might find it easier to make your inventory by writing an imaginary letter telling them how to make your life miserable. One hairdresser wrote such a letter to Ann Landers and with it summed up the most important kinds of work stress for that occupation.

Dear Ann: The life of a hairdresser is not an easy one. As one who has been in the business for a long time, I'd like to submit a list of suggestions for patrons who want to drive their beauticians up the wall. Just do the following:

—Arrive late and throw his (or her) schedule off for the whole day.

—Arrive early. Squirm around in your chair and tap your foot impatiently while you wait.

—Find a picture in a magazine of a hairstyle you admire. Take it along and instruct the operator to fix your hair exactly like the woman's in the picture. (Never mind that the movie queen has a glorious growth of thick hair, and you are nearly bald.)

—Complain that you are tired of the same old hairdo and want something different. When he creates a new style, complain that it "doesn't look like me."

—If your appointment is for a shampoo and set, decide on the spur of the moment that you need a haircut. Ask him to "work it in."

—Request that he leave at least three clips in your hair to make sure it stays in place until you arrive at your destination. Do not, under any circumstances, return the clips. He has plenty. If each customer carries away three, he will only lose 45 clips per day.

—Watch the beautician struggle to please you with the comb-out, then state nonchalantly, "Well, at least it's clean."

—Ask a neighbor to cut your hair for you. She'll make a mess of it. Then go to your hair stylist and ask him to "shape it up."

One last word: Must you smoke cigarettes while I'm working on you? I'm inhaling hairspray eight hours a day. Your
smoke is making me sick.

                                          I Speak for Thousands[5]

Use Your Influence
to Redesign Jobs

Many people accept the structure and content of their job as given.
Stress managers believe in the possibility of change and look for ways
to redesign their jobs and the jobs of those who work for them. An
anesthesiologist who had worked for twenty years as department head
in a large university hospital on the East Coast had mastered the skills
of stress management. He continued to use his influence to improve his
own job and those in the department. "I find my most rewarding challenge," he told us, "in upgrading the competency of the staff and in
updating policies and procedures to make the work a little easier and
more clearly defined for the staff." Whatever your job and no matter
how little formal power you have, you can use your influence to redesign your job. Remember the cocktail waitress who reduced work
stress by redefining her responsibility and calling on the bartender or
bouncer to handle drunks. Once you know the sources of stress, you
can make suggestions, ask others to assist you, and even change the
structure of your own job more than you realize. The stress managers
we studied refused to believe that they had no influence. They pa-
tiently used that influence to work for the reduction of work stress.

Let's consider a job that, on the surface, appears to offer little hope
for change. East-West Insurance Company employs many people like
Kenneth Neiderhoff, a twenty-eight-year-old keypunch operator.[6]
Recently divorced, Ken has custody of his two young children. His
monthly income barely covers the necessities of life and the alimony he
sends to his ex-wife. For seven years he has punched tabulating cards
with information about insurance claims, billings, premium payments,
changes in policy coverage, and cancellations.

Ken has little control over the design of his work. His superiors have planned the last detail of his job description to fit the demands of efficiency, profit, and machines. A service clerk receives typed and handwritten documents from branch offices and insurance agencies scattered around the country. This clerk checks over the material, divides it randomly into batches that will take about one hour of keypunching, then assigns them to one of the several dozen operators like Ken. Each day from nine to five, with two fifteen-minute breaks and a half hour for lunch, Ken sits at his keypunch machine transferring the information to cards. As soon as he completes one batch, he returns it to the service clerk, picks up the next, and punches his keys hour after hour, day after day, year after year.

"It's a mindless job," Ken says disparagingly. "You get so you're punching cards in your sleep." Although he doesn't think about it, nearly every aspect of Ken's job is controlled by others. Someone else sets the standards for the number of cards punched per hour and Ken's supervisor keeps the pressure on him to meet that demand. Someone else decided that work should begin for everyone at nine o'clock each day, whether Ken's two children need special attention or not. Someone else set the time for breaks, whether Ken feels the need for a break then or at some other time. When Ken makes errors, he won't even know about it until his supervisor informs him; someone else finds and corrects his mistakes. Ken doesn't make the decision about which batch of information he will punch on cards. He doesn't know anyone at the branch offices or agencies who have filled out the forms. He will never see the end product of his labors—only the small piles of cards it takes one hour to punch. He can't try out new approaches to his work. He can't vary his pace to break up the routine. It has been more than five years since Ken has learned anything new in his job. It's no wonder that his work has lost any intrinsic interest or meaning it ever held for him.

But Ken's job isn't the only thing he can't control. For several years his own body has begun to react in counterproductive ways to the stress created by the design of his job. He frequently leaves work with a splitting headache. Because of lowered resistance to illness he has used up all his sick leave on bad colds and the flu. His blood pressure has risen to an abnormal level. He often fights depression. "Sometimes I feel completely trapped," he says dejectedly. "I just want to go up to my boss and say, 'I'm through!' and walk out of that insurance company forever!"

East-West Insurance Company employed several dozen keypunch operators like Ken. Many of them had begun to show some of the symptoms of job burnout. Work efficiency was at an all-time low. The speed at which the keypunch operators worked had fallen below the accepted industry standard. The number of errors in one group of about forty keypunch operators had reached an unacceptably high level. Absenteeism, one of the clearest signs of job burnout, had reached the highest level among all departments at East-West.

Although many of the keypunch operators felt powerless, they were able to use what influence they had. They made suggestions on ways to reduce work stress. In a group discussion about the problems, they came up with a list of seventy-three specific suggestions for redesigning their jobs. For example, workers who merely received batches of cards and information to punch said they wanted greater control over their jobs. Why couldn't they receive the information directly from the agencies and branch offices? Why was it necessary to have a service clerk check over this material and then assign it to the keypunch operator? Someone suggested that the keypunch operators could treat certain agencies and branch offices as their own "clients," receive the information directly from them, check it over, call the clients if problems arose, do the keypunching, and accept responsibility for correcting their own mistakes.

Management at East-West Insurance Company accepted many of the recommendations, particularly the ones that gave *greater control* over their jobs to the workers. They sought to give each keypunch operator more responsibility, to turn mindless jobs into challenging ones that allowed for personal growth. For instance, under the new design, workers no longer received batches of work that took about an hour to keypunch. Instead, they assumed responsibility for certain "accounts," the clients that this department served within the company. Now the keypunch operators each had a personal stake in the job; they could go directly to the user departments to clear up mistakes. A new social network developed within the company, giving the jobs more meaning.

Under the old job design, keypunch operators felt frustrated because they had to punch the information exactly as it came to them from the service clerk, even when they recognized mistakes! Lack of control also extended to the fact they could not even plan their own work. The new design gave each keypunch operator the power to correct mistakes, schedule his own work, and correct his own mistakes. The keypunch jobs had previously been dead-end positions in the company. The new design tried to remove this stress by providing for advancement within the department, and more important, transfer and promotion to the user departments that send information to the keypunchers.

In July 1970, a group of keypunchers was selected to institute the changes. Others continued to work at the old jobs to find out which design would enhance the individual worker's life as well as contribute to the overall company goals. East-West Insurance waited one year to see what consequences this redesign would have. The results startled everyone. Absenteeism among the workers in redesigned jobs dropped by 24 percent! A high rate of mistakes in work, a classic symptom of burnout, changed markedly with an improvement of 35 percent. The hourly number of cards that employees punched jumped by nearly 40 percent. In addition, the company could now eliminate supervisory positions, with the result that total savings in one year rose to $64,305!

But this monetary gain couldn't compare with the savings in human morale, sickness, and the prevention of job burnout. A before-and-after survey of employee attitudes showed an overall improved score of 16.5 percent, while keypunch operators following the old procedures remained at the same levels for the entire year. East-West Insurance Company, while saving money, had improved job satisfaction. The work became more interesting. A much higher percentage now said that "the job is worth putting effort into."

Operating keypunch machines under the best of conditions will leave some people bored and frustrated at the end of the day. But the design of keypunch jobs does not come to us on stone tablets. It is possible to change them in ways to effectively manage work stress. Ordinary workers like Ken Neiderhoff can use their influence to redesign stressful jobs. The kinds of changes made at East-West Insurance Company will not eliminate all work stress, but they will bring some relief and, with continued monitoring and redesign, enable more workers to escape the ravages of job burnout.

Although most workers have limited influence to redesign their jobs, others have considerable power. You may have a supervisory role, act as someone's boss, hold a position in middle management, or even work as a corporation president. Consider the power you have to bring relief from work stress to those in your organization, to reduce the causes of job burnout. Even a simple innovation such as providing a way for workers to communicate their suggestions to management could reduce work stress for some.

If you hold a management position, no matter what level, you have an awesome responsibility. You have the power to make work more human. You have the power to allow work to bring rich rewards to the lives of people. You have the power to prevent devastation in the lives of your employees. It is a challenge that more and more enlightened managers are responding to, and in the process they are becoming effective stress managers. Listen to Ted Graves, head of a division in a large East Coast publishing firm. "I watch the people who work for me carefully. If I see someone start to burn out, I do something about it. I talk to him. I might even change the job. Skip Francher had been our marketing manager for several years and did a hell of a job. But then he began to lose interest. His work habits changed. The pressure was getting to him. I'd see him walking up and down the hall, carrying a memo he should have put in the office mail. He avoided the important tasks. I knew something was wrong. So one day I called him in and said, 'How would you like to become an acquisitions editor for this line of books?' It wasn't a promotion or a demotion. It was a new challenge. Within weeks on the new job he was back in high gear. I consider it part of my responsibility to do everything I can to prevent job burnout." And as Ted spoke, we knew that he reaped personal rewards by using his influence to reduce job stress.

The five principles for dealing with the structure and content of your job apply to all occupations and all forms of work stress. In the next three chapters we turn to several forms of work stress that occur so frequently we must give them special treatment. They include the stress of a burnout boss, dead-end jobs, and the helping professions.

Chapter Eight
The Burnout Boss

It comes as a surprise to many people that their boss can have a direct influence on their health. Yet in our research we found that the behavior of the person in charge—the boss, department head, supervisor, section chief, foreman, superintendent, principal, president, chairman of the board—turned up as one of the most frequent sources of work stress. We set out to discover the ways in which bosses behaved in the workplace, whether foreman or company president, and how their behavior caused employees to burn out. Although bosses can make a worker's life miserable, bosses can also change. We found many examples of how bosses, with help from others, redesigned their behavior to lower stress for employees.

Many workers had good things to say about their boss. Others were not so complimentary. In *The 1977 Quality of Employment Survey,* sponsored by the U.S. Department of Labor, 30 percent of all workers were unsure that their supervisor was concerned about their welfare; 52 percent reported that conflicting demands were placed upon them; and another 33 percent indicated excessive work demands. A startling one out of two workers questioned whether their promotions were handled fairly. It's hardly a wonder that one out of every three workers will try and find another employer during the coming year.[1]

Behind these cold statistics are life dramas in which ineffective and incompetent bosses create high levels of frustration for workers. Scrawled on a door in a restroom wall in San Francisco are the words *"Everyone is somebody else's peon."* Implicit in that bit of graffiti philosophy is a depressing fact: your work, your future, and your overall happiness are heavily controlled by somebody else. As a stockbroker crudely put it: "You're always somebody else's nigger. I mean, no matter how well you do or how high up you are, there is always someone who can screw up your career."

The stockbroker's assessment is correct: bosses can screw up your career. More importantly, bosses can dismantle your self-confidence. One of the most important conclusions that emerged from our research was that while many employees like the work they do, they often cannot stand their boss. In this chapter we will study their complaints. The bosses we describe have unique characteristics, yet all possess a common denominator: *each produces an environment of unrelieved stress conducive to burnout.*

The Slave Driver

If you want a glimpse of what life was like on some plantations a century ago, you need only visit the administrative offices of Camden Community Hospital. Chet McGiven, the Hospital Administrator, is called "the General" by hospital employees.

McGiven broke into hospital administration when physicians held the administrative power in hospitals. "I got ahead," he says, "by being twice as smart and three times as savvy as the docs." He paints his world in stark shades of black and white with clear-cut winners and losers, rights and wrongs. McGiven has a low tolerance for government bureaucrats, politicians, chiefs-of-staff, indecisive subordinates, and committees of any kind. His contempt boils over for government health planners. When the local health board disallowed a new addition on his hospital because of the high costs of construction, it was like throwing red meat to a hungry lion. He pounced on the board members, armed with petitions signed by the mayor, city council members, the medical society, and citizens, demanding that they rescind their decision. The health board buckled. The addition was built.

The employees at Camden Community Hospital respect yet fear McGiven. They admire how he has built the hospital into a modern institution with all the latest life-saving technology. On the other hand, story after story circulates about how McGiven the slave driver ruthlessly wields power. Many workers simply cannot tolerate his capricious actions. In fact, McGiven has gone through eight assistants in the past thirteen years.

Slave drivers like McGiven make life unbearable for subordinates. Robert Gressman will carry throughout his life the emotional scars from the fourteen months he worked for McGiven. The son of a Presbyterian minister, Robert graduated with a master of hospital administration degree prior to taking his job at Camden Community Hospital. In his views about work he matched the portrait of the American male worker as researched by Louis Harris and Associates, Inc.[2] Gressman wanted a chance to use his mind and abilities in doing meaningful work. He wanted a chance to grow and obtain a decent salary. However, he also valued leisure. He was willing to work an honest eight-hour day but did not want to bring the briefcase home from the office every night. Work to Gressman was important but, like 64 percent of all working men in this country, he did not find work to be the major source of his satisfaction. Little did Gressman know that these values would stand in sharp contrast to McGiven's expectations.

The first day at the office Gressman arrived at 7:45 A.M., buoyant with enthusiasm. McGiven was waiting for him. The firm handshake seemed to hide what little warmth might lay behind the welcome. Quickly they got down to business as McGiven said, "I try and get here at six-thirty in the morning. That way you're here before the first shift arrives. You're one up on them if they know you are here first."

McGiven spoke with some bitterness about a growing dispute between the head nurses and the hospital pathology department. He told Gressman that he should heal "that festering sore" as soon as possible. He chuckled and added, "I may as well find out if you are worth your salt."

The first week flew by in a whirlwind of activity. The dispute between the nurses and the pathologists became more intense. Each morning Gressman would find hand-scribbled notes from McGiven with new problems and new orders. As the first few weeks passed, the crisis atmosphere remained. One Sunday morning Gressman skipped church in order to go to the office and catch up on things. He was dumbfounded to find McGiven working away behind his desk, something he later learned McGiven did every Sunday.

The following week the hospital's chief pathologist threatened to resign unless the nurses were "put in their places." McGiven promptly walked into Gressman's office and said, "Screw those nurses. You can always get another nurse, but you can't get another pathologist." The next day, against his better judgment, Gressman reprimanded the nursing staff. Later Gressman told his wife, "I felt terrible. Now the nurses are mad at me and I am mad at myself for not standing up to McGiven."

As the months passed, the marching orders continued to flow from McGiven's office. He pulled the strings and Gressman jumped. McGiven demanded obedience. Like a mechanical robot Gressman dutifully tried to solve each problem assigned to him.

Fourteen months later Gressman looked the way he felt. Harassed, nervous, down on himself, questioning his vocation, and angry at his boss, he knew he hadn't lived up to McGiven's expectations. More importantly, he had fallen far beneath his own expectations. He had long discussions with his wife about what was happening to him and to their marriage. "What ever happened to that bright, enthusiastic, forward-looking guy I married?" she asked one day. That made him feel even more guilty. His idealism had faded. His self-confidence was ground down. There wasn't anything that he could point to that he felt good about. Even though he felt anger toward his boss, deep inside he blamed himself for not managing his job more effectively.

To be certain, not all slave drivers act in such a heavy-handed manner as Chet McGiven. Yet the slave-driving mentality sits behind the boss's desk in all too many organizations. As Alfred J. Marrow notes: ". . . managers today rarely admit to being authoritarian. The present posture is verbally to espouse views supportive of democratic procedures and greater self-management. But despite the verbal commitment, the way they relate to others has not changed. This is not to imply that such executives are feigning a democratic point of view. They are seemingly unaware of the contradictions between their professed concepts and their actual behavior. Many executives fail to see how their behavior exploits others. They identify their personal success with the general good. They view the world in terms of their own private needs."[3]

Why do slave drivers supervise in such a debilitating manner? Robert Blake and Jane Mouton, two authorities on managerial behavior, have found that autocratic managers often come from homes where parents place tough demands on their children.[4] They set high levels of achievement, and if the arbitrary standard is not met, they criticize the child. Even success on the part of the child does not bring forth parental praise. Rather, the child is taught to be obedient and not talk back. He must master control of the environment and constantly prove himself.

Unfortunately, as such children move into adulthood and then into management positions, they carry these same rules and attitudes with them. The parents' methods unconsciously become the rules of management. The slave driver demands obedience from subordinates. The slave driver withholds positive reinforcement and ego-satisfying rewards. Punishment is dished out commensurate with the subordinate's failures. The slave driver rules in a world of heavy-handed control, a world of winners and losers, and an environment where employees get used and abused.

It would be a mistake to blame all slave drivers as being intentionally malicious. They simply believe that "a tough boss" ensures an efficient, productive organization. This style of management all too often becomes woven into the fabric of the workplace. It contributes directly to the burnout problem. Contrary to popular belief, the slave-driver mentality does not lead to higher efficiency and profit. More important, no worker *needs* to suffer under a slave driver. The characteristics of a Chet McGiven can change. Because their roots go back to childhood, the boss who treats you like a naughty kid may not realize what he's doing. Making the slave driver *aware* can by itself lead to job improvement for dozens of subordinates.

Here's an example of how one organization started changing supervisory styles. Staff employees at the University of North Carolina rated their bosses on fifteen specific behavior items. Did they show appreciation for a job well done? Were they autocratic? Did they demand too much? As soon as the fifty-six supervisors saw how their employees rated them, they began to manage more effectively. Two weeks later, and again after ten weeks, employees gave higher marks to their bosses on all fifteen items.[5]

Although the autocratic style of the slave driver can undermine the satisfaction of the most dedicated worker, it does not signal a hopeless situation. A large hospital employed thirty-two laundry workers under a single foreman who operated with traditional authority. Discontent among laundry employees led to restructuring the authority system, shifting some decision-making power to a committee of workers. In the weeks and months that followed, two major burnout symptoms changed: absenteeism significantly decreased and productivity improved. The hospital estimated a cost savings of $1,000 per year for each laundry worker.[6]

Both irony and tragedy cloud those organizations where autocratic managers operate. The irony is that while autocratic managers want high productivity, they seldom achieve it. Workers simply don't give 110 percent day after day to a boss they despise. High absenteeism and high job turnover become characteristics of the working staff as morale sinks to low levels. The autocratic manager fails to realize how much more productive the staff would be if they were treated with respect and were significantly involved in management decisions that affect them and the unit in which they work.

The tragedy of the autocratic style of management lies in what it does to subordinates. Workers faced each day with unrealistic demands, lack of support, and disinterest in their welfare will soon feel the symptoms of burnout. It took Robert Gressman three years of experience with Chet McGiven to understand that the problems had come from his boss and not from his ineptitude. Fortunately for Gressman, he recovered from his burnout and found another job, this time with a boss who was not a slave driver. Gradually he put that dark period of his life behind him.

The Silent Boss

One of the most tension-producing bosses is the one who doesn't communicate. In some ways it is easier to work for an openly hostile boss; at least you know where you stand.

Silent bosses produce anxiety. They seldom give praise and rarely involve subordinates in planning. Only reluctantly will they offer help on a work-related problem. The net result is that subordinates are constantly plagued by low-level anxiety.

Silent bosses abound in most organizations. In fact, one out of every ten workers does not know what is expected of her.[7] If that describes you, sooner or later you begin to worry. Am I working on the right tasks? Am I doing it the right way? Am I working fast enough? Does the boss expect something I don't know about?

Butch Langard, a football coach at a midwestern college, works for an athletic director whom the jocks call "The Great Sphinx." When Butch became the coach, he pointedly asked Don Kraften how many games he had to win in order to keep his job. Kraften gave a curt, one-word answer: "Enough." When Butch asked permission to run a football camp for high-school football players, Kraften evasively replied: "The president [of the college] doesn't like people making money on the side. But there isn't any rule that says you can't." When Butch wanted to teach a course on the sociology of American sport, Kraften gave the usual mixed message: "Well, OK, if you really want to. But you'd be better off recruiting some beef for your defensive line."

Not knowing where he stood with his boss made Butch feel uneasy most of the time. As he said to a friend, "It's like you are hooked on the end of his line. You can swim around all you want but you know that hook is buried in your back. Sooner or later he's going to jerk you clean out of the water."

Some bosses are not aware of how their silence puts needless pressure on subordinates. When we confronted a dentist with the bottled-up resentments and hostilities that members of his staff had toward him, he was genuinely surprised and somewhat hurt. "I pay them enough, don't I?" he asked. "I mean, if something is bothering them, why don't they tell me? I stand right by two of them eight hours a day." He completely missed the point. All the hygienists and dental assistants wanted was honest feedback about the quality of their work.

Other bosses know exactly how silence makes subordinates feel. It gives them a sense of power to know that employees cannot predict their behavior or how they will react if the employee "gets out of line." Kraften was such a boss: "I don't want him thinking that I am going to back him up if he has a losing season. Coaching is a tough business. I don't want to feel bad when I fire his ass, which, incidentally, I am about ready to do with Langard."

The silent boss creates three tension-producing problems for you. First, silence places you squarely in a situation that social psychologists call "role conflict." This simply means that you don't know what is expected of you. That was Butch Langard's main problem. He didn't know how many games he had to win, whether it was OK to run a summer camp, or if he should teach a college course.

Studies confirm the fact that the greater the role conflict, the greater the possibility that your health will be adversely affected. Role conflict is significantly correlated with higher pulse rates, abnormal electro-cardiographic readings, and obesity.[8] One study found that foremen were seven times more likely to develop ulcers than shop workers were, primarily because their jobs were riddled with role conflicts.[9]

Second, most silent bosses produce "occasional panics." Since they are noncommunicative, they seldom let subordinates know about future plans and corresponding work-flow patterns. Consequently, new demands hit the subordinate unexpectedly.

Secretaries are often hardest hit by occasional panics as bosses "forget" to tell them about a major report "due tomorrow." As one secretary acidly noted, "What ticks me off is that he never lets me know what's coming. So I make errors and then white them out. Then he glares at me for not having a clean copy. Imagine—he's mad after I have typed for four straight hours without a break."

When a boss does not give subordinates adequate lead time to do certain tasks, a vicious cycle of mistrust is created. After repeated rush jobs, subordinates catch their breath by taking time off on the job. That angers the boss. In retribution the frequency of the panic jobs increases. That angers the employees. Soon the working relationship erodes, work stress increases, and job burnout spreads.

A third point of tension comes from the fact that, except for your paycheck, the silent boss does not provide rewards for working. And a salary alone seldom gives sufficient recompense for any job. Scientific research has clearly demonstrated that positive feedback from your supervisor heavily influences your work satisfaction.[10] Mark Twain once confessed that he could live for three weeks on a compliment, and he was not an exceptionally vain man.[11] He was just admitting candidly what many of us feel in private: we all need a psychological lift from time to time. Unfortunately, silent bosses seldom give such needed rewards.

If you have become the victim of a silent boss, don't blame yourself if you feel fatigued or suffer from splitting headaches. But don't simply blame it on your boss's personality, because every corporation has the power to remedy the problem of noncommunicative supervisors. We now know enough to change work climates, to build in programs that can head off the work stress created by silent bosses.

Take the case of head nurses in seven Veterans Administration hospitals. Realizing the importance of clear goals and positive feedback (the two failings of silent bosses), top management held a two-day workshop for all the head nurses on the medical and surgical wards. They studied how to set clear goals and give positive feedback to their staff. Back on the job, each head nurse, in collaboration with staff nurses, developed written goals they agreed on. This represented a giant step toward eliminating role conflict for more than 380 staff nurses. Then, in the days that followed, the head nurses put into practice what they had learned about letting people know when they did a good job. Researchers tracked the results of these changes. At the end of six months, patient care had improved and these staff nurses felt significantly more satisfied with their jobs than others in the same hospitals.[12]

Silent bosses have a hard time giving praise and recognition, even when they know its importance. Sometimes bosses simply need encouragement to give feedback. When this was done at Emery Air Freight Company, the positive results affected many people. Instead of loading their comments with negative criticisms, bosses were encouraged to tell employees when they did a good job. When the bosses started giving positive feedback, dramatic changes occurred: sales shot up; customer service improved; container use grew more rapidly than expected. At the end of three years, the company estimated direct savings at three million dollars.[13]

But what can you do if you're stuck working for a silent boss? One of the more successful strategies came from a pressman at a dry cleaning establishment. "I *made* him talk to me. I invited him out for a beer. I leaned over the table and told him I'd pick up the tab if he answered one question: 'Am I doing a good enough job for you?' I thought he was going to choke. Nobody at the plant ever talks to him like that. But he told me I was [doing a good job]. Ever since then, whenever I start to worry about my job I just ask him straight out how I'm doing."

When you feel confused about your boss's expectations, ask about them. If you fail to get feedback, ask for it. You'd be surprised at how many silent bosses will start to talk once asked for their opinion.

If you have tried unsuccessfully to talk, your best bet is to focus on the work itself and concern yourself as little as possible with your boss's communication problems. Your problems in having a boss who is silent won't go away, but the amount of energy you invest in worrying about it will surely diminish.

The Backslapper

Managers create insecurity in employees in many different ways. Some, like Chet McGiven, drive their employees fifty, sixty, and even seventy hours per week. Others, like Don Kraften, the athletic director, don't communicate. Still others will put their arm around your shoulder and tell you what a great job you are doing.

If you have never worked for a backslapper it may seem puzzling that a boss who hands out compliments would create stress. But, as Joyce Wagner can attest, backslappers can create immense problems for ambitious, task-oriented subordinates.

After graduating *cum laude* from an Ivy League university, Joyce took a position as a health educator in the Oakview Community Services Department. Her boss, Jim Fry, greeted her warmly on her first day at work. He spent most of the morning chatting with her and then took her out to lunch. "Boy, is he super," she said to her roommate. "He gave me all the time in the world."

Forty-eight hours later she had begun to have second thoughts. She asked for a list of specific tasks on which to work. Fry gave her only a very general description of her duties. "Here's a list of our health programs. Just get acquainted with people and keep things going." When she said that she would really appreciate something more specific, he replied, "Everyone around here kind of figures out for themselves what they need to do. We built a good department that way. I'm sure you'll get along OK, too."

The next day Joyce returned to Fry's office and said half-apologetically, "I'm sorry, but I'm kind of a structured person. I need to know exactly what I'm supposed to do." "Well," he said, "I'll give you some ideas. But you've got to do what you think is right. I trust everyone to do the right thing." After a few general instructions he patted her on the arm as she left and said, "I'm really glad you're part of the team."

Gradually the pressure began to build within Joyce. Without definitive instructions about the job, she felt uneasy about her role. She couldn't understand how Fry could be so friendly to her when he really didn't know what she was doing.

One day she asked Fry why he never called any staff meetings. "Wouldn't it be a good idea to plan collectively for the future?" He said that in his experience he found them pretty much a waste of time. "Furthermore, they usually end up in bitch sessions." His dislike for any type of conflict, well known to all the other staff members, slowly came to light for Joyce. The sign that hung behind Fry's desk aptly summarized his basic value: "If you can't say something nice, don't say anything at all."

Gradually Joyce began to receive messages that Fry didn't altogether appreciate her approach. "You're always talking about how our programs could be improved," he once observed. "You ought to talk about how good they are. We offer outstanding services. I just don't know why you always find fault with things."

Joyce decided that she just couldn't take any more ninety-minute lunch breaks with Fry and members of the staff. The long social lunches where everyone talked about their kids, vacations, and hobbies cut into her work time. But when she skipped, Fry would tell her that they really missed her, which made her feel she had broken another unwritten rule.

"He's killing me with kindness," said Joyce to her roommate. Indeed he was. Her creativity, drive, and ambitions were being stifled by her backslapping boss.

Backslappers can be found in many organizations. Research undertaken by Dr. Gerald D. Bell has demonstrated that 16 percent of managers have such a leadership style.[14] The basic drive that motivates the Jim Frys of the world is a need for love more than for achievement. Backslappers want the members of their staff to like them and, because of that, they place a high premium on loyalty. Every compliment comes with strings attached to a hidden requirement: "I'm such a likable boss; you should really appreciate me."

Backslappers avoid situations where conflict might arise. It was not an oversight that Jim Fry never called a staff meeting in the Oakview Community Services Department. Like most backslapper bosses, he worked to smooth out differences within the staff and help employees stay "happy" in their work.

The backslapper faces a dilemma when an employee makes a mistake. Not wanting to reprimand the employee, the backslapper may make excuses such as, "Well, he's young," or "He's probably doing the best he can." Since even incompetent workers make an effort to carry out their responsibilities, backslappers seldom fire any employee no matter how far short they fall.

The backslapping style of management can generally be traced to strong values developed in childhood. Such managers usually come out of a warm, loving, and overprotective home where the main value centered on avoiding pain, conflict, and suffering. The child slowly learns that the most important thing in life is "to get along." Although such children grow up feeling comfortable, happy, and relatively tension-free, they seldom take on major responsibilities. Unconsciously, says Dr. Bell, the child learns to gauge the feelings of others to ensure that they will react favorably to him much as their parents did.

Not only do backslappers want love, they also want to avoid pressure. That is not to say that they won't be moderately productive. They aim to do an acceptable job, but avoid anything that looks too challenging, too complex, or too difficult. Unfortunately, they also assume that their employees have or should have the same orientation. This can drive goal-oriented, assertive employees straight up the wall, as Joyce Wagner found out. You want to earn your salary, yet your boss will give you little direction. You want to set ambitious goals, yet your boss does not reward you for ambitious work. You want to handle conflicts forthrightly, yet your boss takes great pains to sweep them all under the rug.

The greatest problem for many subordinates is the guilt they have for all the resentments they feel. As Joyce Wagner said: "He'd make me so mad, but then he'd give me basketball tickets, free lunches, and flowers on my birthday. I knew he was manipulating me but I didn't know how to handle it." Some workers deal with a sweet-talking, manipulative boss by simply walking out. Once they recognize that alleged kindness has become a whip to keep them in line, they quickly go to organizations that will reward their talents and hard work.

Other workers simply withdraw and put in their time. "Maybe I should just milk the system," said a department-store sales clerk. "My boss is so nice, she wouldn't say a mean word to anybody. If she wants everything loose and easy, who am I to argue?"

Still others capitalize on the freedom that the backslapping boss gives to subordinates. One year later, Joyce Wagner had ceased to worry about her boss and she decided to plow her creative energy into building one of the finest jogging programs in the city. Occasionally she went out to lunch with Fry and the staff. Always, however, she did her own thing. And she did it competently.

Retired on
Active Duty

His face was flushed. Beads of perspiration glistened as Jim Kraster slammed his fist on the desk. "I can't figure him out. The bureaucratic red tape is killing our clients. They can't get food stamps. They have to wait two months before they can get an appointment in the health clinic. The de-tox center is closed for lack of funds. We've got hundreds of clients on the welfare rolls who we should cut. Yet does he care? Hell no. He just comes in at nine-thirty in the morning, answers a few phone calls, and then drives to his suburban home. Why doesn't he understand what is going on?"

The target of Jim Kraster's assault was Ron Creiter, a fifty-seven-year-old director of a state welfare department. For three years Jim Kraster had tried to get his boss "off his ass." He wanted him to testify at the legislature about the damaging effects of inflation on people who live on fixed incomes. Creiter refused. Kraster tried to persuade his boss to cut red tape associated with the food-stamp program. Again Creiter refused. Angrily he accused his boss of "playing it safe" and "not taking needed action." Creiter dumped all of his subordinate's suggestions into the round file.

On a hot, humid August day, Jim and his boss came to a parting of the ways. One of the ambulances hadn't arrived quickly enough to save the life of an infant who had swallowed a toxic disinfectant. Angrily, Jim shot into his boss's office and demanded to know what he was going to do about it. "Not a thing," Creiter replied. Jim couldn't believe what he was hearing. "Not a thing? Not a thing?" His high-pitched voice reflected his bitterness. "Why don't you do something about it? We have complaints all the time about the ambulance system!"

Creiter's answers were elusive. He cited the low budget that supports the ambulance service, the poor equipment, and the ill-trained drivers. Finally he said, "It's sad when these things happen, but periodically they are going to occur no matter what you or I want."

That night Jim went to his typewriter and pounded out his letter of resignation. After he had cooled down he commented to his wife, "You know I really don't want to leave the department, but what can I do? Working for Creiter is like working for the ultimate government bureaucrat. He doesn't care. He doesn't show emotion. He won't stick his neck out. He strangles you with silly regulations. If you want to try and make the department better he puts his foot on your neck. All he wants to do is collect his pension."

Bosses who are "just putting in their time" can be found in most large organizations. Chief executive officers in major companies can readily identify employees who are "producers" and those who are "deadwood." It is the rare company that doesn't have organizational dry rot brought about by workers who no longer have a commitment to the organization, workers who have slowly burned out in their jobs. As a fifty-five-year-old assistant vice-president told us: "Yeah, I have checked out of here. You only get bypassed [for promotion] so many times before you throw in the sponge. But I am not going to get fired. I'm too smart for that."

Ironically, there are employees in the helping professions who also have "checked out" of their jobs. Social workers, teachers, ministers, and physicians are not immune to pressures that may make them count the days until retirement. As one junior high school principal stated, "The happiest day of my life will come when I don't have to listen to the constant bitching of teachers, parents, and students. When I turn in my key there won't be any regrets."

An army captain put it this way: "Most of us take our jobs seriously. But what really bugs you are those that are hanging on by their fingernails to collect their pension. They've hit the ROAD (Retired *On A*ctive

*D*uty). Not much you can do about them. But it makes you mad as hell that they aren't pulling their weight."

Individuals who have retired on active duty are bad news for an organization that wants high productivity. But such managers also create unrelieved stress for conscientious subordinates and can become a direct cause of burnout. Jim Kraster quit after three and one half years. Idealistic and filled with humanitarian goals, he found that working in a department where the boss put his own interests above his clients' created an intolerable situation.

If you work for an individual who has entered premature retirement, it helps to understand what motivates your boss. A predominant value held by such psychological dropouts is to *survive*. Whether they have two years to go until retirement or twenty-two, they follow the same rule: don't do anything that is going to get you fired. They value their paycheck first and the pension program second. In order to protect their position, psychological dropouts will not take risks. They avoid anything that could have adverse consequences for them. You will almost always find them taking the side of their supervisor in any organizational dispute.

If survival stands out as the most basic value that premature retirees have, a closely related attitude says, "You really can't change the bureaucracy." Ron Creiter often remarked about how all of his friends who had fought the system ended up with ulcers, divorces, and heart attacks. It convinced him that "reformers only get their heads bashed in."

The above values and attitudes have adverse consequences for subordinates. If your boss has signed out on an early retirement, you can count on him looking out for himself but not for you. "Personal involvements just string you out," Creiter often remarked. Such a boss will not reward you for risk taking; in fact you get punished for new ideas or anything that could upset your boss's personal applecart.

If you work for a boss who has retired on active duty, don't be surprised if you and your coworkers begin to burn out. This kind of leadership creates a work environment that seethes with work stress. It can lead to widespread absenteeism and lowered productivity, two of the prime characteristics of burnout. In spite of these consequences, some people who run government agencies, universities, and business corporations frequently reward the noncreativity of managers who retire on the job. As the governor's chief assistant once remarked to Creiter, "You know, we sure like what you're doing with the state welfare department. You don't cause us all the headaches the other departments give us." To put the matter another way: bosses don't retire on active duty unless the organization permits it.

The New York City Welfare Administration had its share of supervisors who had retired on the job. The agency was plagued by inefficiency and absenteeism: workers showed up late, managers failed to carry out innovative programs. The welfare rolls had grown by leaps and bounds, with many cases no longer needing assistance. The top management called in a team of consultants, and at their recommendation revamped the welfare operations. They tightened control over the 600 managers, making sure each one was accountable for achieving certain goals. They fired incompetent managers and those who refused to come out of on-the-job retirement. As a direct result, absenteeism declined 29 percent. Employees began showing up on time; the error rate was cut in half. Productivity climbed by 16 percent. It became possible to reduce the number of welfare cases by 109,000 people at a savings of $200 million in welfare payments.[15] Management had decided they could no longer permit people to retire on the job.

If you work for an organization that allows managers to retire on active duty, any attempt to change your boss will probably meet with failure. You therefore have two choices: you can get out from under your boss or learn to live with ineffective supervision. Either way, reducing this kind of work stress does lie within your grasp. One of the refreshing interviews we had was with a hospital laboratory technician whose boss had retired on active duty. Unable to quit her job, she had chosen the second option. "One day I made up my mind that I was going to quit trying to reform him and, more important, I was going to quit feeling sorry for myself. Soon a big load lifted from my shoulders." This lab tech began to realize how free she was to do the work that she wanted to do. "You know," she said, "I looked around and nearly everyone else in this hospital had a boss that made them go through something called "management by objectives," and then they put you through a "performance review session." They have to jump through administrative hoops all the time. And I had none of that. I began to thank my lucky stars that I woke up in time to realize how good I have it."

The Critic

The ad under "employment opportunities" read:

> Wanted: A hardworking male college student to work as an assistant resort manager from June 14 to September 3. No experience necessary. Call 218-645-6671 for further information.

Greg Britler left his dormitory room and excitedly headed for the pay telephone. Five minutes later he had a job at the Sunny Shores Resort in Park Rapids, Minnesota. After completing final exams he packed his 1964 Ford and headed into northern Minnesota. Greg's pulse quickened as he drove into the driveway of his new summer home.

Dorothy and Matt Kjelstad greeted him as he stepped out of his car. Mrs. Kjelstad, a friendly, white-haired woman, reminded Greg of his grandmother. Mr. Kjelstad, on the other hand, seemed aloof and pre-occupied. He seldom looked Greg in the eye even though they talked several hours that evening.

The following morning, the smell of freshly cooked bacon greeted Greg as he joined the Kjelstads for breakfast. "Ever work in a resort before?" asked Mr. Kjelstad. It was a strange inquiry because Greg had answered that question over the telephone. Mr. Kjelstad grunted and said that he hoped that he was a "fast learner, because the guests would start arriving in two days."

Greg's first task was to get the motorboats running. He had started one of the small fishing motors, when Mr. Kjelstad appeared from behind a pine tree. "I sure hope you have mixed the oil with the gas." Greg hadn't. "You know you could have ruined five thousand dollars' worth of motors?" shouted Mr. Kjelstad in an angry tone. Greg bit his tongue, although it angered him that Kjelstad hadn't given him adequate instructions.

After adding oil, Greg took one of the boats for a test run. He started slowly but felt a sense of exhilaration as he turned the throttle wide open. With the motor working properly, he headed for the boat dock only to find Mr. Kjelstad waiting for him. "Running the engine full blast only costs me money," he said with a scowl.

After lunch Mr. Kjelstad told Greg to paint the numbers on the shuffleboard courts. After completing that project, Greg repaired the basketball hoop by pounding some large nails into the supporting structure. He patched a gaping hole in the volleyball net with some string. He noticed how desperately the lawn chairs needed cleaning, found some S.O.S. pads, and scrubbed them spotless.

As he completed the last lawn chair, Mr. Kjelstad appeared and asked him what he had been doing all afternoon. With a note of satisfaction in his voice, Greg showed his boss the completed projects. Unfortunately, Mr. Kjelstad didn't think Greg had done anything correctly. The lawn furniture should have been put in the sun to dry, "otherwise the wood just rots away." The volleyball net should have been replaced because, "Those strings you put in there won't last a day." They went to the basketball hoops, and, upon closely examining Greg's work, he shook his head and said: "Well, let's hope the nails hold. You really should have used four-inch wood screws."

Greg chafed under each succeeding put-down. However, he couldn't imagine that Kjelstad would have anything bad to say about his painting. But sure enough, he gazed intently at the numbers on the shuffleboard court and after a long silence said, "I bet you only put one coat on those numbers. It will never hold up."

Not a word of thanks. Never a compliment. At best, only silence.

The days that followed seemed a repetition of his first day. Mr. Kjelstad never had a good word to say. Even with jobs done correctly, he always came up with some minor complaint or sang his oft-repeated refrain, "They sure don't teach you college kids nothin'."

On a hot July evening, after a day with Kjelstad on his back, Greg climbed on his bike to head for a little country bar located a half-mile from the resort. The bike wasn't working properly so Greg turned it upside down and began to loosen several bolts. Greg was struggling with a frozen nut when suddenly Mr. Kjelstad appeared. "Haven't you ever heard of a ratchet?" he snapped. Greg shook his head. "How could you have grown up and never used a ratchet? The first lesson you need to learn is to have the right tools. But I guess I have to teach you everything."

The bike incident was the last straw. He walked into the resort office fully prepared to resign. Mrs. Kjelstad quickly noted his dejection and wanted to know what was bothering him. "It's just not worth it. I can't do anything right. I get criticized for not doing enough. Then I get criticized for doing too much. When I finally do something right I don't get a word of thanks. Twelve hundred bucks just isn't worth it."

"He really doesn't mean any harm, Greg," Mrs. Kjelstad tried to reassure him. "I know that he seems gruff as a bear. But he really isn't. In fact, he likes you. After you had been here only one week he told me that you were the best worker he's had in years."

"He sure has a funny way of expressing his gratitude," Greg countered cynically.

"Well, he just has trouble saying nice things to people," Mrs. Kjelstad continued. "His father was just like that. He is the oldest child and—if you think you have it bad—you should have seen how his dad picked on him. He still can't do anything right as far as his dad is concerned."

While unrelenting criticism in itself can cause burnout, there is a more profound reason why critics grind us down. Most of us have clear expectations about how a boss should behave. In childhood we learned that authority figures were usually correct in whatever judgment they happen to make. After all, "Father knows best." We also came to feel that powerful people would look out for us, steer us in the right direction, and reward us when we did well. As adults we superimpose these feelings on our boss as we enter the world of work. The boss becomes the new parent. When the salesman proudly brings to his boss the monthly sales totals, it is not unlike the child who brings home a paper from school. If we don't get our approval needs met by our boss, we often blame ourselves. Under unrelenting and intense criticism, only the rare individual can stand above the battle and say, "Hey, wait a minute. The problem is not with me—the problem is my boss!"

Like Greg Britler, many employees victimized by critical supervisors feel tempted to quit their jobs. In addition to the stress they create for subordinates, this kind of boss adds to the expensive problem of employee turnover. What can an organization do for workers caught under the grinding pressure of such negative critics? They can retrain supervisors, many of whom act in this way without realizing it. Scientific studies show that even a small amount of instruction can change the behavior of bosses who contribute to the burnout problem by undermining subordinates' self-esteem.

General Telephone Company in the Southwest faced up to this problem and reduced the expense of a high turnover rate among employees. One hundred and sixty-six managers and supervisors at several levels participated in a week-long training program. They learned about worker motivation and how negative criticism can damage worker morale. They studied better ways to communicate. During intensive workshops they practiced new skills in giving positive feedback. Back on the job, these supervisors began to treat workers in more constructive ways. Although no one could measure the hidden savings in reducing and preventing burnout, one clear sign of improvement came with a significant drop in resignation rates. The company saved nearly $50,000 dollars simply in the cost of training new workers.[16]

Can you change the behavior of an overly critical boss for whom you work? As a subordinate that is a tough problem. You may never get the boss completely off your back, but two suggestions can diminish the frequency and the intensity of the criticisms.

First, remember that critics usually have low self-confidence. Behind the masks of certainty, rightness, and self-confidence hides a boss with unmet needs for recognition. If you can toss out a few compliments of your own from time to time, admittedly a difficult task, it may have unexpected results. If Greg Britler could have told Mr. Kjelstad how much he had learned from him, or complimented him on the resort he had built over the years, Kjelstad would probably have softened and become less critical.

In addition to your attempts to meet your boss's need for recognition, it's important to assert yourself whenever you are on the receiving end of a barbed criticism. A candid discussion about the put-down may help your boss become more positive. You can use your influence no matter how limited it seems.

Greg Britler stayed on at the resort, and during the last week of the summer he woke up early one morning and went to repair the boat dock. When Mr. Kjelstad saw Greg, he quickly ran to the shore. "What the hell are you doing down here before breakfast?" Greg showed him the new supporting two-by-fours that reinforced the sections of the dock. "How do you like that?" Greg asked. Kjelstad got on his knees to inspect the work. It was solid workmanship and both of them knew it. Kjelstad still didn't say anything. With a twinkle in his eye, Greg looked at him and slowly said, "You got to admit—it's pretty damn good carpentry." Kjelstad couldn't bring himself to say anything but did manage to give an approving grunt as he headed toward the dining room. A big smile crossed Greg's face. The grunt was about all he could have asked for

Almost every workplace includes people who give orders, assign tasks, check up on workers, and provide symbolic rewards. "The boss," by whatever name, can become a major source of work stress. If you work for a *backslapper,* a *critic,* a *slave driver,* or someone who has *retired on active duty,* it can drain your adaptation energy and erode your satisfaction in work. Whether you work for a person who fits one of these types, combines several of them, or creates other kinds of pressures, don't underestimate your boss's effect on you.

Those who want to prevent job burnout and manage the stress created by a boss can take specific steps to that end. We recommend that you begin by reviewing the personal strategies discussed in part 2 of this book, but relate each one specifically to your boss. Two stand out as especially important: take control of your perceptions of the stress caused by your boss, and lower your expectations of the boss. We found some workers who reacted emotionally to their supervisor's personality and magnified conflicts and frustrations all out of proportion. "I simply couldn't stand Sergeant Adams, the top NCO in our company," said an army private. "Every time he came near I'd see red; my heart would begin to pound and I came to hate him for no reason. I knew most of my feelings were irrational, so I started thinking of Sergeant Adams as just another soldier like myself. It took a lot of work, but after several months I had a different view of him." You might evaluate your expectations of your boss by writing down how you think an "ideal boss" would treat you. Then ask yourself if *you* could fill the shoes of such an ideal boss. You may discover that you have secretly longed for a boss who would become the mother or father you had in childhood, or more likely, the ideal one you didn't have. Simply by changing your perceptions of a stressful boss or lowering your expectations, you may turn a seemingly hopeless job into a tolerable one.

The next step in coping with a burnout boss applies the organizational strategies discussed in the previous chapter. However, instead of thinking about your entire job situation, apply them specifically to your relationship to the foreman, supervisor, department head, or other annoying authority figures at work. Begin by looking over your stress inventory and circling each work stress that has a direct connection to your boss. Work on taking a detached view of your boss and analyzing the informal rules that person seems to follow in dealing with you. Taking these simple steps can give you ideas for using your influence to actually change the way your boss treats you and other employees. Keep in mind the following rules as you seek to bring about change:

1. *Work to open up the channels of communication.*   Take advantage of formal conferences with your boss as well as informal times to talk about your job. Busy supervisors often are unaware of the problems subordinates face. Don't overlook written communications as a means of keeping your boss informed about your job.

2. *Avoid arguments and direct attacks.*   Confrontation seldom changes behavior. It often serves to make others defensive and attempt to justify their past actions.

3. *If possible, give your boss positive feedback.*   Let's say your boss fails to give you clear instructions for carrying out a task, then criticizes you for not following his guidelines. You don't feel free to confront your boss on this weakness, but you can wait for a time when she gives instructions more clearly than usual, then say, "I really appreciated knowing how you wanted that report done; it saved me a lot of time and worry." This single statement of appreciation from a subordinate will serve as a better reminder in the future than hundreds of critical comments you might like to make.

4. *If your boss asks for suggestions, don't unload all your frustrations.*   Even when we ask for suggestions and criticism, most of us have difficulty accepting them, especially from subordinates. If you have the opportunity to make written or verbal suggestions to your boss about her behavior, weigh your advice carefully. It's best to use "I" statements rather than "you" statements. Instead of saying, "You never give any feedback to employees about how they're doing," try a less offensive approach: "I don't think we get enough feedback on how we're performing our jobs." Instead of making a dozen suggestions that cover all the shortcomings of your boss, select one or two things you think your boss would be willing to change. Even in making these suggestions, try to give positive feedback about the things you do like about your boss.

Bosses can and do change. No matter how long you've been on the job, your relationship to the person in charge will remain a significant feature of your work. By closely monitoring this relationship and applying the principles we have discussed, you will go a long way toward dealing with the work stress caused by a burnout boss.

Chapter Nine
Dead-End Jobs

Thousands of workers burn out because they get trapped in dead-end jobs. This special form of work stress pervades so many work organizations that we believe it has reached epidemic proportions. Again and again those we talked with told us, "I don't know what to do. I'm locked into a dead-end job and it's driving me crazy." But few people understood the underlying dynamics of their dead-end job; few seemed to grasp the forces that turned good jobs into dead-end jobs. Many workers feel that a dead-end job is a hopeless job and the only alternative lies in quitting. In this chapter we want to analyze the dynamics of dead-end jobs, show you how they create high levels of stress, and discuss ways to manage that stress. We also will show you how to identify when a job is hopeless and terminate your employment while keeping the stress level at a minimum.

Consider the feelings of one worker caught in a dead-end job. "There's no future in my job!" Brian Morrow told us out of deep frustration. "I'm assistant to the purchasing agent at Atlanta Technical Institute. He's a great boss and I don't mind the work, but there's no place to go. He won't retire for twenty years. There's nothing new in the job; I've stopped growing. Five years from now I'll still be processing these same damn purchase orders. And my salary barely keeps up with the cost of living."

Brian's enthusiasm has begun to fade; irritability and fatigue have crept into his life. He is moving slowly into the third stage of job burnout where his symptoms will become chronic. Like millions of jobs, Brian's position at the technical institute has become an endless highway where the future is now. All hope for tomorrow and next month and next year can suffocate under the stifling cloud of a dead-end job. Whether you're a company vice-president or a clerk in the mail room, a dead-end job feels like someone slams the door in your face every time you go to work. A job without a future is a job without meaning. In order to understand dead-end jobs, and how you can keep them from leading to job burnout, we must look at the way work in American culture becomes defined by our expectations about tomorrow.

In many cultures the meaning of work never becomes tied to the future. A Hopi Indian, a Mexican peasant, or a Moroccan villager might find Brian Morrow's concern for the future a strange attitude. For these peoples, the meaning of work flows out of the past. They till the soil, plant their crops, mend their tools, harvest their crops, go to the local market, and do the work their fathers and mothers did. Most cultures of the world foster such connections to the past. Like some giant waterwheel, the endless cycle of clearing land, planting seed, and harvesting crops moves neither forward nor backward. Job satisfaction comes from participating in this work that has roots in past generations.

American culture, on the other hand, teaches us to see the workplace in a radically different way. Change, progress, a better idea, new responsibilities, a promotion, more freedom, a salary increase—these are American staples in the recipe for job satisfaction. Work takes its fundamental meaning from the future, not the past. We admire people who move up in the university, the corporation, or the government agency. We endure unpleasant tasks at work because you "can advance fast in this company," or you "can count on a good raise and better fringe benefits every year."

When the people we interviewed told us, "I'm trapped in a dead-end job," we first interpreted this to mean, "There's almost no chance for advancement in this job." But as we listened more closely we came to see that workers had other reasons for calling a job a dead-end. For example, one woman said, "I've moved right up in this company; I can look forward to more pay raises and promotions in the future. But I've given up all hope of learning anything new. My mind is shriveling up! It's a dead-end job." The essential characteristic of a dead-end job is that it blocks the fulfillment of your hopes for the future. There are five common hopes people bring to their jobs in our society:

1. A hope for advancement
2. A hope for more freedom
3. A hope for increased earnings
4. A hope for learning and doing new things
5. A hope for solutions to enduring work problems

When one or more of these expectations wither and die, your job can become a dead-end and you can burn out. It doesn't matter whether you're a construction worker, a head nurse, a beginning teacher, or a company president.

Few workers tell the boss about these hopes. Indeed, we may not even recognize that they lie hidden within us as powerful forces laid down through long years of growing up in a future-oriented society. Nevertheless, every attempt to tap the attitudes of American workers reveals these hopes. For example, among the top five job priorities in a *Psychology Today* survey of 23,000 people were "a chance to learn new things," "opportunity to develop your skills and abilities," and "the amount of freedom you have."[1] These conditions are frequently missing in dead-end jobs.

From preschool classes through university seminars, we learn to value advancement. First graders proudly march down the hall to the second-grade classroom. As they watch older classmates promoted to still higher grades, they see their own future as one filled with promotions. The child held back a grade, for whatever reason, often feels cheated. But even these unfortunate children will not remain at a dead end in the third or fourth grade. Eventually they too will leave addition and subtraction and move on to multiplication and division.

What happens when you're locked into a job with nothing to look forward to? Let's look at a typical case. Marlene Randler never dreamed that teaching could turn sour. At twenty-three she took a job at Kennedy High School in Kansas City teaching English literature. Excited by her subject, she thrived on the challenge of "turning kids on to Chaucer." By the end of her third year she had hit her stride, developed a notebook full of lectures and lesson plans, and gained considerable popularity with students. She enjoyed the company of the other teachers.

The next three years brought increasing job satisfaction to Marlene. With cost-of-living and merit increases, her salary moved her slightly ahead of inflation. The students voted her "teacher of the year" and the PTA gave her a commendation for "teaching excellence." Each year she came to her favorite classes in Chaucer enjoying the chance to "go into the material in more and more depth."

Then, during her eighth year at Kennedy High, her contentment began to wane. The job had begun to lose its challenge: she decided to explore new areas in her teaching. "I proposed to the department that I drop two sections of Chaucer and teach twentieth-century British novels. But two teachers with seniority voted against the change; they thought they might have to relinquish some of their own academic territory." Back to Chaucer and class after class of surveying all of English literature for tenth graders, Marlene grew increasingly restless.

Fighting staleness, she ordered a new book for the survey class that included an explicit discussion of the sexual motifs in nineteenth-century poetry. Before the end of the semester two parents had complained to the principal, and Marlene received strong suggestions through her department head to go back to the other textbook.

Caught between critical parents and a department policy that would not let her teach in new areas, Marlene tried to remain enthusiastic. Yet her discouragement persisted and the next year her job began to change. A new rule required all teachers to remain at school until four-thirty despite their teaching schedule. The district foresaw a decline in student enrollment and placed a freeze on all promotions. New classes seemed disrespectful and bored with the likes of Byron, Browning, and Yeats.

Marlene grew increasingly resentful of the "system," and it spilled over into her evaluation of the students. After one midsemester exam that she had graded lower than usual, she asked for comments. An eerie silence hung in the room. The usual chatter and laughter were absent as the students filed out and several large male students glared at her as they passed her desk. For the first time in her career, Marlene had a momentary fear for her safety.

As with many teachers, the intrinsic rewards from teaching had evaporated for Marlene. Hemmed in by students, parents, petty rules, a promotion freeze, and department policy, she found little chance for personal growth and new challenge. "It finally grinds you down," she said. "Sometimes I don't think I could enter room one twenty-five one more time, yet I'm faced with that for another twenty-five years." Threats of mass teacher layoffs, reports of violence and vandalism, salary increases that failed to keep pace with inflation—these dashed Marlene's hopes for the future and added to her feeling that she was trapped in a dead-end job.

Marlene Randler is not alone. In fact, nearly one-third of the teachers polled in a National Education Association survey indicated they would not become teachers again if they could start over.[2] The discontent has spread to hundreds of school districts in the United States. As Diana Lindahl, president of the Tacoma, Washington, Teachers Association said, "Teachers in my district are leaving the profession as fast as they can find another job to support themselves."[3] New York City's financial crisis in 1978 threw 9,000 teachers temporarily out of work. When offered a chance to return to their jobs, more than 6,000 called it quits.[4] Thousands of workers feel trapped in factories, offices, government agencies, and corporations. Some jobs, like Marlene's teaching position, have become bankrupt in all five areas—no chance for promotion, no chance for learning and doing new things, no chance for increased earnings, no chance for more freedom, and no chance to solve persistent job problems. Many jobs cancel the worker's hopes in only one or two of these areas, but still create enough stress to bring on the symptoms of burnout. In order to redesign dead-end jobs or cope with the stress they create, we need to look more closely at how such jobs thwart many workers' hopes for the future.

Promotion Barriers
Prevent Advancement

The hope for advancement can fade and die when a company allows or creates promotion barriers. Roadblocks to the future can come through outright discrimination, policies that stereotype workers, personality differences, unfair promotion practices, and jobs that fail to challenge our highly educated work force. The number of college graduates has risen from 286,000 in 1955 to more than 900,000 in 1977. In 1940, for every 220 employees, only one had graduated from college. Today one in four workers holds a college degree.[5]

"I spent four years of my life and borrowed almost $10,000 to finish college, yet the only job I can find is working as a waitress," complains Jill Batten, who holds a degree in English literature. "Some of my friends from college had to take jobs as taxicab drivers, secretaries, and construction workers. They didn't major in fields like biology, music, and political science to get those kinds of jobs." This situation has increased the number of young workers who burn out a few years after graduation. But even if you find a good-paying job that interests you, that's no guarantee it's a job with a future. It's a fact that promotion barriers have reached epidemic proportions in the workplace. Almost half the workers in America feel promotions in their organization are handled unfairly. Nearly 60 percent of all workers express pessimism about their chances for promotion.[6] We can no longer blame this on incompetence or tell workers to get into another field. Most promotion barriers have become chiseled into the edifice of modern work. They come from the structure of a work organization itself, not from the behavior of workers victimized by their dead-end jobs.

Racial discrimination remains a major barrier to promotion for thousands of employees. If you're Black or Chicano or Native American you can easily become locked out of better-paying and more rewarding positions. Twenty-two percent of blacks are either unemployed or underemployed.[7] The "part-time job" has become a classic dead end for minority workers. There are roughly twice as many blacks as whites who want to work full time but cannot find full-time jobs.[8] Racial minorities seldom fill management positions or have responsibility for hiring, so the vicious cycle continues.

Civil rights legislation has reduced formal discrimination to some degree, but has had limited impact on the informal barriers erected by company tradition. Maxwell Jones, a black clerk in the accounting department of a large bank, felt locked in to a dead-end job. At first he felt pleased at landing one of the first jobs offered to blacks in this bank, but as he watched others move to new and challenging positions, he began to wonder why he never heard about openings until *after* someone else was promoted to fill them. "It slowly began to dawn on me what was happening. All the department heads were white; they told each other about openings and handpicked the clerks they liked. Even when they announced positions, you knew they had already made a decision."

This kind of "grapevine discrimination" can affect large numbers of people. News about job openings, the requirements for a position, and who will make the decisions travel along the company grapevine. If you're on the outside of this communication network, you may never know the real reasons you're trapped in your job. As companies grow, more and more people find themselves on the periphery of the grapevine, learning too late about better jobs. This can multiply dead-end jobs, cut into productivity, and send worker morale on a downward spiral.

All too often managers refuse to redesign the communication system because they can manipulate the grapevine to serve their own ends. But redesign can have positive benefits, as the Bank of Virginia Company found. Management introduced a simple procedure that significantly cut problems spawned by dead-end clerical jobs. They set a strict policy in this large bank for weekly posting of all jobs available to clerical employees. They based new promotions on seniority, experience, work performance, interest, and ability. Because the knowledge of new jobs now became available to everyone at the same time, the bank had reduced the chance for informal discrimination. This simple change brought about an increase in employee morale and boosted productivity.[9]

In spite of all the books, political speeches, and sermons about equality, discrimination against women locks them into lower-paying, dead-end jobs. In 1979, the National Commission on Working Women reported that 80 percent of all employed women were in clerical, service, sales, factory, or plant jobs where their work is "undervalued, underpaid, and underappreciated."[10]

Rather than shrinking, the earning gap between women and men continues to widen. In 1965, white women earned only 60 percent of the salary of white men. They had finally reached the original constitutional value of a slave: "Three-fifths of a person." But by 1975, after ten years of efforts to improve the work status of women, their economic value had actually declined to 58 percent of what white males earn.[11] In a survey undertaken by the American Management Association, only 4.5 percent of the women earned between $15,000 and $25,000. Six times as many men took home these higher salaries. Less than one-half of one percent of all women earns $25,000 or more. Twenty times as many men earn that amount or higher![12]

Some workers find that even physical appearance can keep them trapped in dead-end jobs. Due to a thyroid condition, Catherine Laska weighed more than 250 pounds. Although she did outstanding work as a copywriter in a large ad agency, she watched slim, more attractive women promoted ahead of her. Although nothing was said, everyone knew her weight problem influenced promotion decisions. "I have to do twice as well as others to get promoted," she says with a note of bitterness in her voice.

Personality characteristics such as shyness, assertiveness, sociability, and even a sense of humor can also become promotion barriers. And if someone doesn't like the way you act, dress, talk, or look, you won't find the legal recourse available to people victimized by race, sex, or religious discrimination.

Rick Dodler, a twenty-six-year-old fork-lift operator, worked for Salem Trucking Company. At five o'clock every Tuesday and Friday, the dock workers gathered in the warehouse storeroom for a "garage party" with a couple of cases of beer. Rick stayed for fifteen minutes and drank one beer on his first Friday at Salem. The following Tuesday he headed for the parking lot as soon as he had punched out. "Come on, Rick, have a beer!" several other dock workers called, but Rick told them, "Thanks, but I've got to get home tonight."

In the months that followed, Rick avoided the garage parties, preferring to spend the time with his wife and small children. Joking invitations on Tuesday and Friday afternoons about the "henpecked fork-lift operator" soon turned to more caustic remarks. Then, another operator told him at lunch, "You really ought to join us on Friday; the guys think you feel that you're too good for them." More amused than angered, Rick steadfastly refused to take part in the after-hours drinking sessions. In time, the weekly invitations stopped and the social pressure seemed to end. Rick was simply not a part of the Tuesday and Friday ritual.

After four years on the dock at Salem Trucking Company, Rick gained a reputation as one of the most competent workers. During his fifth year, he began to anticipate a promotion. When a foreman position came open, he applied but was passed over. A year later, a similar job went to a crew member with only three years at Salem and a history of minor accidents, but a leader of the drinking parties. Angry and stunned, Rick went to the personnel officer. "Why was I passed over? I got a clean record and no accidents. And with my seniority I thought I was next in line!"

Shifting his weight from one foot to the other, the personnel officer told Rick, "Well, you would have had the job, but when we checked around on the dock, we found that nobody likes you very much. We just couldn't imagine appointing a foreman who had that kind of reputation even before he took the job."

Another promotion barrier comes from policies against promoting inside a company. Those with power to make decisions seem to wear blinders that stereotype regular employees as unfit for higher positions.

A high-ranking attorney for one of the major oil companies told us: "It's amazing how many people get passed over for promotion around here. Some of the guys have sweat blood for the company. Yet when a vacancy opens up, the company goes outside and recruits some hotshot. It's like they just can't break out of the way they see a guy. Like it's impossible for someone to grow into a job. They got 'em pegged for some organizational slot and there isn't much a guy can do about it."

Such stereotypes can crystallize into sacred traditions. A salesperson cannot become a regional manager; a secretary never moves to the position of office administrator; a cab driver never becomes a dispatcher. Even the boss who tries to escape these stereotypes may find company policy won't allow it. Juan Alverez, an interviewer in a western office of the U.S. Census Bureau, impressed the research director with his skill and eagerness. Juan came up with suggestions for improving the return on the monthly agricultural census; he offered to help organize data and always read completed reports. The research director began to ask for Juan's comments on preliminary drafts of reports. After several years, Juan had become a valuable assistant and the director tried to create a position for him as research associate. "But they told me at the regional office it would be impossible. None of the other offices had that kind of position, and if they let us do it, it would only cause problems within the bureau."

An increasing number of organizations have begun to identify and reduce the number of dead-end jobs created by rigid stereotypes. At one publishing company, the secretaries worked for editors, but never moved into editorial positions. This created discontent, since a good secretary, although she learned to do most of the things her boss did, was stuck in a dead-end job. Then the company instituted a change. While continuing their jobs, secretaries could begin a year-long apprenticeship to become assistant editors. Eventually they could move up to the position of editor and beyond as their ability and interest allowed. Overnight their jobs became pathways to the future.

One way you can reduce the stress of a dead-end job that offers little hope of promotion is to examine how you think about the future.

Some workers seem to live with two connected concepts: (1) my present job, and (2) my whole future. If they see little hope for promotion in the present job, it seems as if their *whole future* has become blocked. Yet when we talked to these people, most had decided long ago that their present job would not occupy their entire future. They fully expected to transfer to another job. If you can divide your future into periods of several years, and make your decision explicit about moving on to another job in a few years, the stress may become manageable.

You can also begin examining the hidden structure of your workplace to find promotion barriers. Most barriers tend to stay out of sight in the informal culture of work. At one university a group of women faculty collected statistics on male and female promotion patterns over a ten-year period. Male professors with the same professional degrees and experience had a much better chance of promotion. The women made this information public and brought pressure on the administration to change the hidden policies that had created sexual discrimination. Someone at the publishing company made others aware that secretaries were blocked from becoming editors while outsiders with fewer credentials moved into those positions. Someone at the Bank of Virginia Company studied the hidden structure of that workplace and discovered that the news of job openings traveled by the grapevine, cutting off many workers from applying for those jobs. Perhaps the greatest influence any worker can exert in opening up promotions is to discover how the system works and make that knowledge public. Change in policies has a way of following such public disclosures.

Company Rules
Restrict Freedom

Many people bring to their jobs a hope for more freedom. They want control over how they do their jobs, how they schedule tasks, and the pace at which they work. When you consistently do a good job, you begin to hope for more flexibility. Any job with too many rules can become a dead-end job. Like throwing water on a fire, rigid company rules can extinguish the hope for freedom.

As a night cleanup man at the Ripon Ice Cream Company in Pasadena, California, George Fredrickson enjoyed working the night shift alone. The foreman had explained his job and then said, "Follow the order listed on the bulletin board; that's the way the boss wants it." The list read: (1) Wash down machines; (2) Sweep the floors; (3) Take out trash; (4) Load ice cream cartons into machines; (5) Clean out the coffee room.

Within two weeks George had mastered the cleanup routine. His thoroughness won praise from the foreman. After six weeks, George decided it would simplify his work to load the cartons into the machines first. The foreman walked through on the second night after George had altered his routine and told him, "I don't care if your work does go faster! Around here we go by the book." A small but important part of the future suddenly evaporated for George.

The hope for more freedom probably goes back to our childhood experiences. With each new year, parents and teachers granted us greater leeway in making our own decisions. Strict bedtimes gave way to staying up until we felt tired. Parental choices about clothes gave way to our own decisions. Required courses gave way to electives. Most of us discovered that greater freedom came when we lived up to our promises, held up our end of the bargain, finished our work on time. Mom and Dad told us, "If you complete your homework you can go out tonight." At a deep subconscious level we came to believe that if we did our jobs well, those in authority would lift the petty restrictions that controlled our behavior.

But with the growth of large industrial organizations, rules to control the mass of workers have become commonplace. If you work with only a handful of people, you may have more freedom than those who have jobs at Xerox Corporation or the Ford Motor Company. Giant corporations develop rules to help create uniformity. So do many smaller organizations. Often aimed at the rank-and-file worker, stringent rules are made on the assumption that you will work more efficiently with close supervision and narrow boundaries. When this lack of trust in workers is written down in the company rule book, it becomes necessary to set up penalties for every violation. Then the company has to develop procedures for administering punishment, whether it's a slap on the hands or termination. Although the pinch of rules doesn't squeeze all workers in the same way, many feel so restricted that their jobs seem to be a dead end.

The Time Clock

Although some rules are essential, others make life miserable for workers for no good reason. Even a simple rule like requiring everyone to punch in at 8:30 can create enormous stress because it ignores individual differences. Consider how rigid time schedules foster dead-end jobs while flexible ones enhance worker morale.

Jan Parker, a twenty-nine-year-old secretary, works in the headquarters of a large hotel corporation we can call Midland Hotels. Her first month on the job was a whirlwind of positive experiences. She liked her boss, a young executive who had begun to climb rapidly through the organizational hierarchy. She also reported to an administrative secretary who coordinated the secretarial staff, enabling people to help each other during rush periods.

At first Jan didn't mind the strict rules regarding the time clock. All secretaries punched in by 8:30; they punched out at 4:30. Except for two fifteen-minute break periods and a half-hour lunch, they spent the rest of the day at their desks. If Jan showed up even five minutes late, she lost half an hour of pay. No secretary could make up her time during breaks or at lunch. "And nobody punches in or out for anybody else around here," the administrative secretary told Jan during her first week. "Two girls were fired last year for doing that."

Although Jan's performance was exceptional, she found it difficult to make it to work at 8:30 every day. As a single parent, she had to drop off her three-year-old at the day-care center each morning. It didn't open until 7:45 and Jan raced through freeway traffic to make the starting time; even a small traffic tie-up made her late. She always began work out of breath and tense from the morning rush. She explained her recurrent late arrivals to her boss at the first performance review; he simply said, "Well, it doesn't look too good on your record. Do your best and try to get here on time."

One night her daughter took ill with a painful earache. Jan couldn't see the pediatrician until 9:30 the next morning, so she called the office and told the administrative secretary she would be late. At 10:30 when she walked in, her boss rushed up to her desk and said, "These reports are gonna be late if we don't get them out today." No one asked about her child's health.

The next night her daughter's earache became worse; Jan couldn't see the pediatrician until 10:30. She apologized to her boss for being late, explaining what happened. He said he understood, but that the company "obviously can't have people coming in here whenever they feel like it." Jan could barely contain her anger. Here was a man with a wife at home to care for his children, who took off one afternoon a week for golf, had two-martini lunches that lasted an hour and a half every day, routinely took time off for a haircut. She buried her resentment, however, and didn't say a word. If she complained, she could easily find herself looking for another job; it would take the personnel department less than an hour to have a replacement sitting at her desk. She chafed under the restrictions that slowly turned her position into a dead-end job.

How could the rigid time rules like those at Midland Hotels become more flexible? Can large companies operate successfully and still give employees freedom in setting their own work schedules? We believe that more flexible work schedules could reduce the stress in many dead-end jobs. More than one company has done away with this strict time-clock mentality with surprising results.

Some of the managers at Donnelly Mirrors of Holland, Michigan, resisted the idea of abolishing time clocks.[13] "It will only increase absenteeism," they argued. Donnelly Mirrors employs more than 400 people to manufacture rearview, day-night mirrors, supplying nearly 70 percent of the world market. All clerical and production jobs involved punching time clocks; workers were paid on an hourly basis. In May 1970, employees voted to become salaried employees, eliminating time clocks. As a result of the change, absenteeism dropped by 60 percent and productivity increased. Now when clerical workers at Donnelly Mirrors encounter problems like Jan Parker had, other members of the work team carry the extra load. A new spirit of cooperation has developed with an increase in worker morale.

More and more companies are responding favorably to employee requests for more freedom to design their own work schedules. At Control Data Corporation in Minneapolis, hundreds of employees set their own working hours.[14] Fred Brodbeck likes to jog five miles every morning, and at Control Data he can enjoy a good run, drive to work after the rush hour, and still put in his eight hours by staying later in the afternoon. As a side benefit, he misses the rush-hour traffic again in the evening. While some companies allow employees to choose their own regular eight-hour period, say any time between 6:30 A.M. and 7:30 P.M., others allow flexibility from day to day. As long as you work during the "core hours" of 9:30 and 11:30, and again between 2:00 and 3:30, you can set your schedule. If you have an appointment at the hairdresser's over the noon hour, it creates no problem. If your child needs an early dentist appointment, you don't need to call in or lose several hours' pay. Even if you just want to sleep in some morning, it's your choice.

Flexitime, as these systems are called, has a direct and measurable impact on burnout symptoms. The American Management Association studied thousands of workers and found that in 97 percent of the organizations that used flexible scheduling, worker morale had improved.[15] In 1974, the Business and Professional Women's Foundation surveyed 334 organizations and found that 59 used some type of flexitime.[16] In addition to improved morale, these companies reported substantial reductions in tardiness and absenteeism, with no ill effects on productivity. The social security administration introduced flexible time schedules for 140,000 employees with the result that turnover and absenteeism decreased.[17]

If you feel hemmed in by a rigid time schedule at your workplace, consider using your influence to introduce flexitime. Some employers resist the idea because they've never heard of it; others believe it will only cause confusion and lower productivity. You can begin by researching companies that have used flexitime successfully. New articles appear frequently in *Business Week* and other magazines. Go to your local library and spend a few evenings gathering information. Interview fellow workers to discover the range of problems that a rigid time schedule creates for them. Circulate articles that describe the program at other companies. You might even write to large corporations and ask for information about their experience with flexitime. If you can find a company similar to the one at which you work that has successfully used flexitime, so much the better. Most important: think strategically. Don't yield to the temptation to become a job reformer and ask for too many changes at once. In more than one company, workers with seemingly little power have been able to bring about changes that brought more freedom. In doing so they lowered the risk of job burnout for themselves and others.

The experience with flexitime suggests that we should reevaluate other rules designed to control workers. We have yet to discover the degree of freedom that workers need to enjoy meaningful jobs. If the requirement to punch in at 8:30 every morning had been the only rule that limited Jan Parker's freedom, her job would never have become a complete dead end. But one day, after five months of typing the newsletter for her boss, she collided with the first of several unwritten rules. Feeling certain she could make the newsletter more readable and attractive, she went to work to edit, rearrange, and improve it. Careful not to distort anything, she changed the type size to highlight various paragraphs and reworked several clumsy sentences. Finally she put the newsletter on glossy paper to give it a more professional look.

She showed it to her boss, fully expecting gratitude and approval. Instead he turned an angry red and almost shouted, "Who authorized you to do this?" "Well, I thought I could maybe make it a little better," Jan replied, her confidence shaken. "There wasn't a damn thing wrong with the original," he said; then, regaining his composure, added, "Look, I know you meant well, but you're paid to type. And that's what I want you to do." The rule for Jan was clear: you only do what the boss orders you to do.

In the months that followed, Jan Parker came up against other signposts that marked the limits on what she could do. She discovered, as Dr. Rosabeth Kanter found in studying a large corporation, that secretaries must keep their place. Rewards come from setting up a room for a meeting and serving the coffee, "not for organizing the meeting and writing the agenda."[18] Creativity, responsibility, and initiative are excluded from the secretarial job description. Jan wasn't allowed to work on more complex and challenging tasks because it would have forced her boss to admit that part of his work could be done by a lower-paid employee.[19]

Unwritten company rules that create dead-end jobs can come from your colleagues as well. One afternoon, Jan Parker's boss handed her a sixty-page report and said sheepishly, "I need this yesterday." She had finished typing half of it when the other secretaries headed for the time clock to punch out. Determined to get on the right side of her boss after her blunder over the newsletter, Jan called a friend who would pick up her daughter; she stayed and finished the report. At ten o'clock that night she laid it on his desk.

At nine o'clock the next morning her boss came out of the office and thanked her in a loud voice for "a job well done." Later, when he sent the report out for duplication, she found a personal note that read, "Jan: Thanks a lot for the extra hours. It really helped to have it done so promptly." She sailed through the day only to come crashing down to earth when the administrative secretary warned her on the way out of the office, "Don't know what you were trying to prove with your grandstanding last night. But nobody around here works longer than they need to. Pretty soon they'll think all of us can hang around here after closing. I'd advise you not to do anything like that again." Jan had violated an informal rule: you put in only the hours required by your job description. No more, no less.

Jan Parker endured another restriction during her first two years on the job: she lacked the freedom to be creative. She had enrolled in a college journalism class one evening each week and longed to use her new skills. Then, unexpectedly, during her third year on the job, her boss came to her and said, "I'm really hassled. Would you mind taking a crack at putting together the newsletter?" Jan didn't know whether to laugh or cry, but she went to work on it with a sense of liberation. She redrafted the newsletter at least a dozen times, then took it to her boss for final approval. A week later he began receiving interoffice memos complimenting him about the new look in the newsletter. The next month they worked together on it, and in the following weeks he began to give Jan more responsibilities and authority.

In spite of the satisfaction she now felt, a sense of emptiness still plagued her on the job. One day she realized the source of her feelings. The president of Midland Hotels sent her boss a beautiful letter expressing admiration for the way he ran his department. Jan's boss, elated at the commendation, read Jan the letter, then said, "Well, a lot of the credit goes to you. You've done a lot to improve things around here."

Back at her desk, Jan felt more trapped than ever by her dead-end job. "I'm doing all the work and he's getting all the credit," she thought to herself. And no hint of a raise had come with his verbal recognition of her work. She had run head-on into another corporation rule: *the person at the top gets the credit.* Her hopes faded that increased responsibilities in the future would bring her credit. Jan Parker, without realizing it, had become trapped in a classic no-win dead-end job. During the first phase of her career, the rules stifled her freedom and creativity. When finally given an opportunity to use her skills, the rules prevented her from receiving rewards that matched her responsibilities.

One Monday morning, without any advance warning, Jan came to the office to find her boss had received a promotion to another department. A replacement sat behind his desk. After a few pleasantries, he gave Jan his first instructions: "I take my coffee black and I like my second cup at ten-fifteen." Suddenly Jan felt she had moved back in time almost three years.

Routine Jobs Lose Their Challenge

Many people bring to their jobs a deep hope that they will continue to learn and do new things. Meaningful work makes use of our skills; it challenges us with new opportunities. Almost any job can become a dead end if it becomes boring, repetitive, and lacks challenge.

Routine jobs affect people in different ways. As we've said again and again, you can burn out from too much pressure and stimulation and also from not enough. Not all the secretaries at Midland Hotels found their work as routine as Jan Parker did. Some people on the most repetitive assembly-line jobs find them challenging. But if your job is becoming routine, and you're the type who hopes for personal growth — you want to learn and do new things — it is likely that you'll feel as if you've reached a dead end.

Many workers accept the routine, dead-end job as inevitable. But is it possible we have designed jobs that way without realizing it? Have we created jobs that reach dead ends? Could we, with a little effort, redesign them to answer the deep longing many people feel for challenge and growth? In many cases the answer is a resounding yes. Consider the following example.

Xerox copying machines serve the needs of organizations in every state. At Macalester College, in Saint Paul, Minnesota, a small print shop houses a large copying machine. From dawn to dark, faculty, administration, and students copy memos, papers, letters, articles, lecture notes, class assignments, and dozens of other things. When the copying machine breaks down, someone calls Jerry Blake, the Xerox field representative who drives out to the college and repairs the machine.

Jerry has dozens of similar customers around the city. He visits them on a regular basis as well as in emergencies to clean and service the copying machines. Jerry Blake belongs to a team of more than 7,000 field reps across the country who service the machines rented from the Xerox Corporation.

A few years ago, Xerox field representatives shared with management their on-the-job frustrations.[20] They told them about the repetitive nature of their tasks and how easily the job lost its challenge. As a result of these discussions, it was agreed that an experiment would be conducted in one midwestern branch that had ninety field representatives. The objective of the experiment was to see if the job could be redesigned to make it more interesting. In the first phase of the project the field reps rated sixteen features of their work. All agreed that the job didn't give them enough challenge, recognition, or responsibility.

In the next phase of the project, they asked the field reps for suggestions about redesigning their jobs. They came up with two hundred specific ideas that could improve their work. Field representatives wanted to do new things, such as screening and interviewing job applicants. They suggested that field reps might play an important role in training new technicians. Some volunteered to take an active role in the field-representative-service meetings. They could use their on-the-job experience to help others who might face similar problems. Someone suggested that the representatives each order their own tools and parts. Why should supervisors alone take this responsibility? And why couldn't each field rep decide on the maintenance schedule for places like Macalester College? After all, the field rep knew about individual machines and use patterns better than the supervisors. Taking responsibility for the upkeep of their assigned company car could also add more variety and give them more freedom. The list went on and on, but it came down to a common denominator: changes to give more challenge and responsibility.

Out of the list of two hundred ideas, the Xerox field representatives and management identified fourteen high-priority items for immediate change. When carried out, their dead-end work became transformed into jobs with a future. This group of employees had begun to learn and do new things. After six months a systematic study of the results showed that, in contrast to other branches, the ninety field representatives reported greatly improved morale and positive feelings about their jobs. Absenteeism, that perennial symptom of burnout, had decreased by 40 percent while at other branches it remained the same. Performance measures showed that this one branch had improved more than any of the others.

Some jobs appear so routine as to defy any attempts to make them challenging. Take the job of "bundler" at the Aluminum Company of Canada, in Arvida, Quebec. The man on this job works with a saw-and-shear operator (who cuts ingots of cast aluminum) and a truck driver.

The bundler drives a forklift back and forth to transfer bundles of cast aluminum from the plant to trucks and trains. How can such a job be redesigned to prevent it from reaching a dead end? How can a bundler ever hope to learn and do new things?

In the late 1960s the Aluminum Company of Canada began a re-examination of the work organization that produced cast aluminum.[21] Following accepted theories of workplace design, the total casting process had been broken up into many separate operations. One group of men, each with distinct jobs, worked the furnace and the straight-line casting machine. A "metal pourer," for example, assisted the furnaceman in casting molten metal into solid ingots. Another group (the bundler among them), entirely separate from the first, cut up the ingots and loaded them. Another man from a separate department inspected the work. A survey of employees showed that 91 percent knew only one or, at the most, two jobs. This narrow specialization had created dozens of jobs with no chance for learning new skills.

One of the major changes instituted was the creation of "work teams" that included individuals from all the different groups. Instead of a pay scale tied to single jobs, earnings were linked to the number of jobs each person knew. Individuals on the team were given the responsibility of teaching each other their jobs, and rotating from one job to another as their skills expanded. As Judith Archer, who studied the changes, observed, "The work itself became more interesting because the men shared responsibility for jobs, and as a result fewer errors were made. The men looked forward to rotating on different jobs and, the more actively they rotated, the more interesting they found their work." Job satisfaction increased; men now felt the jobs made use of their potential. Fully 75 percent of the men had mastered five or six jobs, whereas previously not a single worker at the company had such wide knowledge. Doing the work of a bundler may seem like a dead-end job, but when it becomes one of five or six jobs you do, and still others remain to be learned, such a job can give a sense of hope for the future.

What can you do if you're stuck in a routine job that offers little chance to learn and do new things? You can begin by looking for ways to enrich the job yourself. One nurse took a special interest in stroke patients and began to ask questions about them whenever physicians made their rounds. She scoured the nursing and medical journals for reports on rehabilitating those paralyzed by stroke. She stopped wandering through the hospital gift shop at lunchtime and went instead to the hospital library for a brief chance to learn more about strokes. Soon the head nurse, impressed by her knowledge, began to assign her to care for stroke patients on the ward. This specialized interest had transformed a routine nursing job into a learning opportunity.

If people around you have different jobs, try to learn from them. Almost everyone enjoys becoming a teacher of an interested learner. The men who worked as bundlers at the Canadian Aluminum Company could have begun learning other jobs long before the company changed the work organization.

Don't overlook the deep human need for learning new things. If your job doesn't allow you this opportunity, you can reduce the feeling of staleness by taking a night course at a local college or developing an interest in some new area. Fred drove a bus on the night shift for the Metropolitan Transit Company. Inquisitive, he learned what he could about bus engines and the various routes, and still found his job becoming routine. One clear night a regular passenger pointed out the Big Dipper through the front window. That chance comment started an interest for Fred in astronomy. He took courses, built himself a telescope, and began to read astronomy magazines. His job hasn't become more challenging, but his expanding knowledge of planets, quasars, black holes, and constellations has brought deep satisfaction. The routine of bus driving has been offset by the chance to learn about the universe.

Work Problems That Won't Go Away

Whenever you begin a new job it presents you with problems to solve. The new bus driver has to solve the problem of driving fast enough but still not getting ahead of schedule. The new teacher wants to appear warm and friendly, yet has to maintain authority. The new foreman faces the difficulty of giving orders, yet remaining "one of the boys." The new minister must preach challenging sermons without offending a new and strange congregation. Every job has its characteristic problems; finding solutions to them can make work challenging.

Most of us expect to solve work-related problems. We bring to the job a deep hope that eventually, as we learn the ropes, the major difficulties inherent in our jobs will diminish or disappear. A job reaches a dead end when this hope fades; the job has a defect that will not go away. Built into the structure of the job, certain problems trap the worker.

When Robert Wadsworth took the job of production manager for a company making ski jackets, he looked forward to the challenge of his new position. But within six months he discovered that he had two bosses, each with different ideas about what he should do. He couldn't fire or change either one; his hopes for a solution died. This turned his job into a dead end.

Sometimes a double bind occurs, in which conflicting pressures and obligations won't go away. If you please one boss, the other gets on your back. If you satisfy production quotas, the people who work for you will go on strike. If you generate the necessary new ideas, another department head is threatened and will sabotage your efforts. Double binds come in all shapes and sizes. You may be the only employee in your company who feels caught by a particular problem, but don't blame yourself. Like negative fringe benefits, double binds usually come with the job.

Let's look at how a double bind occurs in one occupation. The automobile salesman enters a four-stage process with customers.[22] Each stage contains within it potential frustrations for seller and buyer alike. In the *contact* stage the customer usually comes to the dealership and states that "I'm just looking," a deliberately vague expression that keeps the power in the hands of the customer and keeps the salesman off guard. The salesman can't tell whether the customer just dropped by out of boredom or out of a genuine interest in purchasing a new car.

Often customers will carry a chip on their shoulder as they examine one car after another. A salesman noted, "Every guy who comes in here is sure he is getting cheated, is getting charged $200 too much for the car he's buying. And every guy is sure he's getting $200 too little for the car he's selling you." Another salesman said, "Sometimes you want to grab the guy by the neck and say, 'Hey, I'm not such a bad-ass. I'm just trying to make a living like you.'"

In the second stage the salesman must make the *pitch*. If the salesman comes on too hard he may drive the customer to the dealership down the street. If he comes on too soft the customer might think that he isn't interested. Whatever course he chooses, uncertainty plagues the salesman. Will his pitch help or hurt him in making this sale?

In the third stage the salesman must gently yet firmly move to *close* the deal. The customer might bring in alleged "deals" offered by other agencies that suggest that the salesman is treating him unfairly. They may haggle over a price for days, weeks, or even months. After the salesman has invested hours of time with a customer, the prospective buyer may simply walk out, never to return. The salesman will not have earned one cent for his efforts.

At this point, if the buyer stays, a new threat to the relationship arises: will the floor manager approve the deal? The customer often believes the deal has been completed and then finds out that the salesman must get approval, reviving earlier feelings of mistrust. "Whenever I tell them," said one salesman, "that I got to get our agreement approved, I can just see the resentment. It's like they know they're going to get screwed."

After soothing the resentment of the customer, the salesman must now confront the whims and fancies of the manager. If the salesman lacks information, he might not know whether he has made a reasonable deal. He has made an agreement with the customer that he wants to honor so that he can make a commission. On the other hand, he has to make a profit for the company to remain a good salesman. Often he will end up having to prove to the manager what a good deal he has made only to face the admonition that he "should have been tougher." One salesman put it this way: "The only person harder to convince than the customer is the house . . . to get the house to sign off the car. . . . They always want more money. 'Make him go a little higher' is all they ever think about."[23]

After the manager has approved the deal, the salesman enters into the fourth and last stage of the process. In the *cooling* period the salesman tries to disengage himself from the customer. "The buyer is ushered to the service department where he is literally promoted from the role of buyer to that of owner and presented with the purchased automobile. The salesmen foist the customer on the agency and the service manager now enters into a relationship with the owner . . . The 'cooling' of the buyer becomes a continuing feature of the service manager's role."[24] The customer doesn't realize that the cooling process has set in. If the car turns out to be a lemon, or if the customer wants a free loaner car when he brings it for service, he may well return to the salesman for sympathetic help. This again puts the salesman into a double bind: he has neither the authority nor the resources to help the frustrated customer with his problems. Time invested with an old customer becomes "dead time"; profits come exclusively from talking with new customers.

When the dissatisfied purchaser returns time and time again only to find the salesman either unable or reluctant to give him help, the customer's resentment builds: "Once they make the sale they throw you to the wolves." And so the vicious cycle continues. The next time the customer wants to buy a new car the salesman will have to work all the harder to overcome the mistrust of the buyer.

Cab drivers also face problems that won't go away, although somewhat different from those of automobile salesmen. Sometimes cabbies will go to an address only to find that someone is "playing" with them.[25] This occurs when someone has called the dispatcher, a cab has been sent, but there is no one there who wants a ride. Other customers become "bucket-loads" who simply open the door after arriving at their destination and take off without paying their fare. Others make unreasonable demands on the cabbie, such as asking for a prostitute or requesting a ride into an unsafe area of the city.

Unlike someone who works under restrictive company rules, the cab drivers often don't know the rules under which they have to work. Some customers will give a generous tip because the cabbie breaks the law and speeds to the airport. Another customer's tip depends on a slow and cautious drive. When the customer gets into the car the cabbie must try and find out the customer's expectations: Does he want to be talked to? Does he want to be left alone? Does he have a certain route he likes to take? Is she in a hurry? The customer holds the trump card; if the cab driver guesses wrong, the tip is bound to be meager.

One of the constant irritants for cabbies is that often they are treated as nonpersons. James Henslin describes the impersonal attitudes the public has toward the taxicab driver: "Passengers sometimes do not adjust their behavior to his presence—any more than they would for a steering wheel of an auto. When intimate arguments are fought out in the cab between lovers, for example, it is as though the cab driver was merely a nonhuman extension of the steering wheel, a kind of machine which guides the cab. Such interaction in all its varied aspects—the tones and loudness of voice, the words used, the subjects spoken about—takes place as though the individuals were in private, with no third person present. The effect on the cabbie of some types of non-person treatment is a challenging of the self since others are not acknowledging his self but acting as though he did not exist."[26]

Waitresses often face problems that seem unsolvable. Jan Schmidt, one of the most successful waitresses at the Chateau Supper Club, finally quit her dead-end job in frustration. We talked with Jan less than a week after she resigned. "They (the customers) treat you like a piece of furniture. 'Hey, honey, do this.' 'Hey, doll, what are you going to do after your shift?' I take pride in my work and whenever I get that bullshit it drives me right up the wall. . . . Then they drink. Boy, do they drink. Sometimes you got to calm them down. Like the other night. We had a barbershop convention in town. One of the groups was sitting at the table in the middle of the room and broke into music. One song would have been OK, but they kept it up. The other customers started to get restless. The captain went over and told them to knock it off. But you know who they took it out on? Me. They told me that this was the most uptight place they'd ever been in. Then one guy ordered a

Singapore Sling on the rocks. We have a new bartender and he didn't put enough bitters in it or something. So the guy takes it out on me. He told me he thought it was a pretty low-class joint if you don't know how to make a decent drink. . . . Then I saw a guy raise his hand and wave to me to come. 'Honey, this steak is too rare. I told you *medium* rare.' I took it back to the chef. He was really ticked. That was the third fillet turned back that night and he's got to tell the manager about everything that's returned. When he handed me a new steak he said, 'I hope I don't have to see you again with this same plate.' It was as if it was my fault. I finally got back to the barbershoppers and presented the bill and told them it was a pleasure doing business with them. One guy patted my thigh and told me it would be a pleasure doing business with me too. Right then I decided I wanted out."

A constant source of unrelieved stress has to do with the tips that the waitress may or may not receive. Tipping is absolutely crucial to the waitress's well-being. The waitress is often paid "starvation wages"; management figures that she will make up the difference in tips. The tips can mean the difference between meeting her monthly living expenses or falling farther behind.

Equally important, however, the tip symbolizes the success of the waitress. Yet, as we saw with the taxicab driver, the rules that govern tipping appear as idiosyncratic as the customers. A waitress can knock herself out doing a competent job, only to discover that a 5 percent tip or none at all has been left. On the other hand, as Jan Schmidt said, "Once in a while you get so rushed that you know that you have short-changed the customer. Yet sometimes a guy who I hardly had anything to do with will leave a huge tip. Then you start to wonder, 'Does it make any difference at all what you do?'"

Perhaps the most stressful event for a waitress comes when the tip is used to demean her. One waitress vividly stated her feelings: "Tips? I feel like Carmen. It's like holding out a tambourine and they throw in the coin. (Laughs) There might be occasions when the customers might make it demeaning—the man about town, the conventioneer. When the time comes to pay the check, he would do little things: 'How much should I give you?' He might make an issue about it. I did say to one, 'Don't play God with me. Do what you want.' Then it really didn't matter whether I got a tip or not. I would spit it out, my resentment — that he dares make me feel I'm operating only for a tip. He'd ask for his check. Maybe he's going to sign it. He'd take a very long time and he'd make me stand there: 'Let's see now, what do you think I ought to give you?' He would not let go of that moment. And you know it. You know he meant to demean you. He's holding the change in his hand, or if he'd sign, he'd flourish the pen and wait. These are the times I really get angry. I'm not reticent. Something would come out. Then I really didn't care. 'Goddamn, keep your money!'"[27]

What do automobile salesmen, taxicab drivers, and waitresses have in common that creates enduring problems? The power in their relationship with people lies almost entirely in the hands of the customer. With little effort the customer can deceive them, toy with them, and even demean them. The customer is *always* right. Yet these workers must grin when unreasonable demands are made; they seldom can level when they think the customer is out of line. And they must actually help the customer believe that the customer is the master of the relationship.

This "bottom-dog" position pales before the more terrifying thought that you may never escape from that inferior position. No matter how long on the job, you must continue to take orders, give service, and listen to the demands of the customer.

For many workers, however, the resentments begin to build. The job becomes a dead end. When they no longer play by the arbitrary rules that customers lay down, or when they refuse, as Jan Schmidt said, to "take that kind of bullshit," their effectiveness in making sales or giving service will hit the skids and ultimately so will their employment. But where can you go? One car salesman accurately reflected his insecurity: "Say I've been working at this place twenty years, okay? Most people's jobs, after twenty years you got seniority. You're somebody. After twenty years at this job, I go in tomorrow as if I started today. If I don't sell *x* amount of cars a month, I've gotta look for another job."[28]

Arthur Miller, in *Death of a Salesman,* understood the terror implicit in this situation. Willy Loman, the tragic hero, found that as he aged he could no longer support himself even though he had been successful early in his career. For the Willy Lomans of the world, every day means proving yourself over and over again as the new customer comes through the door.

How to Recognize a Hopeless Job

Some people learn to handle the tensions created by a dead-end job and thereby survive. They keep working to improve their "safety valves" and lower their expectations. Although the job doesn't change, they successfully ward off job burnout in spite of working at a dead-end job. Others follow this route, but in addition manage the work stress by trying to remove the barriers that rob them of hope for the future. They work to reduce the stress of a dead-end job by redesigning that job in small or large ways.

But sometimes both personal and organizational strategies fail. Work stress goes on and on, using up valuable adaptation energy, and you can't seem to escape job burnout. You keep hoping things will change, but almost daily you fight the feeling that you're working in a hopeless job. How can you tell when a job has become hopeless and the time has come to terminate your employment?

The stress of a dead-end job can cloud your judgment, pushing you to one of two extremes. On one hand, many people in dead-end jobs quit impulsively and prematurely. They do so before they have explored other ways to manage the stress created by the job. Then these workers seem surprised to discover that quitting and finding a new job creates new and intense forms of stress. On the other hand, some workers hang on to a dead-end job long after work stress has seriously damaged their health. They get caught in the guilt trap and keep asking, "What's wrong with me that I can't manage this job?" This person hangs on until the bitter end in order to avoid the stigma of personal failure.

If you can first take a detached view of your dead-end job, a strategy discussed in chapter 7, you will neither rush to escape nor refuse to quit. From your detached perspective, recognize that some jobs will defy restructuring. Some jobs will cause job burnout no matter how effectively you manage work stress. Now you can evaluate your situation. From our research we sifted out four major indicators of a hopeless job. Consider any one of these a danger signal that may mean a mismatch between you and your job, but only if you have first employed the personal and organizational strategies discussed in previous chapters. If several of these indicators occur in your job, or if any one becomes extremely serious, you may want to consider other job possibilities.

1. *A hopeless job has a destructive influence on your personal life.* Everyone brings work problems home on occasion; but when those problems constantly spill over into home life and recreation, when they prevent you from ever enjoying nonwork activities, consider looking for another job. You can find out to what extent your job has eroded your personal life through the following exercise. Take out a sheet of paper and write across the top: "Ten Things I Like to Do." Quickly write down the first ten things that come to mind. Now, after each activity, write the date you last did each of them and enjoyed it. If you did all ten at some time during the last few months, and several on more than one occasion, you have kept a healthy balance between your work and personal life. If you can't remember, or several months have passed since you last took a trip, had fun hiking in the woods, enjoyed reading a novel, saw a movie, or did most of the things on your list, indicate the reason for this neglect after each activity. If work pressures are the cause, you may want to consider looking for another employer.

2. *A hopeless job seriously impairs your health.* If your job has left you with a chronic ulcer, weekly migraine headaches, or dangerously high blood pressure, it's time to consider other job options. A serious health problem is one that persists despite your attempts to cope with

the problems at work. It will only disappear when you remove yourself from the cause: work stress.

Each person has a unique tolerance for different degrees of impaired health. Some workers refuse to believe their job is hopeless even when work stress leads them to heavy drinking, or brings on a coronary attack or a bleeding ulcer. These persons chafe to get back to the office even while they lie in an intensive-care unit of some hospital. We believe it's important to place a higher premium on optimum health, to recognize that mild symptoms can foreshadow more serious problems. If you stay on a job that impairs your health, you run the real risk of losing both your job and your health. By quitting one you may save the other.

3. A hopeless job has insufficient rewards.   Whether they realize it or not, most people work for more than salary and fringe benefits. We seldom total up the nonmaterial benefits of our jobs and therefore may not realize when they have disappeared. If your job lacks all of the following potential rewards, you may want to consider looking for a new job: satisfying work, satisfying relationships with your coworkers, and a good relationship with your boss.

If the tasks you do bring satisfaction, and your work load is reasonable, you probably look forward to most days at work. However, if your work provides little intrinsic payoff, if you don't believe in what you're doing, it could mean a mismatch has been made.

The second reward that comes with most jobs is loyalty, friendship, and support from coworkers. "We have a close group at the office," said one engineer. "We help each other move; if someone's sick you know everyone will visit and pitch in to do their work; we're a family and everyone really cares." Friends at work can help make the most miserable dead-end job tolerable. Friends can help you solve work-related problems. Some people who underrate the value of these social relationships quit their jobs in haste and then suffer from loneliness. On the other hand, if your job offers no friends, if you do not enjoy the company of your coworkers, your job probably offers little hope for long-term employment. "I stuck it out for a year and a half," said one woman executive. "I never did feel comfortable with any of the staff. I was an outsider and knew that's the way it would always be."

A final payoff comes in a good relationship with your boss. As we saw in the last chapter, your supervisor plays a crucial role in how you feel about yourself. A competent boss, one interested in your welfare, one who works to keep communication channels open, adds great value to any job. Consider each of these nonmonetary rewards. If all have vanished from your job and you seriously doubt they will return, the value of long-term employment has become questionable.

4. *A hopeless job is one in which you are not taken seriously.* We have talked about the lack of rewards from bad relationships with your coworkers and boss. But one personal affront has such devastating power that we must single it out as a separate indicator of a hopeless job. If you are treated in a roughshod, cavalier manner, if people smile condescendingly but ignore your contribution, you can't escape the pain and rejection. A direct verbal assault from others on the job creates less stress than the pain of not being taken seriously. It can shatter your self-confidence and sense of self-worth long before serious burnout symptoms appear. If you feel caught in a pattern at work in which others who are important to you refuse to take you seriously, it's probably time to get out.

Once you decide a job is hopeless, failure to begin to terminate can only speed up job burnout. However, at this point you are entering a minefield of new stresses. Pick your way carefully. There are good and bad ways to end your employment. If you resign impulsively before finding another position, you invite new and dangerous stresses. Some people make the mistake of giving unsolicited advice to colleagues: "You should get out of this place, it's a graveyard!" Such advice goes unappreciated; coworkers will only withdraw during your remaining weeks and can make your life miserable. Other workers turn against their boss, unleashing long-pent-up fury. They write angry letters of resignation, detailing all the problems they have seen in the organization. They talk to everyone they meet about the injustices they perceive. In a matter of hours they can destroy friendships that took years to build. If you take any of these impulsive approaches, you can also cut yourself off from a valuable support network, one needed in the coming weeks of searching for a new job. Furthermore, you'll probably find your colleagues will silently cheer to see you go.

It's best to make a clear decision to quit a hopeless job and then keep it to yourself or close friends away from work. Consider all your options; don't make your decision in haste. Then, before announcing it to anyone, quietly begin searching for a new position. Don't let yourself get caught by a feeling of panic. Eventually you will find a better working environment. Try to secure a new position before you quit, then offer your former employer a simple reason for quitting. Never blame your employer or you may find future recommendations hurt more than they help. We think it's best not to reveal job-related frustrations, even when asked. Recognize that your responsibility to reform jobs and make changes has ended with your decision to quit. Instead of saying, "This place doesn't have a healthy environment for working," try other reasons: "I found a new job that pays more," "I want to work closer to home," or "I want to develop skills in a new area." Don't forget, no matter how angry you feel, that there are people to thank and people to whom a warm good-bye is in order. If you take this approach, you will escape a hopeless job, but still retain a valuable support network. You may even find that your coworkers throw a good-bye party or two in your honor and you may retain some positive feelings about the years you spent with your former employer.

Chapter Ten
The Professional
Helper

Although people burn out in every occupation, some fields seem to create higher levels of work stress. Very little research to date has systematically compared the levels of stress from one occupation to another. However, there is wide agreement that the helping professions send people into job burnout with unrelenting regularity. We want to examine why this cluster of occupations has such a high risk of job burnout and how the professional helper can survive this hazard.

In the distant past there existed only one social service organization: *the family*. When people were overcome by grief, weakened by illness, demoralized by poverty, or shattered by crisis, the family came to the rescue. Mother, father, grandparents, uncles, aunts, brothers, sisters, cousins—even great-aunts and second cousins pitched in to help in time of need. Yet not a single individual worked in a "helping profession." Those occupations lay far in the future.

The family functioned as hospital, day-care center, rest home, mental-health clinic, welfare agency, boys' club, veterans home, and Red Cross. It was a center for the retarded, a home for unwed mothers, an employment agency for the handicapped, a treatment center for alcoholics, a home for the blind, and a hospice for the dying. Religion and the healing arts were all carried out within the web of kith and kin.

Then came the Industrial Revolution. Momentous changes shook the foundations of society. Slowly a new order emerged. Modern industry became a huge magnet that attracted workers to jobs in cities and towns far from their homes on farms and in villages. Gradually the family lost its central role as a social-service agency; hundreds of new organizations and occupations divided up its former duties. The helping professions were born.

Dr. Daniel Bell believes we have come to the brink of a revolution in the workplace, what he calls the *service revolution,* that could usher in a post-industrial society.[1] The number of jobs that produce goods has continued to decline; by 1981 it will have skidded to an all-time low of 32 percent. At the same time the number of helping professions and other service jobs has mushroomed. These new occupations have brought with them new kinds of job pressures.

It's easy to overlook the growth of helping professions. Yet in a city of 500,000 citizens, there will be dozens of hospitals. The larger ones will have 200 different social-service occupations. Colleges, business schools, and hundreds of primary and secondary schools mean a livelihood for thousands of teachers. Churches dot the tree-lined streets in every neighborhood of the city, each with ministers or priests helping the people of their parish.

But we have seen only the tip of the helping-profession iceberg. Such a city will also have hundreds of physicians, attorneys, counselors, and social workers who deal with "people problems." A glance through the Yellow Pages in an average city reveals a host of social-service organizations. Crime Victims Crisis Center. Home for the Blind. Rape Crisis Center. Migrants in Action. YMCA. Travelers Aid. Shelter for Battered Women. The Bridge for Runaway Youth. Epilepsy League of America. Courage Center for Quadriplegics. Union Gospel Mission. Martin Luther King Center. Crime Prevention Council. Mental Health Association. More than two hundred such organizations serve the needs of people in this one city.

All these professional helpers have one thing in common: *a high risk of burnout.* Hidden beneath the facade of service, obscured by the in-trinsic rewards of helping others, there lurk some of the most deadly job pressures. They can go unrecognized until the teacher quits, the minister becomes depressed, the nurse grows cynical. Burnout in the helping professions can express itself in all of the classic symptoms and often moves through each of its stages at a faster pace than in other types of professions. It's a well-known fact that teachers, social workers, drug counselors, community organizers, nurses, and other people helpers speak of their fields as "burnout occupations." In this chapter we want to show you why these jobs create so much stress, even as the person is trying to relieve stress for others.

Ideals of Service

When you become a nurse, a social worker, a physician, or a rehabilita-tion counselor, you don't merely take a job; you enter a profession with high ideals of service. Professional helpers want to make this a better world in which to live. They hope to restore dignity, health, and happiness to patients and clients.

For many, the initial stimulus for their choice of occupation came from lofty ideals. When we asked professional helpers why they chose their careers, they spoke with a smile and a soft tone of voice. A Peace Corps volunteer said, "I didn't want to be an Ugly American. I wanted to show that we cared." A public-health physician said, "I couldn't think of anything more rewarding than knowing that you are, even if it is in a small way, doing some good." A college professor recalled, "I wanted to work with those eager young minds, to expand their hori-zons, to help them over the hurdles at a crucial time in life." Although it was usually a clergyman who said, "God called me to this work," others revealed their feelings that their occupation was a "high calling." While they respect the businessman, the bricklayer, the carpenter, most professional helpers would not exchange occupational places with them.

The training and education of professional helpers serves a dual purpose: to impart skills and to instill professional ideals. Not everyone in a helping profession starts her career out of love for humanity or a desire to help in time of need. But the weeks at the police academy, the years in nurse's training, and the long seminars on professional ethics for counselors reinforces the commitment to service. A patrolman pointed to his squad car. "At first it was just a job," he said, "but then it became like that sign on the door: 'To Protect and Serve.' That's what it's all about for me." It's difficult to remain in any helping profession without coming to feel deeply that your mission in life is to help solve some basic human problems.

The high expectations people bring to their jobs in the helping professions often have deep roots within their own personal experience. Befriended by the basketball coach in eleventh grade, Carl Baker was drawn to high-school teaching. "That guy did an awful lot for me; I figure I might help some other kids in the same way." Randy Venetian's father was both a policeman and a hero in Randy's eyes. The stories of adventure he told at the dinner table each night left Randy with a profound feeling that "my dad was out there helping people, protecting them from criminals, and that's what I wanted to do."

For others, the pull to the helping professions comes from a wrenching struggle to overcome a personal problem. "I was on skid row for fifteen years before I went on the wagon through AA," a treatment-center counselor told us. "I still have the disease, and always will, but now I'm a *recovered* alcoholic and the best way to stay that way is by helping other alkies." Dr. Adrian Hill fought a long period of depression during her junior year in college. Weekly sessions with a sympathetic counselor had a profound impact on her feelings and also her career. "That was a painful period in my life and I began to realize how many people go through that kind of depression. I decided to get a graduate degree in clinical psychology and eventually open up my own practice."

The idealism of those who enter the helping professions almost always leads to ideas about a mythical "Dream Job." You develop a set of subconscious expectations about serving people. Although often unspoken, these beliefs follow us every day, raising our hopes, challenging us to greater efforts. Here are some of the most common Dream Job beliefs:

—Serving other people is life's highest calling.

—Serving other people will bring its own reward.

—My service will make a significant difference to people in need.

—The people I serve will deeply appreciate what I do for them.

—The sacrifices I make will be outweighed by the intrinsic satisfaction of helping others.

—Serving other people will never become routine.

—My service to people in need will bring me respect and admiration from society.

A word of caution at this point: It's all too easy to blame the individual who holds these Dream Job beliefs, as if he were guilty of a gross misperception or illogical thinking. But these beliefs come from beyond the individual social worker, teacher, or psychotherapist. The Dream Job has its origins in the occupational cultures of every helping profession and is the cornerstone of a helping professional's world view. The admissions brochure for a nursing school announces, "You can make a difference!" The law professor reminds students: "The legal profession is a high calling; you have a responsibility to serve the needs of your clients." Marcus Welby always has a new and intriguing challenge; and he always makes a significant difference to people in need. The social worker goes through a long post-graduate education that inculcates these ideals, often in a setting cut off from reality. And almost every professional association charter, from occupational therapy and medicine to the clergy, reaffirms the tenets of the Dream Job.

Reality Shock

It's hard to imagine a more effective way to set people up for the ravages of burnout. Inculcate the Dream Job. Then assign them to real jobs that daily contradict the respected myths. Back that up with pressures to work hard and sacrifice, and when things go awry the people helper can only ask, "What's wrong with me?"

Whether it takes weeks or years, sooner or later reality shock sets in. The Dream Job, hidden from our awareness, doesn't match the real job. The unwed mother sees you as a custodian, even a prison guard, rather than a Florence Nightingale. The alcoholic doesn't go on the wagon; he writes you off as "a mission stiff who doesn't know what it's like." The students don't appreciate your teaching skill. As one teacher said, "This utter lack of respect and the slamming of doors, using filthy words, telling me to drop dead is really the thing that shocked me these past few months."[2]

And so you work harder. Sacrifice and you will enable others to succeed. The police officer knows that if he intervenes in a domestic argument, the family might turn their wrath against him. Yet he will still try to settle the dispute. The court-appointed attorney will take time from his family to fight for the penniless drifter: "If I don't defend him, who will?" The physician's day can start at 6:30 A.M. with morning rounds and conclude in late evening with a final check on hospitalized patients. In between she will have handled a staggering number of problems in her office. The clergyman is usually on call twenty-four hours a day. His sleep will be interrupted by a telephone call from someone who can't get through the darkness of night without some reassurance. And the more you have to sacrifice, the greater the reality shock. For the Dream Job myth keeps reminding you that all sacrifices should be outweighed by the intrinsic satisfaction of helping others. No matter that those you help don't appreciate your efforts.

Most professional helpers can't even know the specific problems that await them as they drive to work each morning. In that sense, their jobs contrast sharply with the well-defined work of many occupations. A policeman said, "When I kiss my wife good-bye, I often wonder what the day will bring. Maybe all I'll do is give out traffic tickets. But I might also be assaulted. I may never even see my wife again. You just never know. . . ."

As the professional helper arrives at work, the adrenalin starts to flow. A welfare counselor in one of the poorest sections of Chicago said, "I take one look at my desk and there will be a string of phone messages lying there. I try to sort out what are really life-and-death issues that need to be handled immediately from those that can wait. And from that moment until I put the phone down at 5:30 P.M. I will spend most of the time talking with clients who are right on the edge. In fact, I've had clients tell me that they were all prepared to end it all depending on what I would say to them over the phone."

As you plunge into your work, you face an unalterable fact that contradicts your idea of the Dream Job: *Most problems defy easy solution.* Even the nature of the problem can escape your efforts at analysis. Most human concerns have no right or wrong answer, as Betty Hernandez can attest. Betty is a counselor at a family-planning clinic. "Usually the kids that come here are so young and so mixed up and so unsure of themselves that they don't know whether they want an abortion or to bring the pregnancy to term. We spend hours talking about their choice. Inevitably they will turn to me and ask what I would do. That's a heck of a question to ask because I don't know what I would do. On one hand I have seen teenagers carry out their pregnancy and give up the child for adoption. Often there are no visible scars. And sometimes I have seen teenagers make excellent single parents. But I have also seen others give birth to the child, decide to keep it, and then subsequently abuse it morning, noon, and night. There's no computer in this business to tell you what to do."

How do you square this ambiguity with the feeling that if you don't give the right advice the implications could be disastrous? Grace Tesder, a fifth-grade teacher, suspects that one of her students is being sexually abused by her father. She has no proof outside of the cautiously worded comments made by the girl as she lingers after school. "If I even informally pressed the issue I could subject myself and the school to a lawsuit. And if I am wrong I could ruin my reputation as a teacher. But if I don't do anything and if my worst fears are correct, this child will suffer for the rest of her life."

Part of the pressure that professional helpers experience comes from the fact that lay people expect them to be infallible. We attribute powers to doctors and counselors that no human can possibly have. We expect them to make accurate diagnoses of our problems and to find solutions that will work. A forty-three-year-old internist said, "People think of medicine as a science. But it is largely an art. They don't know how imprecise medical science really is." A minister said, "I'm supposed to be some kind of moral conscience. I'm supposed to know the *right* thing to do. And so people come to me for advice. It's heady stuff when you are young. But I've given wrong advice too often. And when you think you have offered good advice it can boomerang on you. Last year I suggested to a husband and a wife that they consider having a trial separation. They were having immense marital problems and I thought it might help them sort out their troubles and . . . give each some space to see how much they needed one another. Well, it didn't work out. The trial separation led to a divorce. The husband had initiated it. And to this day the woman blames me. As she says, I 'gave him an easy way out.' "

The burnout symptoms often begin to appear when the professional helpers cannot meet their own high standards for success, let alone the expectations of clients. And they will burn out when their emotional reserves have been spent and there is no thanks from anyone. We asked an experienced juvenile probation officer whether there were times when he wondered whether it was worth it all. He smiled, looked at the floor, and said: "Yeah, there are lots of times I wonder. . . . One of the most discouraging things that ever happened to me occurred last week. There was this kid by the name of Richie. I helped him when he was hauled in at age nine for shoplifting. He lived with his older brother. His folks had long split. When he skipped school the assistant principal would call me and I would try and find him and get him back in. When he was knifed in some kind of fight he called me and I got him to a doctor. And when he turned thirteen I took him to a Red Sox game. It was his only present. . . . He actually was a good kid. But then I hadn't seen him for a while. And last night I got a call from headquarters. He had committed a felony with some nineteen-year-old punk who needed someone to stand outside the supermarket and alert him if any cops were coming. I went to the judge's chamber the next day and my eyes met Richie's. He couldn't look at me. An hour later the judge threw the book at him, citing a long history of problems with the law. As he went by me I could see his eyes glistening. After everyone had left I slammed my fist on the bench. I was mad at myself for not checking up on him. I saw him through the door as they were leading him to the cell block. I wanted to cry but no tears would come. I felt so hopeless. . . ."

Instead of having their hopes fulfilled by solving the problems of other people, many professional helpers are overwhelmed by the misery, degradation, and absurdity of human problems. In one day most people helpers will experience more of life's insanities than most lay people will experience in a lifetime. A paramedic called to a freeway accident may literally have to pick up pieces of human flesh strewn over the highway. A welfare worker will walk into a house where a baby lies in its own excrement because the mother is strung out on drugs. A surgeon will try to comfort a twenty-eight-year-old woman whose beauty is going to be permanently scarred because cancer has metastasized in her breast.

One physician put it this way: "My God, everyone looks to us as having it made. We drive expensive cars and we live in some exclusive suburb. But what they don't know is that we pay a heavy price for what we have. The other day I visited nine of my patients, each of whom had terminal cancer. And then I had to tell the parents of a seventeen-year-old girl that she had at most a month to live. I felt like shit. I went out to a movie to get my mind off things. In the movie Alan Alda goes into his daughter's room where she is trying to sort out all the pressures in her life. She screamed at him and finally said, 'Life sucks . . .' That's pretty crude, but I sat there nodding my head."

It's a rare person who can touch the most sensitive nerves of life and remain unaffected. "You try and not let it get to you," said a nurse who works in an emergency room. "But sometimes it's a nightmare. . . . And although you do your damnedest to help, your efforts often aren't enough. And then you too become part of that patient's nightmare. . . . Sometimes I just sit in my chair after the day thinking about what's happened. I try to be philosophical and say, 'I did everything humanly possible.' But . . . it's hard not to let the insanity of it all get to you."

You Don't Punch a Clock

In many occupations, when the assembly line stops, the workday ends. The construction crew load their tools in the pickup and head for home. The keypunch machine stops, the office lights go out, the door is securely locked. But human problems don't match eight-hour shifts; they can follow you for twenty-four hours a day, seven days a week. Unlike the work problems an executive in business might carry home, human dilemmas come with such intensity that you can find it impossible to leave them behind. If you put the two-year-old leukemia patient out of your mind, you've given up part of your own human dignity. If, at five o'clock, you cease to care for the young mother who can't find housing, some part of yourself will die.

Perhaps the single greatest cause of burnout in the helping professions comes from this difficulty in getting away from the problems of clients and patients. And because some human needs require round-the-clock care, those who work in residential settings become especially vulnerable to burnout. We met Judy and Jack Carlson at a social-work conference in Michigan. The dark circles under Judy's eyes seemed to confirm the story she told us: "One of the happiest moments of our married life came when we received a telephone call from the executive director of Group Homes, Inc. It's a church-sponsored program. The homes are for mentally retarded adults who can hold down a job. Our combined salary was only $14,200, which wasn't very much, but the director told us we would have free room and board since we would be living with the men in the home."

Judy spoke with animation about their enthusiasm. They looked forward to working with retarded adults. "Society shortchanges these people all the time. They really have a lot of potential. We couldn't think of anything more rewarding than expanding our family and giving six adults a chance at life."

The first hurdle came with the need to find jobs for the six residents. Jack spent eight to ten hours a day talking with prospective employers. The old house needed repair and Judy started fixing it up between the preparation of meals for the "family" and keeping things clean.

Two months later Judy started to experience burnout symptoms, and it's not surprising. Her day began at 5:00 A.M. as she prepared breakfast and didn't end until after 7:00 P.M. with the supervising of the dishwashers. Outside of their official one weekend a month off, this went on seven days a week. Exhausted from the long hours and the constant demands made on her time, Judy became edgy. "One night I flipped on the television. I had looked forward to seeing this movie all week. I barely got into the movie when one of the men sat down and said he needed to tell me something. He said that the people at work were calling him "thumbs" because he was so dumb he couldn't follow instructions. He started to cry. I felt so angry. I was angry at the insensitive slobs where Robbie worked. But I was also angry at him for interrupting my television show. I didn't know what I was saying but I blurted out, "Damn it, Robbie. Life's tough. Nobody is going to do you any favors. You just have to prove to them that you can do the job." As soon as I said it, I could see the hurt in his eyes. He walked away. I tried to watch the movie. I felt so tired and frustrated and guilty. It had taken two months for him to trust me and I destroyed it with one thoughtless comment. So I turned off the TV and looked for him. But he was gone. We spent half the night looking for him and finally found him drinking coffee by himself in a little café. I saw him in the window. He looked so alone."

While Judy struggled with her own feelings of anger at being trapped in the group home, Jack felt ground down by a different set of problems. A deeply religious young man, Jack spent his days visiting the employers of the residents to iron out any difficulties. Evenings filled up with talks to church groups trying to raise financial support for Group Homes, Inc. Invariably he would talk about his joy in the work and about how "God had led them" into this type of work.

But the pressures began to build. Prospective employers of the men seemed interested and polite, but few would actually put themselves on the line to hire retarded individuals. The meager budget for the home raised questions for Jack about the commitment of the church to this type of ministry. The men in the home were likable, but incapable of expressing appreciation in the way the Carlsons wanted. Occasionally Jack worried for Judy's safety at home with several men; although nothing occurred, both knew the dangers.

The bottom seemed to fall out one afternoon for Jack. He had visited a dozen prospective employers, none of whom had job openings for the two men in the home who were still unemployed. He slumped into his chair and opened the mail. A letter from the executive director of Group Homes, Inc., turned down a request for an extra $30 per month to help feed the men. He also denied a request for weekend relief so that he and Judy could have some time alone. Another letter came from Robbie's new employer terminating Robbie's employment. Jack stormed into the kitchen where Judy was preparing yet another meal for her extended family. "Who cares about what we are doing? Who cares that I pound the pavement trying to find them work and you get up every morning to prepare them breakfast? Who cares that we sit and talk with them until midnight trying to help them get enough courage to face another day at work?" One month later the Carlsons resigned, the only escape they could find from the twenty-four-hour-a-day pressure of their work problems.

A minister of a large congregation in Salem, Oregon, said, "One of the deacons in the church said to me, 'Pastor, you need to get some sleep. You're looking awfully tired.' I didn't say anything but I was tempted to unload on him. On Sunday night I was up until one-thirty A.M. with the parents of a teenager who was in a coma because of an overdose. On Tuesday night I got to bed at midnight after spending four hours with a couple who had been physically abusing one another. Last night at one-fifteen A.M. the phone rang. It was the sheriff, who is a member of our church. One of the best kids in the church was killed coming home from a basketball game. He wanted to know whether I would go with him to see the parents. So when that deacon told me I looked tired, I felt like shouting: 'You're goddamn right I am tired. I'm *bone* tired. And all you think I have to do is get up on Sunday morning and sprinkle a few kind words to the congregation. . . .' "

A head nurse who works in an intensive coronary-care unit said, "My husband can't understand why when I come home I just can't shut work off. He says, 'When I get into *my* car at four-thirty I don't even think about my job again until the next morning.' Maybe if I was an electrician like him I could do the same thing. But I know those people in the unit. They are struggling for their lives. And sometimes I have to call in just before I go to bed and see how they are doing and see if there are any problems that the staff can't handle."

The workday seldom ends at 4:30 P.M. for most professional helpers. They have no clock to punch that symbolically releases many workers from their responsibilities. Their jobs have no way to tell them, "Your work is completed—go home and relax." It's hardly a wonder, therefore, that a number of nurses told us that they dream about their patients. As a young physician serving alone in a rural North Dakota community said, "People get sick at night as well as in the day. You just can't order their sickness to arrive conveniently during your office hours."

Red Tape, Low Salaries, Lack of Recognition

Many people helpers competently handle the demands of clients. They manage large numbers of cases and even learn to get away from clients' problems. They enter the arena of human suffering and seldom feel that their own souls are ravaged by what they see. They escape burnout caused by the work itself only to be ambushed from another direction: Increasingly, a major complaint of helping professionals centers on bureaucratic red tape and lack of support from employers. Three interrelated concerns often surface: low salaries, lack of recognition, and an abundance of paperwork, or what one social worker aptly calls "administrivia."

Inflation has created havoc on the already low salaries of many in the helping fields. Nearly a third of the 1,777 teachers polled this year by the National Education Survey indicated that they would not become teachers again if they could start over.[3] Dollar signs permeate most issues that confront teachers and schools.[4] A teacher in Vermont who has a family of four to support makes $11,786. "How can I feel good about my job when I make less than a shop mechanic? I am responsible for taking care of the most important investment parents have and yet I'm not paid a decent salary."[5] A prison guard, who, because he is the third watch commander, is, in effect, the warden of San Quentin prison at night, reports that he makes less money than a *probationary* San Francisco policeman.[6] And yet prison guards put their lives on the line every day for society. A professor in a school of nursing told us: "A highly trained nurse in a neonatal unit may make $12,584 a year. Think about that salary in terms of what other people in society are making. And then think about her responsibilities. If she makes even the slightest error in a medication schedule, that baby could be a vegetable for the rest of his life. And the state could end up paying a million dollars for the care that person would need over a lifetime."

Unfortunately, most people helpers lack power. Nurse's aides, dental assistants, public-health workers, social and welfare personnel are seldom unionized. And if they complain too loudly, they will receive reminders that there are young workers ready to take their places. Some employers would be happy if they quit because the new employee would start at rock-bottom wages. It's a buyer's market.

In addition to low salaries, helping professionals find little recognition from other members of the "helping team." The community of helping professionals has become fragmented into discrete and often isolated disciplines, each fighting for its own identity. A pharmacist said, "I know more about drugs than any other health professional. I can tell you about drug interaction effects; the prognosis, given the unit dosage; and the potential side effects of any medication. But do you think any physician will call me and ask my advice about the medications he prescribes? Never!"

A common complaint of many helpers is that no one really appreciates their skills. A hospital dietician said, "As far as the docs, nurses, and even the hospital administrators are concerned, all we are good for is preparing the meals. You know—keep everyone happy by giving them good cuts of beef. It's infuriating that they know so little about the effect that diet has upon patients' health. And so we sit down here in our little cubicles planning "tasty" meals. Given the fact that most physicians don't have a single course in nutrition in medical school, you would think that they would use our knowledge. But we are seldom called in on any patient consultation."

Part of the difficulty comes from occupations that keep people hidden and isolated. The restaurant inspector, a highly trained technician in food sanitation, makes his rounds to keep food free from contaminating microorganisms. The epidemiologist tracks down possible outbreaks of disease. Yet we seldom hear about the work of these medical detectives until an outbreak occurs of the magnitude of Legionnaire's Disease. The water engineer, the sanitarian, nutritionist, health educator, and laboratory technician perform valuable services to the public. Yet they do it without the recognition that is so essential to a person's well-being.

Many helping professionals can tolerate a system that does not reward them adequately as long as they can work on those things they really enjoy. A nurse said, "No matter what kind of boss I have and no matter how small the salary increases, as long as I have adequate time to give good patient care, I'm happy."

But red tape and bureaucracy have cut these satisfactions for many workers. A doctor said, "Every night I spend three hours going over my records. I dictate something after every patient I see. I despise the paperwork, but you never know who might sue you." A nursing home administrator said, "You can't believe the rules and regulations and the way the state sticks its nose in our business. Every day I have to answer a dozen memos from the department of economic security about some regulation, and invariably I have my weekly conference with the county inspector, who will ask why I don't have a hundred-watt light bulb at the foot of the stairs rather than a seventy-five watt."

When an electrician goes to work, he won't encounter many bureaucratic hassles. In fact, the foreman will serve as a buffer so that the electrician can keep at his work. It's a simple matter of economics. But government agencies, immune from the constraints of the marketplace, will spend valuable energy in meeting the demands of the bureaucracy rather than the needs of the people. A welfare counselor told us, "If I could only spend time with my clients, I'd never complain. But at least 50 percent of my day is spent in unproductive committee meetings and filing reports that will probably never be read. For example, my boss sends a memo asking me to determine the economic status of each of my clients and to submit my report within a week. I stormed into her office and asked, "For Christ's sake, why can't you get off my back? Why can't I spend my time with my clients?'"

Professional helpers entered their careers to help clients, not to serve an impersonal bureaucracy. When their energy goes into meeting meaningless regulations, attending unproductive committee meetings, and coping with bureaucratic inertia, the symptoms of burnout begin to appear.

Increasingly, the most able individuals decide to get out. Lawrence Podell studied social workers who left their employment and found that "those beginning social workers who had achieved the highest scores in the civil-service examination were most likely to leave the agency within nine months or less."[7] When your enthusiasm is shredded by the organization that claims to support you, resignation becomes a viable option.

Helping the Helper

After describing her burnout symptoms, a public-health nutritionist said, "But what makes me even more depressed is that I don't know what to do about it." What do you do when, after helping solve the problems of others, you burn out yourself? Do you quit, hoping to find the grass greener in some other hospital or agency? Should you continue full speed ahead, hoping that the feelings of exhaustion and dissipation will disappear?

There are a number of practical strategies that burned-out professional helpers can use to restore their mental and physical well-being. For some, the use of just one of the strategies will pay big dividends. Others, particularly those in the later stages of burnout, may require all of these strategies before they begin to regain their enthusiasm for work.

Recognize that professional helpers have a high risk of burning out. There's a good chance you work long hours in an environment charged with emotional energy. You probably take your problems home with you and may work in an organization insensitive to your well-being.

Those who fail to recognize that they run a high risk of burning out may find themselves pursuing a maze of blind alleys that only intensify their burnout. Dr. Frank Seeley, a top-flight cardiologist, said, "I got an ulcer before I even knew what was happening. I ignored all the symptoms, pretending that, like Superman, I could work sixty hours a week." Fran Buris, a nurse administrator said, "I was blaming everybody for my problems. Then one day the entire staff threatened to resign. It really shocked me! I suddenly realized all the pressure I had been putting them under." Brad Kanlon, a state welfare caseworker, told us, "I was drowning in a sea of paper. The only way I could manage my case load was to work harder and harder. But the paperwork seemed to consume me and I had to get to work earlier and earlier and stay later and later. It was a no-win situation."

If you find yourself taking an ostrich approach to your problems, blaming others, working harder and harder, and feeling guilty, you could find yourself moving toward the crisis stage of burnout. As you take your own stress inventory, don't overlook one particularly sensitive barometer of burnout in the helping professions: your relationships with the people who need help.

We have found that one of the most accurate indicators of burnout among professional helpers is the extent to which they distance themselves from patients and clients.[8]

Distancing can take the form of becoming impersonal. Instead of referring to the client as Mrs. Smith or Mr. Jones, we use labels such as "neurotic," "paranoid," or even "that old troublemaker." Ann Vanderberg, a nurse supervisor, describes the distancing process in the intensive-care unit. "The main sign of burnout that I've noticed in the ICU personnel is that they become more *technical,* their primary concerns are the *machines,* not the patients. When you ask them how their patients are doing, their first comment is that the machines are okay or the signs are okay, but they don't refer directly to the patients. . . . They won't answer about the whole patient, but rather about one system at a time—his kidneys or heart or blood pressure."[9]

The frustrations of burned-out workers often spill into their relationships with other staff members. They may become supercritical. They may appear negative, cynical, and mistrusting of the motivations of colleagues. Often they will delight in telling others about "how bad things are"; yet they will shoot down every suggestion for improvement as impractical, unworkable, or even naive.

Soon the cynicism wears thin. Other staff members will usually seek to isolate the burned-out colleague, not wanting to hear his constant complaints. Or they may try to bring the cynic back into line, often by putting him down. Rarely, however, will members of the professional staff recognize that chronic cynicism is a cry for help. Ironically, the very people who should be sensitive to such early warning signals may feel so threatened by them that they cannot offer a helping hand.

When burned-out professionals sense rejection from colleagues, they may become angry and bitter, willing to pick a fight with anybody who doesn't agree with them. Some will simply withdraw from their colleagues, firmly convinced that "no one understands." If their clients begin turning to other professional staff members for help, they may resign feeling totally defeated.

Yet even for those who are totally defeated there are signs of hope. Underneath the anger and hostility, the cynicism and depression, the original idealism that motivated them to serve others may remain. A high-school teacher talked almost nonstop for ninety minutes describing the abysmal conditions in his school system. Nobody cared. Nothing turned out right. Everyone was insensitive. But when asked, "Why do you continue to teach?" his eyes glistened with tears. He looked to the floor and hesitantly said, "Because . . . I still love kids."

Set your work priorities.   As we have seen, professional helpers live in a demanding, complex work world. The needs of other people often determine work priorities; schedules can be interrupted at any time by other people. The strong service orientation makes it extremely difficult to set aside time for tasks of their own choosing. Most will respond to the requests of others before they will work on their own priorities.

Some individuals have a keen understanding of the importance of spending time working according to their own agendas. A college professor said, "The best thing about teaching is talking informally with students. But when I look at my calendar and find it filled with faculty meetings and committee assignments and there is not even a single afternoon that I can spend over at the student union, then I know I'm in trouble."

One of the best organizational strategies we discovered for preventing burnout came from a rural social-service agency. The director meets with each program director for thirty minutes every Friday afternoon. She instructs them to bring to the meeting a list of tasks that they intend to pursue during the coming week. The items on each program director's list are ranked according to two criteria: (1) the importance to the agency, and (2) the importance of the tasks to the employee. "When I look over their lists," said the director, "I make certain that they will be working on functions needed by the agency. But I am equally concerned that each employee works on tasks that he finds personally rewarding." It did not surprise us that employee turnover and absenteeism were almost nonexistent in this agency.

Set priorities, making certain you work on some tasks that *you* find rewarding. And don't fall into the trap of thinking that all you can do is respond to the directives of others. Workers have freedom even in structured jobs. Remember Brad Kanlon, the state welfare worker who was drowning in a sea of paper? One day he asked his boss if he couldn't experiment and write a single-page report on his clients rather than the standardized ten-page document. His boss agreed to the suggestion and found the new system more productive. Today Brad Kanlon spends less time pushing papers and more time with clients. And he goes home each night a lot more content with his job.

Pick your wars carefully.   A nursing-home administrator said, "There are only so many battles you can fight. If you are going to survive you have to pick the battles where the outcomes will make a difference."

Many professional helpers encounter human needs at every juncture in the working day. It's easy for them to get drawn into every struggle for improvement of services. Judy Perkins, a junior-high-school teacher, summed up the situation: "You cannot believe the problems in our school. We have abused kids, gifted kids, retarded kids, those who are overweight and the butt of jokes. We have kids sniffing angel dust and smoking pot and kids hangin' around for some affection. It's all so overwhelming." Any attempt to work with these problem kids can drain helpers' energy, but even more frustrating, they invariably meet resistance. When Judy tried to establish special programs for the gifted children in her school she was told that the budget wouldn't permit it. When she tried to set up a self-help group for obese children, the school nurse warned her to "get off my turf." When she suggested that the school needed to do something about the smoking habits of students, other teachers advised her not to stick her nose into the parents' business.

The quickest path toward professional burnout is spreading yourself too thin—taking on too many tasks, trying to solve too many problems. "Yesterday I got hit up with a dozen requests," said a physician who had learned to avoid unimportant battles. "My physicians group asked me to take on more patients. Our office administrator wanted me to chair a committee to look at our billing practices. I got a call from my priest, who wants me to chair their annual fund-raising program. My son called and asked if I could be an assistant coach for his Little League team. Five years ago I would have said yes to all those requests. After all, aren't all those things important? But I've learned the hard way that you can't take everything on and be effective. So I told them I'd think about it and would call them back. Well, I've thought about it and the only additional thing I'm going to take on is Little League coaching. And I know that my physician friends and the office administrator won't like it and the minister will be disappointed. But I'm going to be a bit selfish and think about my own health."

Cultivate at least one good friend who can help you over your burnout hurdles.   Dr. Frank Seeley, the cardiologist, has a standing engagement to meet a physician friend on the third Friday of every month. "We meet at a little German café. I tell him my problems and he tells me his. We try to pool our ideas and help each other. And we always leave that café feeling better." Fran Buris, the nurse administrator, will call up an old professor whenever her stress quotient gets too high.

"She always forces me to look at my problems in new ways. I often think that there are no solutions to my problems, but invariably I'm wrong. Her friendship means everything in the world to me."

The idea of having one really good friend whom you can call when the going gets tough has been pioneered by Alcoholics Anonymous. Often local AA groups will have a buddy system in which all the members have the name and telephone number of someone they can call twenty-four hours a day. Many recovered alcoholics had a buddy who threw them a life preserver when they were about to go under for the third time.

We all need psychological life preservers when the work pressures are mounting. A good friend is about the best insurance policy you can have. We saw many heartwarming situations where colleagues eagerly helped one another. We met three pediatric nurses who have breakfast with one another every Monday morning. "We sit and talk about our weekends, but we also talk about our patients. We work in a tough environment. There are kids with terminal diseases, parents who are extremely worried, and colleagues who demand that we be mentally sharp. But sometimes we don't feel sharp and sometimes we just don't think that we can cope with all the suffering. So one day we decided that we would meet once a week and see if we couldn't assist one another. Last Monday, Jackie told us that she busted up with her boyfriend over the weekend. She was really low. So I agreed to take over her most serious patients. Now next week, depending on how I feel, she may help me out."

Consider professional help.   Many professional helpers find it difficult to ask for help, for "they regard such action as an indication of personal weakness, perhaps even lack of fitness for the profession."[10] Take the case of Father O'Keefe, a parish priest in Philadelphia.

Father O'Keefe's life was his work. He loved it. He was so effective in helping his parishioners solve their problems that his reputation spread to other parishes. Pretty soon he had people from all walks of life and from many different church backgrounds coming to him for help.

Father O'Keefe routinely put in eight hours a day in counseling others and would usually have at least one evening meeting to attend. After his formal day ended he would head for the church's coffeehouse to visit with the teenage crowd.

The long hours began to take their toll. He often found himself snapping in anger at those who disagreed with him. He felt crushed when the parish voted to discontinue support for one of his pet projects. Angrily he lashed out at them in a Sunday morning homily.

As the requests for help poured across his desk, he became cynical about the "picky things people get upset about." At the same time, he lost the healthy detachment from the problems of others. He found himself worrying about a number of teenagers who were on drugs, and when he conducted a funeral for an elderly church member, he broke down and cried uncontrollably shortly before the service was to begin. Increasingly he felt alone and unsupported; he wondered why he had become a parish priest, why he had chosen a life of celibacy.

Late one night after a day filled with people's problems, he had a few drinks and found himself on the floor the next morning. His mind was a blank as to what had happened. He knew that he needed help, but like many professional helpers, could not bring himself to ask for it. "Whom should I turn to?" he asked. "I thought of the bishop, but if I told him my innermost thoughts, any hope of having a larger parish would go down the drain. I thought about going to see another priest. But religious types are the world's worst gossips. The word would have gotten around the diocese that I was having personal problems. I even thought about seeing a psychiatrist. But what if some member of the church saw me? So there was nowhere to go. I drank—and not just in the evening. I lost weight and called in sick. God, I was a basket case. And then I heard that some of the members were asking questions about what was happening to me. The pressure built and somehow I ended up in the hospital. I've been in therapy now for six months and am just now starting to feel like my old self. If only I would have had the courage to ask for help when I needed it."

"I need help" are words foreign to the vocabularies of many in the helping professions. We think that because we have studied other people's problems we should be able to apply such knowledge to ourselves. We fear that others will not be sympathetic. A teacher said, "I wanted to go and talk with the principal and say, 'Look, the kids are driving me up a wall. I need a day or two off.' But I didn't think he would understand." An oncology nurse told us: "I've seen so much death that I wanted to say to the scheduling nurse, 'Please, for God's sake, transfer me to another unit.' But I had second thoughts. They might think that I am unsuited to do *any* kind of nursing."

It is *not* a sign of weakness to ask for help. Such counsel can often produce almost immediate relief. The very act of talking about our problems diminishes their intensity. It changes our perspective on problems that we have viewed in self-defeating ways. New ideas become apparent; new solutions evolve. And finally, remember: "Helpers do not need to be perfect. If they were, there would be very few in the profession."[11]

Part Four
How to Help
Job Burnouts

Chapter Eleven
A Message to Wives, Husbands, Bosses, and Friends

Angelo Marchione and Fred Price went through the Boston Police Academy together. Side by side they sweated out the five-mile runs, watched each other qualify on the pistol range, shared their notes on the legal rights of suspects and prisoners. As rookie cops they went to different precincts, but still stayed close friends.

Six years later Angelo sensed a change: Fred had grown tired, angry, and disillusioned with the department. "Ya gotta relax, Fred, ol' buddy," he told him. "Ya can't take the job so seriously." They even talked about older guys who couldn't handle the stress, cops who had lost their edge, made stupid mistakes, and ended up with routine desk jobs. But Fred couldn't find relief from work stress. He started drinking too much, calling in sick, and taking his frustrations out on his wife and kids.

"The job wore him down," Angelo said later. "I was probably the one person in the department who could have helped him. I tried! My God, how I tried! But either he wouldn't listen or I didn't know what to do. How do you help a guy who's burned out, anyway?"

Like Angelo, hundreds of people ask that same question. For every person who suffers from job burnout, at least a dozen others stand by and watch—often in helplessness. If you're the boss, you may try to intervene, but inadvertently increase the pressure. If you're a husband or wife of a burned-out worker, you can plead and argue without success and even make matters worse. If your friend is suffering from job burnout, you may feel ill equipped to intervene, and do nothing. Most people would like to help; they simply don't know how to go about it. Some even feel they should leave the helping to the experts.

Who Can Help?

In our research, an indisputable fact emerged: people often recovered from job burnout only because *someone helped them.* When burnout sets in, it feels like you're sinking into quicksand. The more you struggle, the faster you sink. You long for someone to reach out, to grab your hand, to pull you to safety. But who? Do you need a psychiatrist? Should you call the family doctor? See a specialist in occupational counseling? Some burnouts will need professional assistance; in most cases it doesn't take an expert. For Betty Janzen, help came in the form of her roommate.

Louise Walker watched Betty go through the honeymoon stage at her new job assisting the director of an alcoholism treatment center. But Betty's boss, although a recovered alcoholic, was still a chronic workaholic. His demands on Betty's time never diminished, and soon the classic burnout symptoms appeared. "I knew what could happen," Louise recalled, "so I just started telling Betty that she was doing herself a disservice by believing there weren't any other jobs in this world. I kept drumming it into her: There *are* other opportunities! There *are* other possibilities! There *are* other options! Pretty soon she started to believe me."

As Betty recalled, "If it wasn't for my roommate, I don't know what would have happened. I was so far down I didn't know which way was up. She listened to me by the hour. I came to realize my boss would never change and so I quit my job, found another, and my whole outlook changed."

For Myron Cooper, escape from the quicksand of job burnout started with his wife. Marge Cooper told us, "Myron felt completely trapped in his job as a real-estate salesman. He was smoking too much, losing sleep, and angry at the world most of the time. We both knew his job would barely make ends meet, and it could go on for the rest of his life. I listened for a long time but finally realized I couldn't help much more.

"One day I said to Myron, 'Why don't you go down and talk to Reverend Jackson about your job?' Now, our minister's not a professional counselor or anything, but he has a lot of good common sense. So Myron went down and pretty soon he was seeing him almost every week.

"Reverend Jackson just listened and listened and listened to how my husband felt. Not once did he blame Myron. Then one day, out of the blue, he says to him, 'Why don't you manage your own agency?' Well, that did it. He just didn't believe it was possible until Reverend Jackson challenged him. Myron started digging up facts, staying up late at night, figuring and figuring. It was like overnight he became a man with a future. He started taking classes in office management."

Today Myron Cooper manages his own agency, works his own hours, and employs the type of people he enjoys working with. As he says philosophically, "I found an out, thanks to my wife and Reverend Jackson."

If you're a boss or colleague, you may provide the essential ingredient for someone to overcome job burnout. When Dr. Freda Alexander took over as principal at Brian Street Elementary School, she soon noticed that Bill Polgar was a less-than-enthusiastic sixth-grade teacher. He looked tired and beaten down as he walked slowly down the school hallway. Checking his personnel file, she discovered that in his ten years at Brian Elementary he had an outstanding record as a teacher. But over the years Bill had been overloaded with after-school duties. He had received little support from a suspicious administration. Long-term stress had brought him slowly but surely to the brink of a burnout crisis.

"I sensed that Bill Polgar had a chip on his shoulder. He needed to hear he was doing a good job," recalled Dr. Alexander. "So I let him know. That was my style anyway. Every chance I got, I'd pass on some parent's comment about his good teaching. I thanked him often for his after-school work. It took months, but after a while it paid off."

If you talk to Bill now, there's a glint in his eye as he enthusiastically talks about the kids in his classroom. And the principal? "She made me feel like Brian Street Elementary School would have to close its doors except for me! I'm sure I would have burned out completely if she hadn't come here when she did."

A roommate, a wife, a minister, a boss—their help was effective because, in addition to good intentions, they had certain skills. Good intentions alone can sometimes add to the stress instead of reduce it. Sheila Barker's husband had the best intentions. When Sheila slipped into a state of emotional exhaustion from her job pressures as a buyer for a furniture store, he wanted to help. Unwittingly, he brought a new pressure into Sheila's life—the pressure to slow down. He kept after her to take time off, to work fewer hours, to rest, to take more time for herself. If she brought work home, because of some deadline pressure at work, he would say, "Why don't you leave that damn work at the office so you can relax while you're at home?" His efforts to help Sheila only delayed her eventual recovery from job burnout.

Effective helping involves a lot more than simply giving advice or lending a friendly ear. It means more than telling someone she is under pressure, the job has become a dead end, or she should take a vacation. Effective helping depends on specific skills, but ones easily within your reach. Let's examine them.

Develop a Helping
Relationship

Here's the single most important advice we can give you for assisting someone who is burning out: *don't try to give help, but try to develop a helping relationship.*

Giving help always carries a hidden danger of making the other person feel helpless. It can undermine his self-confidence. And he needs all of that he can get to cope with his burnout. Giving advice can even imply "You're too stupid to solve your own problems!" And that only erodes self-respect.

A helping relationship involves listening, showing respect, exhibiting deep trust in your friend's capacity to handle work problems. If you concentrate on building a helping relationship, you will avoid jumping to quick conclusions about the problem. The Reverend Mr. Jackson waited for weeks; he didn't blame Myron Cooper, but quietly watered the roots of a helping relationship until it flourished. When he did suggest that Myron consider opening his own real-estate agency, it seemed to Myron as if he had come up with the idea himself. The helping relationship gave him the courage to run with it. Jack Barker, on the other hand, quickly found a pat solution for his wife Sheila's state of emotional exhaustion: rest and relaxation. His quick analysis of the problem led to carping and blame that only intensified the stress for Sheila.

The helping relationship says, "I believe you have the resources within yourself to deal with your problems." That attitude conveys hope to someone who often feels caught in a hopeless situation. It's not unlike the marathon runner who wants to help a novice do well in her first 10,000 meter race. Preaching at the novice to run faster, blaming her for wearing the wrong kind of running shoes, pushing from behind to lengthen her strides, or telling her to quit because she looks tired are all misguided attempts to help. That's the kind of help Jack Barker tried to give his wife. The person who helps the most will simply fall in beside the novice runner, set a steady pace, and run alongside for moral support. Without a word, this kind of action conveys a message of hope: You can do it! I believe in you!

A growing body of scientific evidence has documented the importance of *hope* for surviving and living productively. In a sobering study, Bruno Bettelheim investigated inmates who died in Nazi concentration camps seemingly without physical cause. He found that those inmates who started to believe the guards' predictions that they would never leave the camp except as a corpse died a sudden death.[1]

When animals feel hopeless, they too may die a sudden death. When the tanker *Torrey Canyon* ran aground, it disgorged its oil into the water. People came to pick up the birds and wipe the oil from their wings, but often the birds died in their hands. Some thought that detergent placed in the water caused the sudden deaths. Now at least one scientist is convinced that the birds died "from helplessness produced by the inability of the birds to fly due to the oil."[2]

When hope evaporates and options seem to disappear, lethal results may follow. Of fifty-five individuals who applied for admission into a nursing home, seventeen indicated that they had no alternative but to become a resident. All but one died within ten weeks! On the other hand, only one person among the thirty-eight *who saw an alternative* to going into the same nursing home died during that time period.[3]

In a helping relationship, your optimism transfers, almost by osmosis, to the person who suffers from job burnout. She will begin to feel at a deep level that alternatives exist. The recovery process has then begun. And once the individual feels her internal strength return as she gains control of her life, complete recovery becomes more certain.

Once you've established trust, rapport, and acceptance, you can assess the situation from the other person's point of view. Is your friend burning out from too much work or from too little challenge? Has your husband or wife only begun to feel the symptoms of burnout, or has he or she entered the crisis stage? Does that employee know the major source of unrelieved stress, or does she feel confused about the things that have led to job burnout? A careful diagnosis, made from the perspective of running alongside someone who's burning out, then becomes the basis for giving assistance.

Listen! Listen! Listen!

If you want to help another person, become an active listener. Pay attention to every word, gesture, and facial expression. Listen for the messages hidden between the lines. And when you feel like you've heard it all a dozen times, go right on listening. Nothing seems more difficult; nothing builds a helping relationship so well.

Again and again in our research, burned-out individuals confided that they had not shared their feelings with anybody. No one! Not a wife, husband, friend. Many said that they didn't think others could possibly understand or even want to listen to their problems. A forty-eight-year-old pilot, at the peak of his career, said, "I'm making more money than ever. I have status. I have security. Who could understand my frustrations? If I told anybody, he would think that I had flipped out."

The more acute the burnout, the greater the probability that the individual will feel that "no one understands." This very belief may lead into an isolation cell. Janet Murphy described her husband: "He's a stranger in my house. He gets up, mumbles a few words while gulping down his coffee, then goes to work. He rushes for his scotch and soda the minute he comes home. By early evening it's impossible to carry on a conversation with him."

How can you break through such a barrier of silence? What can you do, if, like Janet's husband, someone near to you has cut himself off from family members, friends, and acquaintances? Janet stumbled across one important principle for helping her husband end his self-imposed silence. She suggested they go see a movie, then stop for pizza on the way home. As they ate, she listened. At first he talked of the movie, then quite naturally turned to his problems. The same thing happened the following weekend after they went to a neighbor's house for supper. "It's funny," she said. "When he's at home he plops down in front of the TV set and doesn't say a word. But when we go out he starts talking about all kinds of important things." Janet had made an important discovery: *certain environments facilitate the honest sharing of feelings.*

A dean of students at a western college always has office hours in the student union. "In that setting the students tell me about what they are *really* thinking." A hospital administrator has a retreat at a plush ski resort each year for his line personnel. "I learn more about what is going on in the hospital by the fireplace or riding the chair lift than I can ever learn in our conference room."

In addition to finding the best time and place for talking, nothing brings someone out of isolation faster than an active listener. Most of us have developed the fine art of halfhearted listening. We've learned to listen to the TV talk show while sewing, reading a book, and carrying on a conversation. We have become experts at "in and out" listening. We tune "in" for a moment of concentration, pick up a few sentences, then tune "out" to read the paper or think about our plans for Saturday night. We have become so accustomed to halfhearted listening that we accept it as normal.

Active listening takes great concentration. But if you listen with your eyes, your ears, your mind, your whole self, it shouts the message: "I'm interested! I want to understand where you're at!"

Active listeners often summarize what the other person has said. This can drastically improve your concentration. John spent five minutes talking about his job, the routine, the boss, and his own lack of challenge. Although tempted to give him advice on how to deal with the job, his wife Marty tried to actively listen. When John paused, she summarized what he had been saying: "You seem to feel trapped in a dull job, and still have to put up with a boss who thinks you ought to be grateful for such a challenging opportunity." Without realizing it, John suddenly thought: "She understands me! Maybe I can risk telling her more about how I feel stuck in this job and how inadequate I am to find anything more challenging." It is this kind of active listening that can help someone leave what Erich Fromm called the prison of aloneness and overcome his separateness from others.[4] As Dr. Elton Mayo said, "One friend, one person who is truly understanding, who takes the trouble to listen to us as we consider our problem, can change our whole outlook on the world."[5]

Ask Questions

You must ask questions if you want to understand what is happening to another person. Often the right question will trigger a whole set of responses. The father of a seventeen-year-old boy said, "We decided to build a sailboat. One night we were struggling with the fit between the centerboard and the hull. Nothing I was doing was making the situation better. Then, without thinking about what I was saying, I half-jokingly said, 'Do you ever feel that you can't do anything right?' Wow—you wouldn't believe what happened. Suddenly I heard his feelings of frustration at not being able to make the basketball team. We kept working on that centerboard, but we were really working on his problems."

You can often start a conversation with someone burning out by asking *information questions*. "What happened at work today?" or "How did the sales meeting go?" will allow someone to talk about nonthreatening events. Some information questions will yield a simple yes or no response. Others can lead to long descriptions of what goes on in the workplace. One of our favorite questions to ask a burned-out person is, "Could you run through the last twenty-four hours and tell us the kinds of things that have happened to you?" Their response often begins with a chronological listing of activities. We try to note areas that seem sensitive or suggest critical problems. Later in the conversation we will return to that sensitive area and probe at greater length.

We suggested this technique to a husband whose wife worked under a great deal of stress. He called the next day to say, "My God, now I realize why she is dragging every night. She goes through more tough problems in one day than I have to face in a month!"

Answers to information questions will give you some of the pieces to the puzzle. Others will come to light when you ask *feeling questions*. Examples of such questions, which tap the frustrations, anger, anxieties, and hopes of the individual, are: "Do you enjoy your job?" "When your boss blew up, what did you feel like doing?" "What feelings do you have when you go to work in the morning?"

Feeling questions tap the inner core of a person's private world. A friend of a physician only had to ask one question that punctured his hard outer shell: "Don't you get tired of listening to everybody's ailments?" Suddenly an avalanche of feelings cascaded out into the open as he described his frustrations in visiting one oncology patient after another.

Asking well-timed information and feeling questions is an art, but one you can easily master. Keep in mind a series of inquiries. Knowing the major kinds of work stress discussed in earlier chapters can offer a springboard into numerous questions. All workers have feelings (good or bad) about their boss, their coworkers, the work that they do, and whether work rewards match their efforts. The more feelings expressed as a result of your questions, the better your understanding of the inner conflicts confronting the individual.

Level

For some people it takes only one or two questions to get them to share their private battles. Others, however, do not take kindly to questions. Marie Rabenherst said, "I married the strong, silent type. You know—never show your feelings. Never cry. Never get emotional. Yet I knew something was bothering my husband deeply. But when I asked, he'd put me down by saying something like 'Oh, nothing for you to get worried about.' He was inscrutable. Yet he was increasingly worried and anxious."

How can you help someone who doesn't want to discuss any part of his problem? He resents your probing. He may even say, as did Marie's husband, "Quit worrying about me. It only makes things worse." His silence can mask a smoldering rage. His frustrations are like unguarded explosives. Your questions seem aimed at igniting the fuse.

If someone locks you out completely, you may have to accept the fact that you cannot help in a direct fashion. Continue to give support; maintain a helping relationship; recognize that each person has the right to control his own life.

However, *leveling* does offer an effective strategy with some people. To level means to make a direct statement about how you feel in the impasse situation. Leveling places a mirror to someone so he can see himself. It's as if you intentionally light the fuse that allows for a controlled explosion that will harm no one.

"One evening while finishing dinner," said Marie Rabenherst, "I asked my husband a whole bunch of things. I really wanted him to open up. So I asked him how things were going at work and what he wanted to do on vacation and whether he ever thought about taking a different kind of job. All I got was the cold shoulder.

"Finally I said, 'Do you want to hear what *I* think about you and what you're doing to your family?' He seemed startled and responded defensively by saying, 'Sure—go right ahead. Everybody else is taking potshots at me.' I felt myself get flushed but I regained my composure and said, 'Look, I don't want to add to your problems. I thought maybe I could help.' Well, that seemed to simmer him down and we started talking. I tried to be as honest as I could.

" 'I feel cut off from whatever is bothering you. I've sat by for months and watched you lose all the sparkle in your life!' Suddenly I looked at him and saw tears welling up in his eyes. I stopped talking. He smiled a bit and told me that I probably knew him too well! We started laughing because we do know each other well. And then he told me about how his promotion fell through and that the handwriting was on the wall as to his future in the company. Suddenly it was out in the open. He felt better and so did I. We started to make some plans."

As with asking questions, effective leveling is an art. You must use it carefully to avoid two dangers. The first uses leveling as an excuse to attack. Without realizing it, you have been collecting real and/or imagined grievances against the person for weeks, months, or even years. Suddenly at a critical time when you want to help, leveling becomes a chance to get rid of *your* frustrations rather than *his.* When this type of leveling is used, the results are usually destructive. People become defensive and outright conflict usually follows.

The other extreme comes if you level in a halfhearted, indirect manner; you're "walking on eggshells." You secretly hope to avoid any explosion, to keep from offending the other person. Halfhearted leveling stems from fear; it is almost always ineffective and can make the problem worse rather than better.

To avoid both destructive and halfhearted leveling, *talk only about the here-and-now.* Examples of here-and-now leveling are:

1. "You seldom have anything good to say about your job. Is everything going OK at work?" (Husband to wife)

2. "You seem to be a bit irritated lately with me and the kids. Are we doing something that is bothering you or is something else the matter?" (Wife to husband)
3. "We've worked together now for four years and have always gotten along well. But for some reason I think we are getting on one another's nerves lately. Do you feel that way?" (Worker to worker)
4. "You've always been so efficient. But lately I have noticed that we are falling behind in our correspondence. Is everything OK?" (Boss to secretary)
5. "When you have a few minutes, I would like to talk with you about my workload and the increased demands on my time." (Worker to foreman)

Listening, questioning, and leveling all aim to help the individual verbalize her frustrations. The very act of talking about her problems opens the release valve to the human pressure cooker. Slowly the destructive forces begin to escape.

Plan Ahead

You can help a person move out of his burned-out state by encouraging him to plan for the future. We can all minimize stressful events by preparing for them. Every college teacher can identify students who have mastered the art of planning for examination week. Some students come to their final examinations with little sign of distress. They planned from the beginning of the semester, then kept up their assignments, read their textbooks. Others come to the final exam tense, with dark circles under their eyes, feeling the full stress of the test.

Anyone who can look ahead and say, "Boy, that's going to be a rough week (or month or year), I'd better plan for it," has headed off a stress attack. Those who simply plunge blindly ahead will suffer the consequences. Try to get into clear focus how the burned-out person sees the immediate future. If she anticipates an easier schedule, help her to capitalize on her freedom. Suggest she avoid the temptation to fill her calendar simply because the schedule is less demanding. On the other hand, if the next couple of weeks will bring great pressures, help her to identify ways that she can make those weeks as tolerable as possible.

One of the best examples of how planning can bring a sense of stability was given to us by the wife of a tax accountant. "For the first nine years of our marriage, the months of January through April were horrendous. During the first two weeks of April, I thought my husband would lose his mind. Everyone wanted to see him in order to meet the April fifteenth tax deadline. One Christmas I mentioned how I dreaded the next four months. He agreed. We started to plan ahead. He brought his calendar home. We scheduled some evenings for the family. Then he crossed out one Friday in every month that was going to be a long weekend for the two of us. All we did was make some simple adjustments in his calendar, but it was one of the best things we have ever done. And it didn't cost us many clients. In fact, he told me that he was feeling so much more relaxed about things that he was getting more referrals than ever."

Dr. Alaman Magid, a San Diego psychiatrist, assists patients under stress with a set of techniques he calls "Time Therapy," based on written goals. "I zero in on three kinds of time: work, leisure, and health time. Patients write out their goals and I program the goals with a form of self-hypnosis in which each day, before getting out of bed, they visualize what the whole day is going to be like. It's like transcendental meditation, but this can take as little as five minutes."[6]

It is important for burnout victims to set *realistic* goals. To do otherwise only heightens frustration. You may recall Dr. Brian Simpson, the college history professor from an earlier chapter. Bored by the courses he taught, angry at the apathy of the students, upset by the dean who gave him too much work to do, Brian had an advanced case of job burnout. In trying to come to grips with his situation, Dr. Simpson, with the aid of a concerned friend, wrote the following goals. It marked the beginning of his recovery from burnout.

Within two months, Dr. Simpson had had productive meetings with the dean of the college and with his students. Together with his wife he

I. Work Goals

1. Set aside 8:00–10:00 A.M. to prepare for my classes. Do not allow interruptions.

2. Invite my students for supper in my home. Try to get to know each student by name.

3. Read the student evaluations of my courses. Share the evaluations with Jim Hardgrove and determine what I can do to improve my teaching.

4. Talk with the dean about next year's teaching load.

II. Leisure Goals

1. Subscribe to *Fishing Facts* and *Sports Illustrated*.

2. Read a novel during the month.

3. Invite Chuck and Grace to our home for a long weekend this spring.

4. Begin planning the family vacation.

III. Health Goals

1. No longer skip breakfast.

2. Walk twenty minutes each evening.

3. Play racquetball at least twice during the month.

planned an exciting family vacation. His evening walk brought new energy and he renewed an old friendship while playing racquetball. But, work goal number 3 became the major key to his recovery.

Jim Hardgrove, a crusty, slightly cynical, but absolutely charming biology professor, had fought all the wars in academia for almost forty years. He had taught veterans in the forties, the silent generation of the fifties, war resisters in the sixties, and now the apathetic students of the seventies.

As Brian Simpson shared his frustrations, the elder colleague listened with great intent. A deep understanding grew, the kind that only comes when one shares his weaknesses with another person. They laughed about their similar struggle, and Brian choked up when he talked about his sense of failure. But Brian felt that someone whom he deeply respected had understood his problems. Now they talk at least once a month. The elder professor, acting like a senior statesman, has a sense of pride, knowing that his junior colleague trusts his judgment. And Brian has the benefit of the wisdom of someone who knows exactly what he is going through.

Although there is no single best strategy for helping someone to recover from job burnout, sometimes an effective beginning is to help the person *regain control over her leisure time.* "There isn't much I can do about work," said a twenty-three-year-old hospital laboratory technician, "but there is a lot I can do about the sixteen hours that I'm away from it."

In helping people find new options, suggest that they reexamine their leisure activities. Often they will first want to talk about their problems at work, but eventually you may discover they have lost the joy of swinging a golf club, reading a novel, walking in the woods, sewing a new dress, or spending an evening with friends. Your objective will be to help them make contact with *past* joys and connect them with *future* joys.

A pharmacist on the verge of suicide recovered within a year. If you were to see him today you would barely recognize him in contrast to his burned-out state of a year ago. "I will never forget last Thanksgiving. I felt like a complete failure. I was barely holding my own financially and, what was worse, I was bored to death. Then I started to rethink a few of my values. I lowered my expectations. I changed a few things at work. But most importantly, I started doing something that I hadn't done in years. Every Saturday morning I now get up at four-thirty A.M., stop for breakfast, then drive to Forest Lake as the sun rises. I'm out in the fishing boat just as daylight can be seen. It's beautiful. Often I'm the only one out on the lake. Somehow my work problems don't seem quite so bad on Monday morning."

Search for an Achilles' Heel

Like Achilles, most of us have a particular point of vulnerability to stress. Achilles, the hero of Homer's *Iliad,* had great strength except for the weakness of his heel. Paris, his enemy, shot an arrow that fatally wounded Achilles by piercing his heel. If you can help a burned-out individual find his point of weakness, his Achilles' heel, you can then help him develop strategies of protection. For one person it might come from constant telephone interruptions; another might find he has so little actual work to do that time drags. Still another person's point of vulnerability may come from an over-critical boss. Let's look at one example in detail. One widespread problem for white collar workers is *meetings.*

In a survey conducted by Alec Mackenzie and Associates, executives from nine nations including the U.S. stated that meetings were the fourth biggest time waster of all. The other three were telephone interruptions, drop-in visitors, and ineffective delegation of responsibilities. Professor Henry Mintzberg of McGill University has noted that on the average, 60 percent of the executive's time is spent in meetings with two or more people.[7]

We are a nation of meetings. Government, business, and educational institutions have created ad hoc committee meetings, standing committee meetings, informational meetings, advisory meetings, and problem-solving meetings. We even have committees formed only to find members for other committees. The landslide of committee meetings keeps people from completing their work, creates boredom, and often leads to needless interpersonal conflict.

The problem comes with unnecessary meetings and meetings that are run inefficiently. When an employee suddenly finds himself going from one meeting to another, fully aware that he would rather work on other tasks, the individual becomes angry. "I feel powerless to call a stop to all this committee nonsense," said one social worker. "I'm burned out on meetings!" It's hardly a wonder that researchers have found that with frequent meetings, employees develop negative and dehumanized attitudes.[8]

If you suspect that someone is vulnerable to too many meetings, ask to go over his calendar with him. Ask him to evaluate whether every scheduled and unscheduled meeting he had during the previous week was necessary. Then examine the following week's calendar and ask the same question. Gradually he will begin to see that the more time he spends in meetings, the less productive time he will have for himself.

Janet Kriften, a frustrated executive, was amazed at how many hours she was spending in unproductive and unnecessary meetings. But she took corrective action that quickly changed the situation. The first meetings that she cut out were those that were routinely scheduled but that did not need to be held. Then she carefully examined the agenda of other meetings and only went to those where she could make a contribution. Before scheduling staff meetings, she would ask: "Does this meeting really have to be held?" By asking that question she eliminated 50 percent of the meetings in her department. When she did schedule a meeting, however, everyone knew that it was going to be an important one. They seldom missed. In fact, they looked forward to the meetings, for they knew that there would be productive outcomes.

Give TLC (Tender Loving Care)

No matter what suggestions you may give to a burned-out person, always make certain that *tender loving care informs your advice.* A kind word, a reassuring glance, a gentle touch—these say, "I value you for yourself." Tender loving care remains the most powerful healing medicine for job burnouts.

TLC can do much to counterbalance the lack of support most people find in the workplace itself. As the Swiss psychiatrist Paul Tournier has noted: "A worker can spend years in a factory, shop or office, without meeting anyone who takes the slightest interest in him as a person. The daily routine, together with the prevailing atmosphere of our times, make it possible for him to associate with companions whom he really does not know and who do not know him."[9]

Tender loving care has a direct influence on our health and ability to cope with job-related stress. Quite by accident, researchers in Ohio State University discovered that rabbits that were touched, fondled, and talked to had far less chance of developing arteriosclerosis as compared with rabbits treated as experimental subjects.[10] Studies of individuals who have lost their jobs demonstrate that if workers receive support from family members and friends, they can survive and move into another era in their lives. If, however, workers do not have such support systems, the news that they will lose their job will cost them dearly in terms of their physical and mental health.

But how does one give tender loving care? The answer rests, in part, in the suggestions given in this chapter. Show interest, listen, develop a helping relationship, ask questions, express your feelings honestly, help the person set goals. These all demonstrate your support. In addition, however, we must develop a new ethic of concern for our colleagues as we work side by side on the assembly line, in the office, and the boardroom.

Fortunately, a new breed of managers has begun to understand that good worker morale means good business. Nic Braston, a strapping, two-hundred-pound vice-president of a hospital corporation, has a reputation for tough, no-nonsense management. His steel-blue eyes seem to look right through you as he talks. The bottom line for Nic is the monthly profit-and-loss column. Yet on the third afternoon of every month, he sits down with subordinates without any agenda. "I look at them and see how they walk into my office. If something is bothering them I ask them to get it out in the open. If they are screwing up I tell them. But most of all I keep telling them that I am glad that they are working with me. Everybody feels better after those meetings. We are always more like a team." Nic has never had a personnel administration course in his life. Yet he has learned a powerful management principle: Subordinates function more productively if they are given support and help on their work-related problems.

Can tender loving care be given by bosses in the competitive world of business? The answer is a resounding yes. You can give support in many ways that will help employees *and* the employer. Often the quickest way to help a burned-out worker is to change his work routine. Ask him to work on a new project or have him develop a new proposal. If he is overwhelmed by paperwork, assign it temporarily to someone else. If the worker has lost creativity, put him in contact with someone who overflows with enthusiasm. If he is good at a particular task, free him from other responsibilities so he can find satisfaction in what he does best. And, like Dr. Alexander, the principal at Brian Street Elementary School, don't hesitate to tell the workers they are doing a good job. Hardly a worker exists who doesn't want to hear that from his boss.

Make Use of Resources

You are not alone in your efforts to help the person suffering from job burnout. If you want to help someone drowning at an ocean beach, take a few seconds to look for backup support before you dive in the water. Your deep concern and the immediate crisis can cause you to ignore the life preserver hanging on the pier, the lifeguard sitting in a nearby tower, the group of swimming instructors playing volleyball on the beach, and the local first-aid station with resuscitation equipment. But your success in rescuing a drowning victim could well depend on making full use of all these resources. The same is true for burnout.

Begin by using the most readily available resources. For example, you might give this book to the person caught under the burden of work stress. Tell her, "Here's a book that I found useful. After you read it, I'd really like to talk together about some of the ideas it discusses." It could serve as a life preserver, helping the person to stay afloat until the lifeguard rows out and helps her into a boat.

Try to find other books and pamphlets on work stress, career renewal, and job opportunities. Ask the local librarian for references to books in this area. You might look through the *Reader's Guide to Periodical Literature* in your local library for topics like "stress," "burnout," and "career." This might lead to brief articles on specific fields like "teacher burnout" or "executive burnout." Check your local bookstore, which will probably have a section of books on career development and job opportunities. If a nearby bookstore doesn't stock such books, call the college or university bookstore in your town and continue your search there. Look through the reference notes at the end of this book, which list many additional sources of information on job burnout.

A word of warning: *Don't overwhelm the person you hope to assist with too much information.* A single book or well-chosen article is more likely to be read than a pile of books and pamphlets. Read the material yourself to improve your understanding of work stress and job burnout, but use it selectively with your friend or spouse.

Many work organizations offer a variety of resources. In several school districts "teacher burnout resource centers" provide reading material as well as counseling help. We know of at least one church that has a regular "job-transition support group." Each week people from the community meet to discuss their work problems, how to deal with stress, and how to renew their careers. With a few telephone calls you might discover a similar group in your city or town.

Employee-assistance programs are now available in many companies. Ten years ago, fewer than 300 firms offered any help beyond a nurse who handed out Bandaids, aspirin, and recorded the absences of workers. Today there are over 2,400 employee-assistance programs, including those located in some of the *Fortune* 500's most prestigious companies: General Mills, Control Data, Minnesota Mining and Manufacturing, and General Motors.[11] Even smaller firms have such programs. For example, at the Tennat Company of Minneapolis, a manufacturer of floor-maintenance products with about 1,000 employees, approximately 30 employees a year will use their assistance program to help solve personal problems, such as alcoholism, family conflict, and problems arising at work.

Many corporations now recognize that giving assistance is in the best interest of the company. Bob Jones of the Control Data Corporation's personnel office puts it this way: "Say you have an employee and you're paying him $10,000 a year for 10 years. That's $100,000 you've invested in him and that doesn't even count all the training and insurance and other benefits. Some employee relations people say that would bring it up to $200,000. Now, if that employee started missing work, the manager typically would raise hell, and if you let it run, the employee's work keeps deteriorating and finally you have to fire him or he quits, and there goes your investment. But if you had a computer worth about $100,000 and one day it started making mistakes, you wouldn't get rid of it, would you? You'd call in an engineer to look it over and see what's wrong and you'd be willing to spend a lot to get it fixed and save your investment."[12]

"What we are learning," said the director of an employee-assistance program in a large university, "is that you shouldn't punish people when they are having problems. When you punish them you only add to your own problems. They will miss more work, they will be tardy more often, and they will be more inefficient."

In every community, agencies exist that specialize in helping people. Some will charge you for their services, but most will not if you are unable to pay. There are agencies designed for people who are at a dead end in their career and who want career counseling. There are agencies that will help those who have turned to alcohol as an escape from their problems. And there are usually a host of agencies that can help with family problems, including separation and divorce. These agencies are at your doorstep. They have highly competent staff who chose their careers because they care about people struggling with life's problems. They can offer assistance to you as well as to the burnout victim you want to help. You can find a listing of such agencies in the white pages of most telephone books under the county's community service programs.

Postscript: Take
Care of Yourself

Conversations with burned-out people are emotionally draining. The very act of helping another person transfers your strength to the depleted well of the other person. Unless you take care of yourself, you can end up exhausted and emotionally spent.

The best way to maintain your own strength and vitality is to keep your identity separate from the person you help. The better you feel about your own life, the better your ability to give assistance. When Dr. Brian Simpson reached the depth of his despair, Mrs. Simpson rekindled an old hobby of making pottery. She also started to take twenty-minute walks in the evening, and to do volunteer work in the community hospital. "I love him," she told us, "but I had to get away from him once in a while. I was determined not to let his depression become my depression."

In *The Prophet,* Kahlil Gibran stated that the cyprus and the oak must not grow too close together. They would then stifle one another and neither could grow and soar to the heavens. It's wise advice to ponder—particularly when trying to help someone else.

The National Job Burnout Survey

The scientific study of job burnout has only recently begun. Scholars in many fields have started to examine the way jobs create stress. The National Institute of Occupational Safety and Health has initiated a study of job stress in the last few years. The search goes on—to identify the symptoms of burnout, to plot the stages of burnout, to discover better ways to cope with burnout, and to redesign the structure of work.

You can help. More information is needed. This national job burnout survey will broaden our understanding of the problem. It can provide new insights on how you cope with stress, how people in different occupations solve the problem of job burnout.

You can also benefit from answering these survey questions. By filling out the national job burnout survey on the following pages, you will discover some things about your job. It can help you take a stress inventory. It can give you ideas about how to deal with stress and how to keep from burning out yourself.

THE NATIONAL JOB BURNOUT QUESTIONNAIRE

The purpose of this questionnaire is to better understand work stress and how it affects the health of workers. We want to know how people like yourself have learned to cope with job pressures.

This questionnaire is for people in every occupation. We hope to hear from welders, college professors, housewives, students, bank clerks, farmers, bus drivers, corporation presidents, and people in all the 30,000 occupations.

You don't have to be burned out to answer these questions. In fact, if you cope well with stress, you can help us understand the most important issue—how to survive!

You may answer this questionnaire anonymously; you don't need to sign it or give us your address. Clip out these pages or make a copy of the questionnaire, answer the questions, then mail to:

The National Job Burnout Survey
Dr. James Spradley
Department of Anthropology
Macalester College
St. Paul, Minnesota   55105

The answers to all questions are *voluntary*. If you don't want to answer a question, feel free to skip it and go on to the next one. The answers will be kept *confidential*. We will not identify individuals or where they work.

PART ONE

Answer the following questions briefly, or circle the appropriate response.

1. What is the title of your present occupation (or if unemployed, the last occupation you held)?

2. How long have you worked in that position? ___ years
3. How long have you spent in each of the following types of employment?

	10 years or more	6–9 years	2–5 years	1 year or less	never employed in this field
Executive or manager	1	2	3	4	5
Professional	1	2	3	4	5
Salesperson	1	2	3	4	5
Foreman or skilled worker	1	2	3	4	5
Housewife	1	2	3	4	5
Clerical worker	1	2	3	4	5
Semiskilled or unskilled	1	2	3	4	5
Other ___	1	2	3	4	5

Place a number beside each of the following items according to the following scale:

1 — **strongly agree**
2 — **agree**
3 — **neither agree nor disagree**
4 — **disagree**
5 — **strongly disagree**

___ 4. All in all, I am satisfied with my job.

___ 5. Doing my job well gives me a good feeling.

___ 6. If I were free to go into any type of work, I would choose my present job.

___ 7. My work is interesting.

___ 8. I feel bored with my work most of the time.

___ 9. If a friend were interested in a job like mine, I would encourage him/her.

___10. If I had enough money to live comfortably for the rest of my life, I would continue to work.

___11. If I had enough money to live comfortably for the rest of my life, I would continue to work at my present job.

___12. On most days, time drags on the job.

___13. I often feel trapped in my present job.

___14. In general I don't like my job.

___15. My job requires that I keep learning new things.

___16. My job requires that I work very fast.

___17. What I do at work is more important to me than the money I earn.

___18. My job requires that I work very hard.

___19. I have a lot to say about what happens on my job.

20. Have you ever burned out from job stress?   ___ yes
                                                ___ no

21. How long after your present job began did you start to experience symptoms of burnout?

   ___ by end of first month

   ___ by end of first year

   ___ by end of third year

   ___ after five years

   ___ other _____

22. On the following scale, indicate by circling a number where you feel you are:

0	1	2	3	4	5	6	7	8	9	10

not   **completely**
burned ————————————————————————— **burned**
out   **out**

23. Before you read this book, how much knowledge did you have

about work stress, job burnout, and how to cope with it? (Circle a number.)

0	1	2	3	4	5	6	7	8	9	10
none					some					a great deal

24. Job burnout often goes through stages. Indicate which stage you feel you are in:

    ___ **Stage One:** My job is exciting and I have no burnout symptoms.

    ___ **Stage Two:** Occasionally I am under stress but don't feel burned out. I don't always have as much energy as I once did.

    ___ **Stage Three:** I am definitely burning out and have one or more symptoms of burnout, such as emotional exhaustion or physical symptoms.

    ___ **Stage Four:** Burnout has reached a crisis stage. I am obsessed with work frustrations. I think my job is bad for me. The symptoms of burnout that I'm experiencing won't go away.

    ___ **Stage Five:** I am in need of help. I feel completely burned out. I'm completely devastated by job burnout and I often wonder if I can go on.

    ___ **Other:** (explain) _____

    _____

25. Read each of the following symptoms that can signal job burnout. Place a number before each one according to the following scale:

    0 – **I have not experienced this**
    1 – **Mild**
    2 – **Moderate**
    3 – **Severe**

    ___ I feel emotionally and physically exhausted.

    ___ I can't enjoy my leisure.

    ___ I have lost my efficiency on the job.

    ___ I feel jaded and lack interest in my work.

____I have trouble getting to sleep.

____I have trouble waking up.

____I get headaches.

____I get neck aches.

____I have shoulder aches.

____My eyes itch.

____I have lost my appetite.

____I have shortness of breath.

____I experience nausea.

____I feel dizzy.

____I have stomach upset.

____I have a drinking problem.

____I smoke too much.

____I get frequent backaches.

____I have ulcers.

____I have colitis.

____I get constipated.

____I get canker sores.

____I get frequent colds.

____I have high blood pressure.

____My heart skips beats.

____My heart races.

26. What level of formal education do you have?

____none

____grades 1–7

____grade 8

____grades 9–11

____grade 12

____some college without degree

____a college degree

____graduate or professional education

27. What is your age?_____
28. What is your annual income before taxes?_____
29. Do you work full time or part time?_____
30. Are you self-employed?_____
31. What is your sex: male_____ female_____
32. What is your marital status?

   ____single
   ____married
   ____living together
   ____separated
   ____divorced
   ____widowed

PART TWO
Open-Ended Questions

In this part of the questionnaire, we would like to have your ideas and opinions on a number of questions. We suggest that you answer these questions on a separate sheet of paper. We are interested in how you feel and what you think about your job, about work stress, and about job burnout. We encourage you to answer these questions in as much detail as you can.

1. Describe the three most stressful things about your job.
2. How would you feel if you had to continue working at your present job for the rest of your life?
3. In general, how do you feel about your job? What do you like or dislike about the work you do?
4. Could you describe the kind of work you do? Tell us about a typical day at the job.
5. Could you give us an example of a particularly difficult day or a stressful experience connected with work?

6. Could you describe how you feel after a particularly stressful day on the job?

7. Many people describe their work as "a dead-end job." If you think you are in a dead-end job, can you tell us what it is about your job that contributes to this feeling?

8. Many people have to juggle work responsibilities with housework, going to school, family life, and even a second job. Could you describe the way your job affects these other aspects of your life?

9. Have you ever felt "burned out" from the pressures and problems of your present work or any other job? Could you describe your experience of being burned out? What were your symptoms?

10. Have you ever recovered from job burnout? What did you do to feel better? How long did it take? Could you describe your recovery?

11. Could you list and explain all the ways you have found to effectively reduce stress or release tensions, both on and off the job?

12. On the basis of your own experience, what advice can you give to people under considerable work stress or burning out from their job?

13. Is there anything else about your job, working conditions, work stress, or coping with pressures that you would like to tell us?

Mail your completed answers to:

The National Job Burnout Survey
Dr. James Spradley
Department of Anthropology
Macalester College
St. Paul, Minnesota   55105

Notes

Chapter One: What Is Job Burnout?

1. Our own work on stress and occupations covers many topics and our results have been published in a variety of books and periodicals. The study of Peace Corps volunteers–James P. Spradley and Mark Phillips, "Culture and Stress: A Quantitative Analysis," *American Anthropologist* 74 (1972): 518–529. The work with skid-row bums and police department problems–James P. Spradley, *You Owe Yourself a Drunk: An Ethnography of Urban Nomads* (Boston: Little, Brown, 1970). *See also* James P. Spradley, "Public Health Services and the Culture of Skid Row Bums," *Proceedings of Conference on Public Inebriates,* National Institute on Alcohol and Alcohol Abuse (Washington, D.C.: U.S. Government Printing Office, 1975): 1–19. Research on women's occupations–James P. Spradley and Brenda Mann, *The Cocktail Waitress: Woman's Work in a Man's World* (New York: John Wiley & Sons, 1975). An intensive study of family stress and coping–Thomas S. Spradley and James P. Spradley, *Deaf Like Me* (New York: Random House, 1978). Articles by Robert L. Veninga focusing on stressful organizational problems confronting health professionals–"The Management of Disruptive Conflict in Hospitals," *Hospital and Health Service Administration* (Spring 1979): 8–29; "The Management of Change in Health Agencies," *Public Health Reports* (March–April 1975): 149–153; "Defensive Behavior: Causes, Effects, and Cures," *Journal of Environmental Health* (July–August 1974): 5–8; "Communications: A Patient's Eye View," *American Journal of Nursing* (February 1973): 320–322.

2. The etymology of the term *burnout* is unclear. *Webster's Third New International Dictionary* defines the verb *burn out* as "to fail, wear out, or become exhausted by reason of excessive demands on energy, strength, or

resources." *Burnout* is a word commonly used by teenagers to describe someone who is atypical and out of step with his peers. It may also be used to describe one who habitually uses drugs (even marijuana), or someone who has been "fried" by an overdose of drugs. When used by adults, the term *burnout* usually refers to someone who has lost vitality, the ability to cope with everyday pressures, and the ability to function effectively and efficiently.

A wealth of studies is available to help the reader understand the burnout syndrome, or some aspect of it. Edwin Locke notes that 3,350 articles, books, and dissertations have been published to date on topics related to job satisfaction. Among the articles that we found particularly helpful are the following:

   a. Stanislav V. Kasl, "Mental Health and Work Environment: An Examination of the Evidence," *Journal of Occupational Medicine* 15, no. 6 (June 1973): 509–518.
   b. Phyllis Lehmann, "Job Stress: Hidden Hazard," *Job Safety and Health* 2, no. 4 (April 1974): 4–10.
   c. David Coburn, "Job-Worker Incongruence: Consequences for Health," *Journal of Health and Social Behavior* 15 (1975): 198–212.
   d. Cary L. Cooper and John Crump, "Prevention of and Coping with Occupational Stress," *Journal of Occupational Medicine* 10, no. 6 (June 1978): 420–426.
   e. Lennart Levi, M.D., "Occupational Mental Health: Its Monitoring, Protection, and Promotion," *Journal of Occupational Medicine* 21, no. 1 (January 1979): 26–32.

Among the studies reported in the popular press that are particularly relevant to the concept of burnout are:

   a. Patricia A. Renwick, Edward E. Lawler, and the *Psychology Today* staff, "What You Really Want from Your Job," *Psychology Today* (May 1978): 53–66.
   b. "The Playboy Report on American Men," *Playboy* (March 1979): 89–94, 232, 235–237.

3. Carroll M. Brodsky, M.D., "Long-term Work Stress in Teachers and Prison Guards," *Journal of Occupational Medicine* 19, no. 2 (February 1977): 133–138.
4. Carla Marie Rupp, "Press Stresses Aired at ANPA Encounter," *Editor and Publisher* 110 (30 April 1977): 15.
5. J. R. P. French and R. D. Caplan, "Organizations Stress and Individual Strain," in *The Failure of Success,* ed. A. J. Marrow (New York: AMACOM, 1972), pp. 30–66.
6. James Robins, "Firms Try Newer Way to Slash Absenteeism as Carrot and Stick Fail," *Wall Street Journal,* 14 March 1979.

7. Jim Hampton, "Stress: A Little Helps, But Too Much Is Disabling," *National Observer* 1, 8 February 1975.
8. *Minneapolis Star,* 23 July 1979.
9. National Commission on Working Women, news release (Washington, D.C.: 23 April 1979).
10. Among the scholarly papers that have focused attention on the burnout syndrome are:
    a. Herbert J. Freudenberger, "Staff Burn-out," *Journal of Social Issues* 30, no. 1 (1975): 159–165.
    b. Herbert J. Freudenberger, *The Staff Burn-out Syndrome,* Drug Abuse Council, Washington, D.C. (1975).
    c. Christina Maslach, "Burned-out," *Human Behavior* 5 (September 1976): 16–22.
    d. Robert Kahn, "Job Burnout: Prevention and Remedies," *Public Welfare* (Spring 1978): 61–63.
    e. A. Pines and Christina Maslach, "Characteristics of Staff Burnout in Mental Health Settings," *Hospital and Community Psychiatry* 29, no. 4 (April 1978): 233–237.
    f. Seymour Shubin, "Burnout: The Professional Hazard You Face in Nursing," *Nursing 78* 8, no. 7 (July 1978): 22–27.
    g. Robert L. Veninga, "Administrator Burnout: Causes and Cures," *Hospital Progress* (February 1979).
    One of the best reviews of the vast literature on stress, jobs, and the psychological and physiological symptoms is edited by Cary L. Cooper and Roy Payne: *Stress at Work* (New York: John Wiley & Sons, 1978).

Chapter Two: The Stress Response

1. Sally Reed, "Teacher 'Burnout' a Growing Hazard," *New York Times,* 7 January 1979.
2. Jeffrey Elliot, "The Roots of Alex Haley's Writing Career," *Writer's Digest* (August 1980): 20.
3. W. B. Cannon, *Bodily Changes in Pain, Hunger, Fear, and Rage,* 2nd ed. (New York: Appleton, 1929), p. 27.
4. Hans Selye, M.D., *Stress Without Distress* (New York: McGraw-Hill, 1969), p. 4.
5. Phyllis Lehmann, "Job Stress: Hidden Hazard," *Job, Safety and Health* 2, no. 4 (April 1974): 5.
6. S. Cobb and R. M. Rose, "Hypertension, Peptic Ulcer, and Diabetes in Air Traffic Controllers," *Journal of the American Medical Association* 224 (1973): 489–492.
7. David A. Hamburg, "The Relevance of Recent Evolutionary Changes to

Human Stress Biology," in *Social Life of Early Man,* ed. S. L. Washburn, Viking Fund Publication in Anthropology (1961): 284.

8. John R. P. French and Robert D. Caplan, "Psychosocial Factors in Coronary Heart Disease," *Industrial Medicine* 39, no. 9 (September 1979): 31–45. *See also* James House, "Occupational Stress and Coronary Heart Disease: A Review and Theoretical Integration," *Journal of Health and Social Behavior* 15 (March 1974): 13–27.

9. Joe Blade, "'Blues' of the Job Collaring Many," *Minneapolis Star,* 2 May 1977.

10. The work of Dr. Thomas Holmes and his colleagues has been published in numerous places. One of the original reports that discusses the methodology and outcome is Thomas H. Holmes and Richard Rahe, "The Social Readjustment Rating Scale," *Journal of Psychosomatic Research* 11 (1967): 213–217.

11. Robert P. Quinn and Graham L. Staines, *The 1977 Quality of Employment Survey,* Survey Research Center, University of Michigan, Ann Arbor (1979): 2–5.

12. Letty Cottin Pogrebin, "Stress on the Job," *Ladies' Home Journal* 94 (6 September 1977): 31–32.

Chapter Three: Stages of Job Burnout

1. Robert P. Quinn and Graham L. Staines, *The 1977 Quality of Employment Survey,* Survey Research Center, University of Michigan, Ann Arbor (1979): 216–217.

2. Kenneth Larsen, *The Workers* (New York: Bantam, 1971), p. 50.

3. Joe Blade, "'Blues' of the Job Collaring Many," *Minneapolis Star,* 2 May 1977.

4. Quinn and Staines, p. 56.

5. Patricia A. Renwick, Edward E. Lawler and the *Psychology Today* staff, "What You Really Want from Your Job," *Psychology Today* (May 1978): 55.

6. Phyllis Lehmann, "Job Stress: Hidden Hazard," *Job, Safety and Health* 2, no. 4 (April 1974): 8.

7. Jack Anderson, "Crew Fatigue Imperils Airliners," *St. Paul Dispatch,* 20 March 1979.

8. Quinn and Staines, p. 51.

9. Ibid., p. 9.

10. Ibid.

11. Herbert J. Freudenberger, *The Staff Burn-out Syndrome,* Drug Abuse Council, Washington, D.C. (1975): 13–14.

12. Quinn and Staines, p. 235.

13. Gerald Fisher, interview, *U.S. News and World Report* (6 November 1978): 66.
14. Renwick et al., p. 60.
15. Quinn and Staines, p. 235.
16. Christina Maslach, "Burned-out," *Human Behavior* 5 (September 1976): 19.
17. Lehmann, p. 10.
18. Carroll M. Brodsky, M.D., "Long-term Work Stress in Teachers and Prison Guards," *Journal of Occupational Medicine* 19, no. 2 (February 1977): 136.
19. Seymour Shubin, "Burnout: The Professional Hazard You Face in Nursing," *Nursing 78* 8, no. 7 (July 1978): 24.
20. Brodsky, pp. 133–138.
21. Ibid., p. 135.
22. James P. Spradley, *You Owe Yourself a Drunk: An Ethnography of Urban Nomads* (Boston: Little, Brown, 1970).

Chapter Four: Taking Control of Job Burnout

1. Suzi Ehrman, "Lord of the Rings: An Ethnography of a Directory Assistance Operator" (unpublished paper, Macalester College, St. Paul, Minnesota, 1977).
2. "Ma Bell's Family Lets Off Steam over Pressures," *Minneapolis Star,* 15 June 1979.
3. There is a large literature on cognitive-behavior therapy. For an introduction to this approach as well as a guide to other references, *see* A. T. Beck, *Cognitive Therapy and Emotional Disorders* (New York: International Universities Press, 1976); and Albert Ellis and R. A. Harper, *A New Guide to Rational Living* (Englewood Cliffs, N.J.: Prentice-Hall, 1975).
4. Albert Ellis, "What People Can Do for Themselves to Cope with Stress," in *Stress at Work,* ed. Cary L. Cooper and Roy Payne (New York: John Wiley & Sons, 1978), p. 221.
5. Robert P. Quinn and Graham L. Staines, *The 1977 Quality of Employment Survey,* Survey Research Center, University of Michigan, Ann Arbor (1979): 277.
6. Darrell Sifford, "Some Methods of Coping with Stress," *Philadelphia Inquirer,* 4 April 1978.
7. Ibid.

Chapter Five: Stress Safety Valves

1. Robert P. Quinn and Graham L. Staines, *The 1977 Quality of Employment Survey,* Survey Research Center, University of Michigan, Ann Arbor (1979): 237.

2. Ibid., p. 298.
3. Ibid.
4. Ibid., p. 91.
5. Ibid., p. 268.
6. "How to Deal with Stress on the Job," *U.S. News and World Report* (13 March 1978): 80–81.
7. James F. Fixx, *The Complete Book of Running* (New York: Random House, 1977), p. 28.
8. Ibid., p. 16.
9. Ibid., p. 6.
10. Malcolm Carruthers, "Antidotes to Stress," in *Human Behavior and Adaptation,* ed. N. Blurton Jones and V. Reynolds (New York: Halstead Press, 1978), pp. 279–284.
11. Quinn and Staines, pp. 193–203.
12. National Commission on Working Women, news release (Washington, D.C., 23 April 1979).
13. Eugene C. Walker, *Learn to Relax* (Englewood Cliffs, N.J.: Prentice-Hall, 1975), p. 10.

Chapter Six: Burnout Blind Alleys

1. Flora Davis, "How to Live with Stress–and Thrive," *Woman's Day* (22 May 1979): 80.
2. Hans Selye, M.D., *Stress Without Distress* (New York: McGraw-Hill, 1969), p. 4.
3. "Stress Gets Drop on City Policeman," *Minneapolis Star,* 15 June 1978.
4. Gerald Caplan, *Principles of Preventive Psychiatry* (New York: Basic Books, 1964), p. 288.
5. John Papanek, "A Rocky Mountain Low," *Sports Illustrated* (19 March 1979): 50–53.
6. Herbert J. Freudenberger, *The Staff Burn-out Syndrome,* Drug Abuse Council, New York (1975): 15.
7. "Do You Work Too Hard? An Expert Explains the Dangers," *U.S. News and World Report* (26 March 1979): 73.
8. Ibid.
9. Christina Maslach, "Burnout: A Social Psychological Analysis" (Paper presented to the American Psychological Association, San Francisco, August 1977): 3.
10. Lester Davis, "The Many Faces of Guilt," *Family Health* (July 1977): 22.
11. Robert P. Quinn and Graham L. Staines, *The 1977 Quality of Employment Survey,* Survey Research Center, University of Michigan, Ann Arbor (1979): 257.
12. Maslach, p. 15.

13. Quinn and Staines, p. 196.
14. Maslach, p. 14.
15. Ibid., p. 15.

Chapter Seven: Managing Stressful Jobs
  1. Those interested in a step-by-step guide to making observations and studying the culture of the workplace may wish to examine the following books by James P. Spradley (New York: Holt, Rinehart and Winston): *The Ethnographic Interview* (1979); and *Participant Observation* (1980). Each book outlines a method used by anthropologists, which the author has applied to cultural scenes in our own society, including many occupational settings.
  2. James P. Spradley and Brenda Mann, *The Cocktail Waitress: Woman's Work in a Man's World* (New York: John Wiley & Sons, 1975).
  3. Ibid.
  4. Robert P. Quinn and Graham L. Staines, *The 1977 Quality of Employment Survey,* Survey Research Center, University of Michigan, Ann Arbor (1979): 40.
  5. "Ann Landers," *Minneapolis Tribune,* 15 May 1979.
  6. This example is based on Robert Janson's study, "A Job Enrichment Trial in Data Processing—in an Insurance Organization," in *The Quality of Working Life,* vol. 2: *Cases and Commentary,* ed. Louis E. Davis and Albert B. Cherns (New York: The Free Press, 1975), pp. 300–314. Janson does not identify the name of the company, which we have called East-West Insurance Company.

Chapter Eight: The Burnout Boss
  1. Robert P. Quinn and Graham L. Staines, *The 1977 Quality of Employment Survey,* Survey Research Center, University of Michigan, Ann Arbor (1979): 218–219.
  2. "The Playboy Report on American Men," *Playboy* (March 1979): 235–236.
  3. Eugene Louis Cass and Frederick G. Zimmer, *Man and Work in Society* (New York: Van Nostrand Reinhold Company, 1975), p. 39.
  4. Robert Blake and Jane Mouton, *The Managerial Grid* (Houston: Gulf Publishing Company, 1964), p. 43.
  5. W. H. Hegarty, "Using Subordinate Ratings to Elicit Behavior Changes in Supervisors," *Journal of Applied Psychology* 6 (1974): 764–766.
  6. J. E. Bragg and I. R. Andrews, "Participative Decision Making: An Experimental Study in a Hospital," *Journal of Applied Behavioral Science* 9 (1973): 727–735.
  7. Quinn and Staines, p. 196.

8. Cary L. Cooper and Roy Payne, ed., *Stress at Work* (New York: John Wiley & Sons, 1978), pp. 86–87.

9. Ibid.

10. Robert L. Veninga, "Interpersonal Feedback: A Cost Benefit Analysis," *Motivating Personnel and Managing Conflict,* 2nd ed. (Wakefield, Mass.: Contemporary Publishing Company, 1976), pp. 32–35.

11. "Praise Is a Good Way to Lift the Self-esteem of Others," *Minneapolis Tribune,* 18 December 1978.

12. E. D. Dyer, M. A. Monson, and M. J. Cope, "Increasing the Quality of Patient Care Through Performance Counseling and Written Goal Setting," *Nursing Research* 24 (1975): 138–144.

13. Dyer, Monson, and Cope, "At Emery Air Freight: Positive Reinforcement Boosts Performance," *Organizational Dynamics* 1, no. 3 (1973): 41–50.

14. Gerald D. Bell, *The Achievers* (Chapel Hill, N.C.: Preston-Hill, 1973), p. 15.

15. A. H. Spiegel III, "How Outsiders Overhauled a Public Agency," *Harvard Business Review* 53, no. 1 (1975): 116–124.

16. D. D. Ely and J. T. Morse, "TA and Reinforcement Theory," *Personnel* 51, no. 2 (1974): 38–41.

Chapter Nine: Dead-End Jobs

1. Patricia A. Renwick, Edward E. Lawler and the *Psychology Today* staff, "What You Really Want from Your Job," *Psychology Today* (May 1978): 56.

2. "School Troubles Causing More Teachers to Leave Profession," *Minneapolis Tribune,* 6 July 1979.

3. Ibid.

4. Sally Reed, "Teacher 'Burnout' a Growing Hazard," *New York Times,* 7 January 1979.

5. Eli Ginzberg, "The Professionalization of the U.S. Labor Force," *Scientific America* 240, no. 3 (March 1979): 49.

6. Robert P. Quinn and Graham L. Staines, *The 1977 Quality of Employment Survey,* Survey Research Center, University of Michigan, Ann Arbor (1979): 219.

7. Herman P. Miller, "Measuring Subemployment in Poverty Areas of Large U.S. Cities," *Monthly Labor Review* 96 (1973): 13.

8. Robert W. Bednarzik, "Involuntary Part-Time Work: A Cyclical Analysis," *Monthly Labor Review* 98 (1975): 16.

9. *Banking* 65 (June 1973).

10. "National Survey of Working Women: Perceptions, Problems, Prospects," Center for Women and Work (Washington, D.C., 28 June 1979): ii.

11. *Women's Advocate* 5, no. 8 (December 1977): 3.

12. Martha Burrow, *Developing Woman Managers: What Needs to Be Done?* (New York: AMACOM, 1978), p. 2.

13. Stephen C. Iman, "The Development of Participation by Semiautonomous Work Teams: The Case of Donnelly Mirrors," in *The Quality of Working Life*, vol. 2: *Cases and Commentary*, ed. Louis E. Davis and Albert B. Cherns (New York: The Free Press, 1975), pp. 216–231.
14. "Sylvia Porter," *Minneapolis Tribune*, 12 July 1978.
15. Lucia Mouat, "Flexible Work Schedules Are Gaining Popularity," Christian Science Monitor News Service, *Minneapolis Tribune*, 28 January 1979.
16. Jo Hartley, "Experience with Flexible Hours of Work," *Monthly Labor Review* (May 1976): 41.
17. Mouat.
18. Rosabeth Moss Kanter, *Men and Women of the Corporation* (New York: Basic Books, 1977), p. 86.
19. Ibid., p. 92.
20. Carl D. Jacobs, "Job Enrichment of Field Technical Representatives – Xerox Corporation," in *The Quality of Working Life*, vol. 2: *Cases and Commentary*, ed. Louis E. Davis and Albert B. Cherns (New York: The Free Press, 1975), pp. 285–289.
21. Judith T. Archer, "Achieving Joint Organization, Technical, and Personal Needs: The Case of the Sheltered Experiment of Aluminum Casting Team," in *The Quality of Working Life*, vol. 2: *Cases and Commentary*, ed. Louis E. Davis and Albert B. Cherns (New York: The Free Press, 1975), pp. 253–269.
22. George Ritzer, *Working: Conflict and Change* (Englewood Cliffs, N.J.: Prentice-Hall, 1972), pp. 247–248.
23. Joy Browne, *The Used Car Game: A Sociology of the Bargain* (Lexington, Mass.: Lexington Books, 1973), p. 68.
24. Ritzer, p. 249.
25. Ibid., p. 289.
26. James Henslin, "The Underlife of Cabdriving: A Study in Exploitation and Punishment" in *Organizational Reality: Reports from the Firing Line*, ed. Peter J. Frost, Vance F. Mitchell, and Walter R. Nord (Santa Monica: Goodyear Publishing Company, 1978), pp. 159–171.
27. Studs Terkel, *Working* (New York: Pantheon Books, 1974), p. 295.
28. Ibid., p. 227.

Chapter Ten: The Professional Helper

1. Daniel Bell, *The Coming of Post-Industrial Society: A Century in Social Forecasting* (New York: Basic Books, 1973).
2. Elizabeth M. Eddy, *Becoming a Teacher: The Passage to Professional Status* (New York: Columbia University Teachers College Press, 1971), p. ii.
3. "School Troubles Causing More Teachers to Leave Profession," *Minneapolis Tribune*, 6 July 1979.
4. "Why Teachers Are Unhappy," *Changing Times* (September 1979): 13.

5. Ibid., p. 14.
6. "I Didn't Bring Anyone Here and I Can't Send Anybody Home," *Saturday Review* (22 July 1979): 12.
7. Lawrence Podell, "Attrition of First Line Social Service Staff," *Welfare Review* 5 (1967): 12.
8. Christina Maslach, "Burned-out," *Human Behavior* 5 (September 1976): 18.
9. Seymour Shubin, "Burnout: The Professional Hazard You Face in Nursing," *Nursing 78* 8, no. 7 (July 1978): 25.
10. Arthur W. Combs, Donald L. Avilia, and William W. Purkey, *Helping Relationships* (Boston: Allyn & Bacon, 1978), p. 207.
11. Ibid., p. 208.

Chapter Eleven: A Message to Wives, Husbands, Bosses, and Friends

1. Martin E. P. Seligman, *Helplessness* (San Francisco: W. H. Freeman & Company, 1975), p. 184.
2. Ibid., p. 173.
3. Ibid., p. 185.
4. Floyd Matson and Ashley Montague, *The Human Dialogue* (New York: The Free Press, 1967), p. 159.
5. Ernest Borman, William Howell, Ralph Nichols, and George Shapiro, *Interpersonal Communication in the Modern Organization* (Englewood Cliffs, N.J.: Prentice-Hall, 1969), p. 178.
6. "Man and Work," *Playboy* (August 1979): 187.
7. Herbert Meyer, "The Meeting-Goer's Lament," *Fortune* (22 October 1979): 95.
8. Ayala Pines and Christina Maslach, "Characteristics of Staff Burnout in Mental Health Settings," *Hospital and Community Psychiatry* 29, no. 4 (April 1978): 235.
9. Paul Tournier, *The Meaning of Persons* (New York: Harper and Brothers, 1957), p. 42.
10. "Cholesterol? Try a Little Tenderness," *Minneapolis Star,* 8 October 1979.
11. An excellent description of physical fitness programs is found in "As Companies Jump on Fitness Bandwagon," *U.S. News and World Report,* (28 January 1980): 36–39.
12. George Monaghan, "Enter the Corporate Welfare State," *Minneapolis Star,* 10 April 1979.

Index

About the Authors

James P. Spradley is an urban anthropologist and a writer. He was born in Baker, Oregon, in 1933 and grew up in Los Angeles. He received his Ph.D. in anthropology from the University of Washington. The author of more than a dozen books, he has researched and written about skid-row alcoholics, culture and stress, cocktail-waitress culture, childhood deafness, American family life, and Kwakiutl Indian culture. In 1969 he received the Stirling Award in Culture and Personality given by the American Anthropological Association for his paper "Adaptive Strategies of Urban Nomads: The Ethnoscience of Tramp Culture." He has taught at Seattle Pacific College and the University of Washington Medical School. At present he is DeWitt Wallace Professor of Anthropology at Macalester College, Saint Paul, Minnesota.

Robert L. Veninga is associate professor in the Program of Health Education at the School of Public Health, University of Minnesota. He holds a Ph.D. from the same university in Speech-Communication, specializing in communication processes within hospitals and health organizations. He has written widely on health education and health administration and was presented by the American College of Hospital

Administrators with the 1980 Edgar C. Hayhow Award for his article on "The Management of Disruptive Conflict." He is a frequent speaker at national and regional conventions and a regular particpant at the New England Hospital Assembly. His courses at the University of Minnesota attract students from many disciplines, including public health, nursing, pharmacy, social work, dentistry, and business administration. He is listed in *Who's Who in Health Care*.